Internet Fire

— and —

Network Security

Karanjit Siyan, Ph.D.

Chris Hare

New Riders Publishing Indianapolis, Indiana

NRP
NEW RIDERS
PUBLISHING

Internet Firewalls and Network Security

By Karanjit Siyan, Ph.D., and Chris Hare

Published by:
New Riders Publishing
201 West 103rd Street
Indianapolis, IN 46290 USA

Printed in the United States of America 2 3 4 5 6 7 8 9 0

```
Hare, R. Christopher E., 1962-
    Internet firewalls and network security / R. Christopher E.
  Hare, Karanjit Siyan.
      p.   cm.
    Includes index.
    ISBN 1-56205-437-6
    1. Internet (Computer network)  2. Computer networks--Security
  measures.  I. Siyan, Karanjit, 1954-    . II. Title.
  TK5105.875.I57H36  1995
  005.8--dc20                                      94-48196
                                                        CIP
```

Warning and Disclaimer

This book is designed to provide information about the Internet. Every effort has been made to make this book as complete and as accurate as possible, but no warranty or fitness is implied.

The information is provided on an "as is" basis. The author and New Riders Publishing shall have neither liability nor responsibility to any person or entity with respect to any loss or damages arising from the information contained in this book or from the use of the disks or programs that may accompany it.

PUBLISHER	*Don Fowley*
ASSOCIATE PUBLISHER	*Tim Huddleston*
PRODUCT DEVELOPMENT MANAGER	*Rob Tidrow*
MARKETING MANAGER	*Ray Robinson*
DIRECTOR OF SPECIAL PROJECTS	*Cheri Robinson*
MANAGING EDITOR	*Tad Ringo*

ABOUT THE AUTHORS

Karanjit Siyan, Ph.D. is president of Kinetics Corporation. He has authored international seminars on Solaris & SunOS, TCP/IP networks, PC Network Integration, Novell networks, Windows NT, and Expert Systems using Fuzzy Logic. He teaches advanced technology seminars in the United States, Canada, Europe, and the Far East. Dr. Siyan had published articles in *Dr. Dobbs Journal*, *The C Users Journal*, and *Databased Advisor*, and is actively involved in Internet research. Dr. Siyan has been involved with Unix systems programming and administration since his graduate days at the University of California at Berkeley when BSD Unix was being developed. He holds a Ph.D. in Computer Science and his dissertation topic was "Fuzzy Logic and Neural Networks for Computer Network Management." Before working as an independent consultant, Karanjit worked as a senior member of technical staff at ROLM Corporation. As part of his consulting work, Karanjit has written a number of custom compiler and operating system developmental tools. His other interests include Novell-based, Windows NT-based, and OS/2 networks. He holds an ECNE certification for Novell-based networks and Microsoft Certified Professional for Windows NT, and has written a number of books for Macmillan Computer Publishing. Karanjit Siyan is based in Montana where he lives with his wife, Dei.

Chris Hare started working with Unix in 1986 as a programmer learning and writing C language code. Since that time, he has worked as a system administrator, written Unix course materials, and authored numerous programs. In 1988, he became the first SCO Authorized instructor in Canada. He has spent the last few years focused in PERL and TCP/IP, while writing numerous technical articles for *Sys Admin* and testing programs for *UNIX World*'s Wizard's Grabbag column. Chris is currently working as Operations Manager for i*internet Inc., which is a Canadian Internet Services Provider.

TRADEMARK ACKNOWLEDGMENTS

All terms mentioned in this book that are known to be trademarks or service marks have been appropriately capitalized. New Riders Publishing cannot attest to the accuracy of this information. Use of a term in this book should not be regarded as affecting the validity of any trademark or service mark.

PRODUCT DIRECTOR
Emmett Dulaney

SENIOR ACQUISITIONS EDITOR
Jim LeValley

PRODUCTION EDITOR
Amy Bezek

TECHNICAL EDITOR
William M. Steen

COPY EDITORS
Geneil Breeze
John Kane
Cliff Shubs
John Sleeva
Steve Weiss
Lisa Wilson

EDITORIAL ASSISTANT
Karen Opal

COVER DESIGNER
Jay Corpus
Roger S. Morgan

BOOK DESIGNER
Kim Scott

PRODUCTION TEAM SUPERVISOR
Katy Bodenmiller

GRAPHICS IMAGE SPECIALISTS
Dennis Sheehan
Clint Lahnen

PRODUCTION ANALYST
Angela D. Bannan
Dennis Clay Hager

PRODUCTION TEAM
Elaine Brush, Mary Ann Cosby
Maxine Dillingham, Mike Henry
Michael Brumitt, Cheryl Cameron
Charlotte Clapp, DiMonique Ford
Louisa Klucznik, Ayanna Lacey
Brian-Kent Proffitt, Erich Richter
Jackie Thompson, Jill Tompkins
Dennis Wesner, Jeff Weissenberger

INDEXER
Greg Eldred

ACKNOWLEDGMENTS

From Karanjit Siyan

One of the more pleasurable tasks of being an author is to thank the people responsible for the success of a book. My heartfelt thanks to my wife Dei for her love and support. I wish to thank my father Ahal Singh and my mother Tejinder, my brothers Harjit and Jagjit, and my sisters Kookie and Dolly. Thanks also to Margaret Cooper Scott, Cathryn and Bob Foley, Craig and Lydia Cooper, Robert and Janie Cooper, Heidi and Steve Bynum, Barbara and Edward L. Scott (Scotty), and Jacquelyn McGregor for their love and support. Special thanks to Mother. Without her spiritual support, this book would not have been possible.

I wish to thank Jeffrey and Nancy Wintroub for their many thoughtful actions and support during the intense period of development of this book. Others who deserve credit are Bob Sanregret and Anders Amundson, who initially got me interested in writing teaching materials on computer networks. I also wish to thank the many people at Learning Tree for their help and support and permission to use some viewgraphs from the courses I have authored for them. In particular, I would like to thank John Moriarty, Rick Adamson, Dr. David Collins, and Eric Garen. I wish to thank John Rutkai for his advise in selecting server components that I needed for writing this book.

I wish to acknowledge the many people who have helped me along the way: Harpreet Sandhu, Bill Duby, Angela, Michael Anaast, Janice Culliford, my students Lisa, Debi, Sheri, Rondi, and Linda, Edward and Mary Kramer, Daniel Gottsegen, David Stanfield, Dr. Wagner, Bill Joy, Professor Ramamoorthy, Professor G.S. Sanyal, Professor "M," Professor Kumar Subramaniam, Professor Mahabalipuram, Marti Lichtanski, Rex Cardinale, Dave Ford, mathematician D.R. Kaprekar, Mr. Gadre, Mr. Misra, and Mr. Hoffman.

I also wish to thank the following individuals for their help in providing me with information on their firewall products: Maurius Nacht of CheckPoint Corporation; Rick Kuzuski and Bob Harvey of Internet Security Corporation for the FireWall-1 Gateway product; Robert M. Darden and Keith Ker of Trusted Information Systems, Inc. for the InterLock product. I also wish to thank Ravi Shankar of Cisco Corporation for his help in providing the documentation on Cisco's Internet firewall solutions.

Many thanks to the staff of Macmillan Computer Publishing. In particular, I wish to thank Emmett Dulaney, Product Director, and Jim LeValley, Senior Acquisitions Editor, for their encouragement throughout the development of this book. Thanks to the lead editor, Amy Bezek, for her editorial skills, and to Ray Robinson, the marketing director, for his patience and willingness to listen to my suggestions.

From Chris Hare

The year 1994 will always be remembered for me as one of personal triumphs. Having worked on two books for New Riders Publishing and other successes will always cause the year to stand out in my mind.

I would like to thank Jim LeValley and Emmett Dulaney at New Riders for their encouragement and support, and Martha Masinton and Robert Ward at R&D Publications who got me started in a writing career through *Sys Admin* magazine. This book marks the beginning of a new cycle, as during its development I changed jobs and moved into an environment where the content of this book will have a daily effect on my life.

Finally, a special thank you to my wife Terri for being supportive in all situations, and our children Meagan and Matthew, who realize that Dad's computer is for more than just playing games!

CONTENTS AT A GLANCE

TABLE OF CONTENTS

PART II ✣ SCREENING ROUTERS AND FIREWALLS

4 An Introduction to Screening Routers

5 Packet Filters

INTRODUCTION

INTERNET FIREWALLS AND NETWORK SECURITY is designed for system administrators and interested users who realize the risks involved in connecting a computer system to the Internet.

In days of old, brick walls were built between buildings in apartment complexes so that if a fire broke out, it would not spread from one building to another. Quite naturally, the walls were called "firewalls."

When you connect your LAN to the Internet, you are enabling your users to reach and communicate with the outside world. At the same time, however, you are enabling the outside world to reach and interact with your LAN. Firewalls, in their barest sense, are routers through which the data traffic flows. If intruders attempt unauthorized access to your network, you stop them at the firewall and do not allow them any further into the system.

WHO SHOULD READ THIS BOOK

Internet Firewalls and Network Security is designed for advanced users and system administrators. It contains information and procedures for the average networked site and represents many hours spent troubleshooting and administering that environment.

HOW THIS BOOK HELPS YOU

The information presented in Part One provides an overview of security and TCP/IP. Being the protocol of the Internet, it is important to understand how TCP/IP works and what utilities are available. It also is important to understand the concept of security and why it is necessary to limit access to resources.

Part Two covers firewalls and screening hosts. Not only are various theories and hypothetical examples discussed, but real world examples are given. Over-the-counter products are discussed, as well as tool kits that enable you to build your own firewall from scratch.

The appendix section offers a quick way to locate key information. Appendix A lists the sample worksheets contained in the chapters and where they can be found. Appendix B lists locations of more information, while Appendix C provides a list of vendors.

CONVENTIONS USED IN THIS BOOK

Throughout this book, certain conventions are used to help you distinguish the various elements of firewalls, system files, and sample data. Before you look ahead, you should spend a moment examining these conventions.

- ❖ Shortcut keys and key combinations are found in the text where appropriate. In most applications, for example, Shift+Ins is the shortcut key combination for the Paste command.

- ❖ Key combinations appear in the following formats:

    KEY1+KEY2. When you see a plus sign (+) between key names, you should hold down the first key while pressing the second key. Then release both keys.

    KEY1, KEY2. When a comma (,) appears between key names, you should press and release the first key and then press and release the second key.

❖ Information you type is in **bold**. This convention applies to individual letters and numbers, as well as words or phrases. This convention, however, does not apply to special keys, such as Enter, Esc, or Ctrl.

❖ New terms appear in *italic*.

❖ Text displayed on-screen but not as part of an application, such as system prompts and messages, appear in a special, `computer`, typeface.

SPECIAL TEXT USED IN THIS BOOK

Throughout this book you will find examples of special text. These passages have been given special treatment so you can instantly recognize their significance and easily find them for future reference.

NOTES, TIPS, AND WARNINGS

Internet Firewalls and Network Security features many special sidebars, which are set apart from the normal text by icons. The book includes three distinct types of sidebars: Notes, Tips, and Warnings.

A *note* includes "extra" information you should find useful, but which complements the discussion at hand instead of being a direct part of it. A note might describe special situations that arise when you use a firewall under certain circumstances, and tell you what steps to take when such situations arise. Notes also might explain ways to avoid problems with your software and hardware.

A *tip* provides quick instructions for getting the most from your firewall implementation as you follow the steps outlined in the general discussion. A tip might show you ways to conserve memory in some setups, speed up a procedure, or perform one of many timesaving and system-enhancing techniques.

WARNING

A *warning* tells you when a procedure might be dangerous, that is, when you run the risk of losing data, locking your system, or even damaging your hardware. Warnings generally explain ways to avoid such losses, or describe the steps you can take to remedy them.

NEW RIDERS PUBLISHING

The staff of New Riders Publishing is committed to bringing you the very best in computer reference material. Each New Riders book is the result of months of work by authors and staff who research and refine the information contained within its covers.

As part of this commitment to you, the NRP reader, New Riders invites your input. Please let us know whether you enjoy this book, if you have trouble with the information and examples presented, or if you have a suggestion for the next edition.

Please note, though, that New Riders' staff cannot serve as a technical resource for firewalls, security, or questions about software- or hardware-related problems. Please refer to the documentation that accompanies your products or to the application's Help systems.

If you have a question or comment about any New Riders book, there are several ways to contact New Riders Publishing. We will respond to as many readers as we can. Your name, address, or phone number never becomes part of a mailing list or is used for any purpose other than to help us continue to bring you the best books possible. You can write us at the following address:

New Riders Publishing
Attn: Associate Publisher
201 W. 103rd Street
Indianapolis, IN 46290

If you prefer, you can fax New Riders Publishing at (317)581-4670.

You can send electronic mail to New Riders from a variety of sources. NRP maintains several mailboxes organized by topic area. Mail in these mailboxes is forwarded to the staff member who is best able to address your concerns. Substitute the appropriate mailbox name from this list when addressing your e-mail:

ADMIN	Comments and complaints for NRP's Publisher
APPS	Word, Excel, WordPerfect, and other office applications
ACQ	Book proposals and inquiries by potential authors

CAD	AutoCAD, 3D Studio, AutoSketch, and CAD products
DATABASE	Access, dBASE, Paradox, and other database products
GRAPHICS	CorelDRAW!, Photoshop, and other graphics products
INTERNET	Internet
NETWORK	NetWare, LANtastic, and other network-related topics
OS	MS-DOS, OS/2, and all other operating systems except UNIX and Windows
UNIX	Unix
WINDOWS	Microsoft Windows (all versions)
OTHER	Anything that doesn't fit into the preceding categories

If you use an MHS e-mail system that routes through CompuServe, send your messages to the following:

> *mailbox* @ NEWRIDER

To send NRP mail from CompuServe, use the following address:

> MHS: *mailbox* @ NEWRIDER

To send mail from the Internet, use the following address format:

> *mailbox*@newrider.mhs.compuserve.com

NRP is an imprint of Macmillan Computer Publishing. To obtain a catalog of information, or to purchase any Macmillan Computer Publishing book, call (800)428-5331.

Thank you for selecting *Internet Firewalls and Network Security*!

PART I

BACKGROUND INFORMATION

UNDERSTANDING
TCP/IP

TCP/IP IS A SET OF DATA communications protocols. These protocols allow for the routing of information from one machine to another, the delivery of e-mail and news, even the use of remote login capabilities.

The name TCP/IP refers to the two major protocols, Transmission Control Protocol and Internet Protocol. While there are many other protocols that provide services that operate over TCP/IP, these are the most common.

THE HISTORY OF TCP/IP

Internetworking with TCP/IP has been around for many years—almost as many years as Unix has been available. TCP/IP, or Transmission Control Protocol/Internet Protocol, grew out of the work that was done with the Defense Advanced Projects Research Agency, or DARPA. In 1969, DARPA sponsored a project that became known as the ARPANET. This network mainly provided high-bandwidth connectivity between the major computing sites in government, educational, and research laboratories.

The ARPANET provided those users with the ability to transfer e-mail and files from one site to another, while DARPA provided the research funding for the entire project. Through the evolution of the project, it became clear that a wide range of benefits and advantages were available, and that it was possible to provide cross-country network links.

During the 1970s, DARPA continued to fund and encourage research on the ARPANET, which consisted chiefly of point-to-point leased line interconnections. DARPA also started pushing for research into alternate forms of communication links, such as satellites and radio. It was during this time that the framework for a common set of networking technologies started to form. The result was TCP/IP. In an attempt to increase acceptance and use of these protocols, DARPA provided a low-cost implementation of them to the user community. This implementation was targeted chiefly at the University of California at Berkeley's BSD Unix implementation.

DARPA funded the creation of the company Bolt Beranek and Newman Inc. (BBN) to develop the implementation of TCP/IP on BSD Unix. This development project came at the time when many sites were in the process of adopting and developing local area network technologies, which were based closely on extensions of the previous single computer environments that were already in use. By January 1983, all the computers connected to the ARPANET were running the new TCP/IP protocols. In addition, many sites that were not connected to the ARPANET also were using the TCP/IP protocols.

Because the ARPANET generally was limited to a select group of government departments and agencies, the National Science Foundation created the NSFNet that also was using the successful ARPANET protocols. This network, which in some ways was an extension of the ARPANET, consisted of a backbone network connecting all the super-computer centers within the United States and a series of smaller networks that were then connected to the NSFNet backbone.

Because of the approaches taken with NSFNet, numerous network topologies are available, and TCP/IP is not restricted to any single one. This means that TCP/IP can run on token ring, Ethernet and other bus topologies, point-to-point leased lines, and more. However, TCP/IP has been closely linked with Ethernet—so much so that the two were used almost interchangeably.

Since that time, the use of TCP/IP has increased at a phenomenal rate, and the number of connections to the Internet, or this global network of networks, has also increased at an almost exponential rate. A countless number of people are making a living off the Internet, and with the current trends in information dissemination, it likely will touch the lives of every person in the developed world at some time.

TCP/IP, however, is not a single protocol. In fact, it consists of a number of protocols, each providing some very specific services. The remainder of this chapter examines how addressing is performed in TCP/IP, network configuration, the files controlling how TCP/IP can be used, and many of the various administrative commands and daemons.

A daemon is a program that runs to perform a specific function. Unlike many commands that execute and exit, a daemon performs its work and waits for more. For example, sendmail is a daemon. It remains active even if there is no mail to be processed.

N O T E

EXPLORING ADDRESSES, SUBNETS, AND HOST NAMES

Each machine on the Internet must have a distinctly different address, like your postal address, so that information destined for it can be successfully delivered. This address scheme is controlled by the Internet Protocol (IP).

As of the time of this writing, the Internet Engineering Task Force (IETF) has almost completed the specification for the next version of IP, which will include a much larger address space. The larger address space is needed in response to the large number of computers that now are being connected to the Internet.

N O T E

Each machine has its own IP Address, and that IP address consists of two parts: the network portion and the host portion. The network part of the address is used to describe the network on which the host resides, and the host portion is used to identify the particular host. To ensure that network addresses are unique, a central agency is responsible for the assignment of those addresses.

Because the original Internet designers did not know how the Internet would grow, they decided to design an address scheme flexible enough to handle a larger network with many hosts or a smaller network with only a few hosts. This addressing scheme introduces address classes, of which there are four.

IP addresses can be expressed in several different forms. First is the dotted decimal notation, which shows a decimal number with each byte separated by a period, as in 192.139.234.102. Alternatively, this address also can be expressed as a single hexadecimal number such as 0xC08BEA66. The most commonly used address format, however, is the dotted decimal notation.

ADDRESS CLASSES

As mentioned, there are four major address classes: class A, B, C, and D. Classes A, B, and C are used to identify the computers that share a common network. A class D, or multicast address, is used to identify a set of computers that all share a common protocol. Because the first three classes are more commonly used, this chapter focuses on them. Regardless of the address class, each address consists of 32 bits, or 4 bytes. Each byte is commonly referred to as an *octet*, so an IP address consists of four octets.

Each octet can have a value from 0 to 255. Certain values, however, have a special meaning that is shown in Table 1.1 later in this chapter.

CLASS A ADDRESSES

In a class A address, the first octet represents the network portion, and the remaining three identify the host (see fig. 1.1).

FIGURE 1.1

The class A address format.

This address class means that this network can have millions of hosts because there are 24 bits available to specify the host address. In figure 1.1, you see that the first bit of the first octet is set to 0. This means that the network portion of the address must be less than 128. Actually, the network portion of a class A address ranges from 1 to 127.

CLASS B ADDRESSES

A class B address is similar in structure to a class A, with the exception that a class B address uses two octets for the network portion and two octets for the host portion (see fig. 1.2). This means that there can be more class B networks, each with thousands of hosts.

```
Bits  1        9        17         25       31
      |1|0|    netid    |          hostid          |
```

FIGURE 1.2

The class B address format.

As illustrated in figure 1.2, the configuration of the class B address is such that each portion shares the same amount of the address. The first two bits of the network address are set to 1 and 0, meaning that the network address ranges from 128 to 191. With this format, each network can have thousands of hosts.

CLASS C ADDRESSES

A class C address uses three octets for the network portion, and one octet for the host. The result is that there can be more class C networks, each with a small number of hosts. Because the maximum value of a single octet is 255, and there are two reserved values, there can be 253 hosts for a class C network. This network format is illustrated in figure 1.3.

```
Bits  1      9          17           25       31
      |1|1|0|        netid          |  hostid  |
```

FIGURE 1.3

The class C address format.

As illustrated in figure 1.3, the first two bits of the network address are set to one. This means that the network address for a class C network ranges from 192 to 223. The remaining values from 224 to 255 are used in the fourth address class.

SPECIAL ADDRESSES

It has been mentioned that there are several different addresses reserved for special purposes. These addresses are listed in table 1.1.

TABLE 1.1
Reserved Addresses

Dotted Decimal Address	Explanation
0.0.0.0	All hosts broadcast address for old Sun networks.
num.num.num.0	Identifies the entire network.
num.num.num.255	All hosts on the specified network. (Broadcast Address)
255.255.255.255	All hosts broadcast for current networks.

These reserved addresses cannot be used to address any host or network. They have been specifically reserved. There can be other reserved addresses depending upon other factors, which you will see later in this chapter.

SUBNETS

Each host on a network has a specific IP address to enable other hosts to communicate with it. Depending upon the class of network, there can be anywhere from 253 to millions of hosts on a network. It would not be practical, however, for a class A or class B address to be restricted to one network with thousands or millions of hosts. To solve this problem, subnets were developed to split the host portion of the address into additional networks.

Subnets work by taking the host portion of the address and splitting it through the use of a netmask. The netmask essentially moves the dividing line between the network and the hosts from one place to another within the address. This has the effect of increasing the number of available networks, but reduces the number of hosts that can be connected to each network.

The use of subnets does provide advantages. Many smaller organizations can only obtain a class C address, yet they have several distinct offices that must be linked together. If they only have one IP address, a router will not connect the two locations because the router requires that each network have a distinct address. By splitting the network into subnets, they can use a router to connect the two networks because they now have distinctly different network addresses.

The subnet is interpreted through the netmask, or subnet mask. If the bit is on in the netmask, that equivalent bit in the address is interpreted as a network bit. If the bit is off, it is considered part of the host address. It is important to note that the subnet is known only locally; to the rest of the Internet, the address looks like a standard IP address.

As noted in the following table, each class of IP addresses has a default netmask associated with it.

TABLE 1.2
Standard Netmasks

Address Class	Default Netmask
A	255.0.0.0
B	255.255.0.0
C	255.255.255.0

In order to understand fully and appreciate how this works, you need to consider an example. Assume that you have a network address of 198.53.64.0, and you want to break this up into subnets. To further subdivide this class C network, it is necessary for you to use some of the bits in the host portion, or last byte, of the address as part of the network portion. While this increases the number of networks you can have, it decreases the number of hosts that can be on each subnet.

The Internet RFC 950 also requires that the first and last division of each subnet be reserved. This means that the actual number of useable subnets is two less than the total number of divisions. For example, if you want to split your class C network into two divisions, you cannot connect any hosts! If you want to have six subnets, then you must split your network into eight divisions.

The following example illustrates how the bits in the last octet are set, and how many subnets and hosts can be created for each. The variable portion that represents the bits used for the host portion is identified by the letter V.

8	7	6	5	4	3	2	1	Divisions	Subnets	Hosts/Subnets
F	V	V	V	V	V	V	V	2	0	0
F	F	V	V	V	V	V	V	4	2	62
F	F	F	V	V	V	V	V	8	6	30
F	F	F	F	V	V	V	V	16	14	14
F	F	F	F	F	V	V	V	32	30	6
F	F	F	F	F	F	V	V	64	62	2
F	F	F	F	F	F	F	V	128	126	0

The preceding example shows that you can effectively only use a minimum division of four with two subnets and 62 hosts per net, or a maximum of 64 divisions which results in 62 subnets of two hosts each. The first example could be used for two separate ethernets, while the second could be used for a series of point-to-point protocol links.

However, the selection of the type of subnets that should be chosen is determined by the maximum number of users that will be required on any subnet, and the minimum number of subnets required.

The possible network portions formed in the development of your divisions are formed by evaluating the values of the fixed portion of the last byte. Looking back to the last example, you see that to split our class C address into eight divisions, or 6 subnets, you need to fix the first three bits in the last octet. The network portions are formed through the evaluation of the non-fixed portion of the last byte. Consider the following example, which lists the bit combinations and illustrates how the Class address is split into the subnets.

```
Network    Host
8  7  6 ¦ 5  4  3  2  1      Decimal Values
- - - - - - - - - - - - - - - - - - - - - - - - - -
0  0  1 ¦ 0  0  0  0  0           32
0  1  0 ¦ 0  0  0  0  0           64
0  1  1 ¦ 0  0  0  0  0           96
1  0  0 ¦ 0  0  0  0  0          128
1  0  1 ¦ 0  0  0  0  0          160
1  1  0 ¦ 0  0  0  0  0          192
```

As shown in the preceding example, the top three bits—8, 7, and 6—are fixed in that they are used as part of the host address. This means that the available networks become the following:

Network
N.O.P.32
N.O.P.64
N.O.P.96
N.O.P.128
N.O.P.160
N.O.P.192

The standard netmask for a class C address is 255.255.255.0. For our subnetted network, the first three bytes remain the same. The fourth byte is created by setting the network portion to 1s and the host portion to zero. Looking back at the preceding example, you see what the network addresses will be. You use the same format for determining the netmask. This means that the netmasks for these subnets are the following:

Network	Broadcast	Netmask
N.O.P.32	N.O.P.31	255.255.255.32
N.O.P.64	N.O.P.63	255.255.255.64
N.O.P.96	N.O.P.95	255.255.255.96
N.O.P.128	N.O.P.127	255.255.255.128
N.O.P.160	N.O.P.159	255.255.255.160
N.O.P.192	N.O.P.191	255.255.255.192

The end result is that you have split this class C address into six subnetworks, thereby increasing your available address space without having to apply for an additional network address.

When looking at the netmask, it is easy to see why many administrators stick with byte-oriented netmasks—they are much easier to understand. By using a bit-oriented approach to the netmask, however, many different configurations can be achieved. Using a netmask of 255.255.255.192 on a class C address, for example, creates four subnets. The same netmask on a class B address, however, creates more than a thousand subnets!

HOST NAMES

Each device connected to the Internet must be assigned a unique IP address, but IP addresses can be difficult to remember. Consequently, each device is generally assigned a host name, which is used to access that device. The network does not require the use of names, but they do make the network easier to use.

For TCP/IP to work properly, the host name must be translated into the corresponding IP address. This can be accomplished through several different methods, including looking up the host name up in a file called the host table or resolving it through the use of the Domain Name Service (DNS).

Methods for translating the host name into the corresponding IP address and DNS are discussed later in this chapter.

N O T E

Within each organization, the host name must be unique. The host name consists of two pieces: the actual host name and the TCP/IP domain. The domain is assigned by a central registry depending on the country you are in and the type of organization you are registering. The most commonly used domains are .com, .edu, and .gov for commercial, educational, and government institutions within the United States. While it is possible to obtain a domain using these outside the United States, it is best not to.

For organizations outside the United States, there may be other rules governing how domains are assigned. For example, a company in Canada named Widgets Inc. could apply for widgets.ca, where .ca denotes that the organization is in Canada. If the same company was in the United Kingdom, then the domain would likely be widgets.co.uk, indicating that it is a commercial organization within the United Kingdom.

Regarding the actual names for the given hosts, the Internet Request for Comments (RFC) number 1178 provides some excellent guidelines regarding how to name systems. Here are some guidelines you should remember:

❖ Use real words that are short, easy to spell, and easy to remember. The point of using host names instead of IP addresses is that they are easier to use. If host names are difficult to spell and remember, they defeat their own purpose.

❖ Use theme names. All hosts in a group could be named after human movements such as fall, jump, or hop, or cartoon characters, foods, or other groupings. Theme names are much easier to think up than unrestricted names.

❖ Avoid using project names, personal names, acronyms, or other such cryptic jargon. This type of host name typically is renamed in the future, which can sometimes be more difficult than it sounds.

> The only requirement is that the host name be unique within the domain. A well-chosen name, however, can save future work and make the user community happier.

The host name of your computer can be determined by using the hostname command, as shown in the following:

```
$ hostname
oreo.widgets.ca
$
```

On some TCP/IP implementations, the hostname command does not print the information as shown above, but only prints the actual name of the system. The output of hostname is the name of the system and the TCP/IP domain name.

WORKING WITH NETWORK INTERFACES

Each device that is to be connected to a network must have a network interface. This network interface must be consistent with the media on which the network is running. A network card for token ring, for example, cannot be connected to a thin coaxial cable network.

The following are the commonly used network types:

Media Type

Token Ring

Thinnet (RG-58U Coax Cable)

Ethernet (RG-8U Coaxial cable)

Twisted Pair Cable

Fiber Optics

Each network interface has a name for the device and an IP address. If there is more than one network interface in a device, each network interface must be part of a different network. That is, the IP addresses must be different, as shown in figure 1.4.

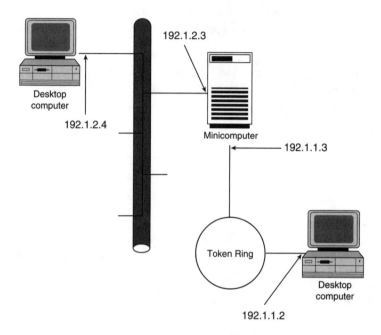

FIGURE 1.4

Network interfaces.

The exact name used for each device is vendor implemented, and often is different depending upon the type of interface that is in use. Table 1.3 lists some of the network interface names that are used, and on what systems those names are found.

TABLE 1.3
Network Interface Names

Interface Name	Operating System
le0	SunOS 4.1.3
wdn0,e3a,sl0,ppp1	SCO Unix
du0	DEC Ultrix

Consequently, as the system is configured, the network administrator must decide what the name of the device is, or must understand how to query the system to determine the name of the device. Having this information is essential to successfully configuring the network interface.

19

CONFIGURATION USING IFCONFIG

Except for Serial Line Internet Protocol (SLIP) and Point-to-Point Protocol (PPP) interfaces, the ifconfig command is used to configure the interface, including its IP address, broadcast address, netmask, and whether or not the interface is operational. There are some variations to this command, so it is wise to check out your system's documentation when setting up your interface.

Normally ifconfig is used at boot time to configure the interface. ifconfig also can be used after the system is running to change the IP address, or other interface configuration information.

The command syntax for ifconfig is:

```
ifconfig interface address-family address destination-address parameters
```

The interface value identifies the name of the interface that is being configured—wdn0, for example. The address family identifies the type of addressing used for this interface. Currently, the only value supported for this argument is inet.

The address value can consist of a host name that is found in /etc/hosts, or an Internet address expressed in dot notation. If the name form is used and the host name is not found in the /etc/hosts file, an error is returned.

Table 1.4 lists the commonly available parameters that can be configured with ifconfig.

TABLE 1.4
ifconfig Commands

Command	Function
up	This marks the interface as being up, or operational. When the first address of the interface is configured, the interface is marked as up. It also can be used to reset an interface after it was previously marked down.
down	This marks an interface down. When the interface is marked down, the system does not attempt to transmit messages through that interface. If possible, the interface will be reset to prevent the reception of incoming packets as well. Use of this command does not automatically disable the routes that use this interface.

Command	Function
trailers	This requests the use of a trailer-link-level encapsulation when transmitting. If the interface is capable of supporting trailers, the system encapsulates the outgoing messages in a manner that minimizes the number of memory-to-memory copy operations performed by the receiver.
-trailers	Disables the use of trailer encapsulation.
arp	This enables the use of the Address Resolution Protocol in mapping between network-level addresses and link-level addresses.
-arp	This disables the use of the Address Resolution Protocol.
metric N	This sets the routing metric for this interface, which is by default 0. The routing metric is used by the route daemon, routed. The higher the metric, the less favorable the route is.
debug	This enables network-driver-level debugging.
-debug	This disables driver-dependent debugging code.
netmask MASK	This specifies how much of the address is used for the division of a network into subnets. The netmask contains 1s for the bit positions that are used for the network and subnet parts, and 0s for the host portion.
dest-address	This specifies the destination address of the correspondent on the other end of a point-to-point link.
broadcast	Specifies the address to use when sending a packet to all of the hosts on a network. The default value is the network portion and all 1s for the host portion. If the network portion is 192.139.234, for example, then the broadcast address is 192.139.234.255.

The following illustrates using ifconfig on an SCO system that has only one interface.

```
ifconfig lo0 localhost
ifconfig wdn0 198.73.138.2 -trailers netmask 255.255.255.0 broadcast
➥198.73.138.255
```

The preceding code has two lines. The first illustrates defining the localhost loopback interface, and the second defines an interface named wdn0 using an IP address of 198.73.138.2. The trailer encapsulation option is turned off (-trailers), the netmask is 255.255.255.0, and the broadcast address is the default, using all 1s for the host portion.

The following code illustrates using ifconfig on a SunOS 4.1.3 system.

```
ifconfig le0 198.73.138.6 -trailers netmask 0xffffff00 broadcast 198.73.138.6
```

The options used on the SunOS system are the same as with SCO systems, except that the netmask defined on the Sun system uses a hexadecimal notation rather than the dot notation.

N O T E

> The use of the ifconfig is restricted to the super-user when used to configure the interface. A normal user can use the ifconfig command to query the status of the interface.

REVIEWING THE NETWORK CONFIGURATION FILES

A large number of files assist in the configuration and control of TCP/IP on the system. Next, this chapter examines those files, their use, and their formats. Understanding the services that are controlled from these files is essential to locate hidden security problems later. Some of these files also have inherent security problems, which will also be discussed.

THE /ETC/HOSTS FILE

The purpose of the /etc/hosts file is to provide simple host name to IP address resolution. Remember that TCP/IP only requires the use of IP addresses. The use of host names is for your convenience and ease of use. When a host name is used, TCP/IP examines the contents of the /etc/hosts file (assuming that Domain Name Service is not in use) to find the IP address for the host.

The format of an entry in the /etc/hosts file is:

```
address     official name     alias ...
```

The columns refer to the IP address, the official or fully qualified domain name (FQDN), and any aliases for the machine. This is illustrated in this sample hosts file shown here:

```
# IP ADDRESS     FQDN                    ALIASES
```

```
127.0.0.1          localhost
192.139.234.50     gateway.widgets.ca      gateway
142.77.252.6       gateway.widgets.ca      router
142.77.17.1        nb.ottawa.uunet.ca
198.73.137.1       gateway.widgets.ca      ppp1
198.73.137.2       newton.widgets.ca       newton
198.73.137.50      gateway.widgets.ca      net2
```

The aliases include the short form of the host name, as well as any other names for the host. The routines that search this file skip text that follows a "#", which represents a comment, as well as blank lines.

> The network configuration files all support the use of comments with the "#" symbol. This allows the network administrator to document changes and notes.

N O T E

THE /ETC/ETHERS FILE

After the IP address is known, TCP/IP converts this to the actual ethernet hardware address when the host is on the local network. This can be done by using the Address Resolution Protocol (ARP), or by creating a list of all of the ethernet addresses in the file /etc/ethers. The format of this file is the ethernet address followed by the official host name, as illustrated here:

```
# Ethernet Address      Host Name
8:0:20:0:fc:6f          laidbak
2:7:1:1:18:27           grinch
0:aa:0:2:30:55          slaid
e0:0:c0:1:85:23         lancelot
```

The information in this file actually is used by the Reverse Address Resolution Protocol daemon, rarpd, which is explained later in this chapter. The ethernet address notation used is x:x:x:x:x:x, where x is a hexadecimal number representing one byte in the address. The address bytes are always in network order, and there should be an entry in the hosts file for each device in this file.

THE /ETC/NETWORKS FILE

This file provides a list of IP addresses and names for networks on the Internet. Each line provides the information for a specific network, as shown here:

```
# NETWORK NAME          IP ADDRESS
loopback                127
Ottawa.widgets.ca       192.139.234
```

```
Toronto.widgets.ca        192.139.235
WAN.widgets.ca            198.73.137
Lab.widgets.ca           198.73.138
Montreal.widgets.ca      198.73.139
```

Each entry in the file consists of the network IP address, the name for the network, any aliases, and comments.

THE /ETC/PROTOCOLS FILE

The /etc/protocols file provides a list of known DARPA Internet protocols. This file should not be changed, as it gives the information provided by the DDN Network Information Center. As shown here, each line contains the protocol name, the protocol number, and any aliases for the protocol.

```
# Internet (IP) protocols
#
ip       0     IP      # internet protocol, pseudo protocol number
icmp     1     ICMP    # internet control message protocol
ggp      3     GGP     # gateway to gateway protocol
tcp      6     TCP     # transmission control protocol
egp      8     EGP     # Exterior Gateway Protocol
pup      12    PUP     # PARC universal packet protocol
udp      17    UDP     # user datagram protocol
hello    63    HELLO   # HELLO Routing Protocol
```

THE /ETC/SERVICES FILE

The /etc/service file provides a list of the available services on the host. For each service, a line in the file should be present that provides the following information:

> Official service name
>
> Port number
>
> Protocol name
>
> Aliases

As with the other files, each entry is separated by a space or tab. The port number and protocol name are considered a single item, as a slash (/) is used to separate them. A portion of the /etc/services file is shown in the following:

```
#
# Network services, Internet style
#
echo      7/tcp
echo      7/udp
discard   9/tcp    sink     null
discard   9/udp    sink     null
```

```
systat      11/tcp      users
ftp         21/tcp
telnet      23/tcp
smtp        25/tcp      mail
time        37/tcp      timserver
time        37/udp      timserver
rlp         39/udp      resource        # resource location
whois       43/tcp      nicname
domain      53/tcp      nameserver      # name-domain server
domain      53/udp      nameserver
```

It's obvious that this file relies upon information from /etc/protocols to function. If the service is not available, or you want to remove support for a specific service, then the appropriate line can be commented out using the comment symbol. In many cases, however, the file /etc/inetd.conf also has to be updated to disable support for a given protocol.

THE /ETC/INETD.CONF FILE

The inetd.conf file is used to provide the information to the inetd command. As discussed later in the chapter, inetd is the Internet super-server. It listens on a specified TCP/IP port and starts the appropriate command when a connection is requested on that port. This saves system resources by only starting the daemons when they are needed.

The following illustrates an inetd.conf file from an SCO system, along with the file format.

```
#
ftp         stream    tcp     nowait    NOLUID    /etc/ftpd -l -v    ftpd
telnet      stream    tcp     nowait    NOLUID    /etc/telnetd       telnetd
shell       stream    tcp     nowait    NOLUID    /etc/rshd          rshd
login       stream    tcp     nowait    NOLUID    /etc/rlogind       rlogind
exec        stream    tcp     nowait    NOLUID    /etc/rexecd        rexecd
# finger    stream    tcp     nowait    nouser    /etc/fingerd       fingerd
```

The SCO inetd.conf file differs from the format of most systems because of the C2 security components found in the SCO Unix operating system. Specifically, SCO requires the Login UID, or LUID, to be set for each user who accesses the system. Because setting the LUID should not be done until a user actually logs in, the LUID must not be set when the daemon starts up. This is accomplished by using the NOLUID parameter in the file.

The following illustrates the standard inetd.conf file that is found on most other Unix systems.

```
#
ftp         stream    tcp     nowait    root      /usr/etc/in.ftpd      in.ftpd
telnet      stream    tcp     nowait    root      /usr/etc/in.telentd   in.telentd
shell       stream    tcp     nowait    root      /usr/etc/in.rshd      in.rshd
login       stream    tcp     nowait    root      /usr/etc/in.rlogind   in.rlogind
exec        stream    tcp     nowait    root      /usr/etc/in.rexecd    in.rexecd
# finger    stream    tcp     nowait    nobody    /usr/etc/in.fingerd   in.fingerd
```

Understanding the Network Access Files

Two files can have a significant impact on the security of your system. These files are the /etc/hosts.equiv and the .rhosts files.

The /etc/hosts.equiv File

The /etc/hosts.equiv file contains a list of trusted hosts. This file is used by the r* commands rlogin, rcp, rcmd, and rsh, and is discussed in detail later in this chapter. The format of this file consists of a list of machine names, one per line, as illustrated here:

```
localhost
oreo
wabbit.widgets.ca
chare
chelsea
widgets
pirate
```

> It's a good habit to use a fully qualified name, but if the domain is omitted, TCP/IP adds it to the host name when validating the remote system.

The .rhosts File

The .rhosts file that is used in the users HOME directory accomplishes a similar purpose to /etc/hosts.equiv. The file format is the same, with one notable exception. The hosts.equiv file is used to provide equivalence between hosts, while the .rhosts file is used to provide equivalence between users. The .rhosts file is appended to the information found in /etc/hosts.equiv when checking for equivalence.

> The hosts.equiv file is not used for the root user. The only file processed in this case is /.rhosts.

USER AND HOST EQUIVALENCY

Host Equivalency, or Trusted Host Access, is configured by the system administrator by using the file /etc/hosts.equiv. This file consists of host names, one per line.

> It is a good idea to document in the file who the network administrator is, as comments can be included by using the comment symbol (#).

Each entry in the hosts.equiv file is *trusted*. That is, users on the named machine can access their equivalent accounts on this machine without a password. This is not applicable for root, however, as will be explained later. Figure 1.5 will be used in our discussion of user equivalency.

FIGURE 1.5

A sample network.

The two machines shown in figure 1.5, oreo and wabbit, both have a user named chare. If the user chare currently is logged into wabbit, and issues the command

```
$ rlogin oreo
```

with host equivalency established, then chare will be logged into oreo without being asked for his password. If host equivalency is not there, chare will be asked for his password on the remote machine.

The following must be considered with /etc/hosts.equiv.

❖ It assumes that you trust ALL the users on the remote machine.

❖ Root is *never* trusted through the use of this file.

There is a second format for the hosts.equiv file, known as .rhosts, which was shown previously. This format lists a system name and a user name. With the addition of the user name, the user is allowed to log in with any user name found in /etc/passwd.

User equivalence is a mechanism in which the same user is known to all of the machines in the network. This makes the network administrator's job easier in the long run. It should be considered absolutely necessary for environments where NFS is used or is planned.

To configure user equivalence, the user creates a file in his home directory called .rhosts. This file must be writeable only by the owner of the file. If it is not, then the file is ignored for validation purposes. As with the hosts.equiv file, this file contains a system name per line, but generally also includes the name of the user who is being equivalenced. The issue of host and user equivalence will be presented again in more detail in Chapter 2, "Security."

EXAMINING TCP/IP DAEMONS

Because of the varying implementations of TCP/IP that are available, a wide range of daemons can comprise the system. As many as possible are listed here along with a brief explanation of what they do. If they are operating system specific, the operating system version information also is included.

Many of the TCP/IP daemons are named with the name of the service they provide followed by the letter "d," as in bootpd. This convention is used to indicate that this command is a daemon.

THE SLINK DAEMON

The slink daemon provides the necessary components to link the STREAMS modules required for streams TCP/IP. When the system is started, a configuration file, typically /etc/strcf, is processed, thus establishing the links between STREAMS modules for each of the network devices present in the system.

This daemon is only found on versions of Unix that use STREAMS based TCP/IP, such as most System V derivatives.

THE LDSOCKET DAEMON

The ldsocket command initializes the System V STREAMS TCP/IP Berkeley networking compatibility interface. This daemon also is found only on System V based implementations of TCP/IP, as the BSD-based versions do not use a STREAMS-based implementation. As the ldsocket program is loaded, a file, generally /etc/sockcf, is processed, and the streams modules are loaded and configured to provide the socket style interface.

THE cpd DAEMON

This is a copy protection daemon that is specific to the Santa Cruz Operation versions of TCP/IP. When TCP/IP starts, it registers with the copy protection daemon. When the cpd receives a datagram from a remote system with the same serial number, a warning message is printed advising the system administrator of the problem. SCO is the only system with this feature.

THE LINE PRINTER DAEMON (LPD)

The lpd is the line printer daemon, or spool area handler, and is executed at boot time. It accepts incoming print jobs on a specific TCP/IP port, and queues the print job for printing on the local or remote system. The printer configuration information is stored in the file /etc/printcap, and the access control to the printer is maintained through the file /etc/hosts.lpd.

THE SNMP DAEMON (SNMPD)

The SNMP daemon is an implementation of the Internet Simple Network Management Protocol, as defined in RFCs 1155-1157, 1213, and 1227. While this daemon is capable of receiving information from SNMP agents on other systems, many systems do not include SNMP Management software.

THE RARP DAEMON (RARPD)

The RARP command is a daemon that responds to Reverse Address Resolution Protocol (RARP) requests. Other systems typically use RARP at boot time to discover their (32 bit) IP address given their (48 bit) Ethernet address. The booting machine sends its Ethernet address in an RARP request message. For the request to be answered, the system running rarpd must have the machine's name-to-IP-address entry in the /etc/hosts file or must be available from the domain name server and its name-to-Ethernet-address entry must exist in the /etc/ethers file. Using the above two sources, rarpd maps this Ethernet address into the corresponding IP address.

THE BOOTP DAEMON (BOOTPD)

The BOOTP daemon implements an Internet Boot Protocol server as defined in RFC 951 and RFC 1048. The bootpd daemon is started by the inetd super-server when a boot request arrives. If bootpd does not receive another boot request within 15 minutes of the last one it received, it exits to conserve system resources. The Internet Boot Protocol server is designed to provide network information to the client. This information can include, but is not restricted to, the client's IP address, netmask, broadcast address, domain server address, router address, etc.

THE ROUTE DAEMON (ROUTED)

The route daemon is invoked at boot time to manage the Internet Routing Tables. The routed daemon uses a variant of the Xerox NS Routing Information Protocol to maintain up-to-date kernel Routing Table entries. In normal operation, routed listens on the UDP socket 520 to provide the route service for routing information packets. If the host is an internetwork router, it periodically supplies copies of its routing tables to any directly connected hosts and networks.

The netstat command, which is discussed later in this chapter, is used to print the routing tables on a host. The netstat command is shown here:

```
$ netstat -r
Routing tables
Destination          Gateway            Flags   Refs   Use       Interface
nb.ottawa.uunet.     gateway            UH      0      1         du0
localhost.0.0.12     localhost.0.0.127. UH      3      0         lo0
topgun               gateway            UH      1      3218      du1
default              gateway            UG      1      669360    du0
Lab.widgets.ca       gateway            U       8      3340413   wdn0
Ottawa.widgets.ca    gateway            U       10     2083505   iat0
$
```

The list identifies the gateway that is used to reach a specific destination network, along with the status of the route (flags). It also includes how many connections are in use through that gateway, the number of packets through the gateway, and the name of the interface in this machine that connects the machine to the network.

Most systems are capable of handling dynamic and static routes. The dynamic routes are handled by the routed daemon. As the routes change, the routed daemon updates the tables and informs other hosts as needed. The static routes generally are manipulated by hand using the route command, and generally are not controlled by the routed daemon.

THE DOMAIN NAME SERVICE—NAMED

named is the Internet Domain Name Server, and it is the second mechanism available to provide host name to IP address resolution. The daemon can serve in a variety of roles, including primary, secondary, caching, and as a slave, depending upon the requirements of the network administrator. If the /etc/hosts file is not used, and domain name service (DNS) is configured, then the system makes requests to the DNS to provide the IP address for a host name. If the local DNS does not know the IP address for the specified host, it queries other name servers until it obtains the address.

The user command nslookup is used to query the DNS server for a given piece of information. The following illustrates using the nslookup command to find the IP address for the host name gatekeeper.dec.com.

```
$ nslookup gatekeeper.dec.com
Server:  gateway.widgets.ca
Address:  192.139.234.50
Non-authoritative answer:
Name:    gatekeeper.dec.com
Address:  16.1.0.2

$
```

In this output, the domain name server gateway.widgets.ca cannot provide an authoritative response because it is not the authoritative master for the dec.com domain. The end result is that you learn the IP address for gatekeeper.dec.com is, in fact, 16.1.0.2.

THE SYSTEM LOGGER—SYSLOGD

This daemon is responsible for logging various system messages in a set of files described by the syslogd configuration file /etc/syslog.conf. Each message is saved on a single line in the file and can contain a wide variety of information. The syslog daemon receives information sent to it and saves the messages in its log file. Information can consist of informational, error, status, and debug messages. Each message also can have a level of severity associated with it.

INETD—THE SUPER-SERVER

The inetd super-server listens on multiple TCP/IP ports for incoming connection requests. When the request is received, it spawns the appropriate server. The use of a super-server allows other servers to spawn only when needed, thereby saving system resources. When the connection is terminated, the spawned server terminates.

Typically, servers that are started through inetd include fingerd, ftpd, rexecd, rlogind, and others. inetd, however, cannot be used for servers like named, routed, rwhod, sendmail, or any RFS or NFS server.

THE RWHO DAEMON (RWHOD)

The RWHO daemon maintains the database used by the rwho and ruptime commands. Its operation is predicated by its capability to broadcast messages on a network. rwho operates by periodically querying the state of the system and broadcasting that information on the network. It also listens for rwho messages produced by other systems, so it can update its database of remote server information.

It is important to note that this service takes up more and more bandwidth as the number of hosts grows. For large networks, the cost in network traffic becomes prohibitive.

EXPLORING TCP/IP UTILITIES

TCP/IP commands can be split into three categories: those that are used to administer the TCP/IP network at one level or another, user commands that can be considered applications unto themselves, and third-party applications that have been implemented by using one or more of the services provided by TCP/IP, such as client-server databases.

ADMINISTRATION COMMANDS

This section examines some of the commands that are used to administer the TCP/IP services provided in a system. Many of the commands can be executed by either a regular user or the super-user, but some features are restricted due to the nature of the command. An understanding of the commands available to administer TCP/IP, however, is important for the administrator and helpful for the user.

THE PING COMMAND

The ping command is used to send Internet Control Message Protocol (ICMP) packets from one host to another. ping transmits packets using the ICMP ECHO_REQUEST command and expects to get an ICMP ECHO_REPLY in response to each transmitted packet. The name ping comes from the sonar detection device that uses a sound pulse resembling a ping to locate targets in the surrounding area. In this case, the sound pulses are ICMP packets to a target host.

The following illustrates using ping with a responding host and using ping with a nonresponding host. Under normal circumstances, ping does not terminate, but broadcasts packets until the user stops it, typically through an interrupt signal such as Control+C.

```
$ ping shylock
PING shylock (192.139.234.12): 56 data bytes
64 bytes from shylock (192.139.234.12): icmp_seq=0 ttl=254 time=10 ms
64 bytes from shylock (192.139.234.12): icmp_seq=1 ttl=254 time=10 ms
64 bytes from shylock (192.139.234.12): icmp_seq=2 ttl=254 time=10 ms
64 bytes from shylock (192.139.234.12): icmp_seq=3 ttl=254 time=10 ms

-- shylock ping statistics --
4 packets transmitted, 4 packets received, 0% packet loss
round-trip min/avg/max = 10/10/10 ms
$
```

The ping command has a wide variety of options that can be used to help locate potential problems in the connections. These options and their explanation are shown in table 1.6.

Table 1.6
ping Command Options

Option	Description
-c count	This instructs ping to continue sending packets until count requests have been sent and received.
-d	This option turns on the debug option for the socket being used.
-f	This is a flood ping. It causes ping to output packets as fast as they come back from the remote host or 100 times per second, whichever is faster. In this mode, each request is shown with a period, and for each response, a backspace is printed. Only the super-user can use this option. For obvious reasons, this can be very hard on a network and should be used with caution.
-i seconds	This option instructs ping to wait the specified number of seconds between transmitting each packet. This option cannot be used with the -f option.
-n	Numeric mode only. Normally ping attempts to resolve the IP address for a host name. This option instructs ping to print the IP addresses and not look up the symbolic names. This is important if for some reason the local name server is not available.
-p pattern	This enables the user to specify up to 16 pad bytes to be added to the packet. This is useful for diagnosing data-dependent problems in a network. Using -p ff, for example, causes the transmitted packet to be filled with all 1s.
-q	Normally, ping reports each response received. This option puts ping into quiet mode. The result is that it prints the summary information at startup and completion of the command.
-R	This adds the ICMP RECORD_ROUTE option to the ECHO_REQUEST packet. This asks for the route to be recorded in the packet, which ping then prints when the packet is returned. There is only room for nine routes in each packet, and many hosts ignore or discard this option.
-r	This causes ping to bypass the normal routing tables that would be used to transmit a packet. For this to work, the host must be on a directly attached network. If the target host is not, an error is printed by ping.

continues

TABLE 1.6, CONTINUED
PING COMMAND OPTIONS

Option	Description
-s packetsize	This enables the user to specify the number of data bytes that are to be sent. The default is 56 bytes, which translates into 64 ICMP data bytes when combined with the 8 bytes of ICMP header of data.
-v	This puts ping into verbose mode. It instructs ping to print all ICMP packets returned other than ECHO_RESPONSE packets.

The following demonstrates the -q option for ping. With this example, ping prints only the startup and summary information.

```
$ ping -q ftp.widgets.ca
PING chelsea.widgets.ca (198.73.138.6): 56 data bytes

-- chelsea.widgets.ca ping statistics --
7 packets transmitted, 7 packets received, 0% packet loss
round-trip min/avg/max = 0/0/0 ms
$
```

These examples are not representative of all implementations of ping. The following illustrates the output of ping on BSD versions of Unix.

```
% /usr/etc/ping gateway
gateway.widgets.ca is alive
%
```

For the BSD Unix users, the ping command generally does not print the information that was illustrated in preceding code. The preceding example serves to illustrate that even different versions of TCP/IP have been implemented differently.

When ping is used for fault isolation, it should first be run on the local host to ensure that the network interface is up and running. The ping program is intended for use in network testing, measurement, and management. Because of the load it can impose on the network, however, it is not wise to use ping during normal working hours or from automated test scripts.

THE RUPTIME AND RWHO COMMANDS

The ruptime command uses the facilities of the rwhod server to show the status of the local machines on the network. It prints a status line for each host in its database. This database is built by using broadcast rwho packets, once every one to three minutes. Machines that have not reported a status for five minutes are reported as down. The output of ruptime is shown here.

```
$ ruptime
chelsea        up 17+01:28,    0 users,   load 0.00, 0.00, 0.00
daffy          up 29+06:11,    0 users,   load 1.00, 1.00, 1.00
gateway        up 16+14:34,    1 user,    load 1.00, 1.05, 1.02
mallow         up  5+12:46,    0 users,   load 0.00, 0.00, 0.00
oreo           up 19+13:13,    1 user,    load 2.00, 2.00, 1.33
ovide          up  4+04:54,    1 user,    load 1.14, 1.16, 1.17
wabbit       down 107+01:33
$
```

If the rwhod server is not running on any of the hosts in your network, then ruptime reports the status message no hosts!!! and exits. In the preceding example, the system wabbit appears to be down. This might be accurate, but it also might be that the rwhod server has exited or is no longer running on the system.

Normally, the ruptime output is sorted by host name, but the following options alter the output format of ruptime.

TABLE 1.7
ruptime Options

Option	Description
-a	Includes all users in ruptime output. (Users idle for more than an hour are not usually counted in the user list.)
-l	Sorts the output by load average.
-t	Sorts the output by uptime.
-u	Sorts the output by the number of users.
-r	Reverses the sort order.

The rwho command lists the users who currently are logged in on each of the servers in the network. The rwho command reports the users who are logged in on hosts that are responding to and transmitting rwhod packets. The output of the rwho command is shown in here:

```
$ rwho
chare      oreo:ttyp0     Oct  9 14:58 :01
root       ovide:tty08    Oct  4 18:05
topgun     gateway:tty2A Oct  9 13:54
$
```

In this output, the name of the user is shown as well as the system name, the port he is logged in on, and the date he logged in to the system. This looks like the output from the who command, except the system name is included in the port information.

THE IFCONFIG COMMAND

The ifconfig command has been presented in some detail, but this section illustrates some additional uses for it. By using ifconfig, for example, it is possible to query the interface to find out how it has been configured, as shown here:

```
$ /etc/ifconfig wdn0
wdn0: flags=23<UP,BROADCAST,NOTRAILERS>
        inet 198.73.138.2 netmask ffffff00 broadcast 198.73.138.255
$
```

This output shows that the interface is up, it does not use trailer encapsulation, and it identifies the addresses and netmask currently used by the interface. Any interface that is configured on the system can be queried in this manner.

The following illustrates marking an interface down, verifying that information, and then marking the interface up.

```
# ifconfig du0
du0: flags=51<UP,POINTOPOINT,RUNNING>
        inet 142.77.252.6 --> 142.77.17.1 netmask ffff0000
# ifconfig du0 down
# ifconfig du0
du0: flags=50<POINTOPOINT,RUNNING>
        inet 142.77.252.6 --> 142.77.17.1 netmask ffff0000
# ping toradm
PING toradm.widgets.ca (142.77.253.13): 56 data bytes
ping: sendto: Network is unreachable
ping: wrote toradm.widgets.ca 64 chars, ret=-1
ping: sendto: Network is unreachable
ping: wrote toradm.widgets.ca 64 chars, ret=-1
ping: sendto: Network is unreachable
ping: wrote toradm.widgets.ca 64 chars, ret=-1

-- toradm.widgets.ca ping statistics --
3 packets transmitted, 0 packets received, 100% packet loss
# ifconfig du0 up
# ifconfig du0
du0: flags=51<UP,POINTOPOINT,RUNNING>
        inet 142.77.252.6 --> 142.77.17.1 netmask ffff0000
# ping toradm
PING toradm.widgets.ca (142.77.253.13): 56 data bytes
64 bytes from toradm.widgets.ca (142.77.253.13): icmp_seq=0 ttl=251 time=610 ms
64 bytes from toradm.widgets.ca (142.77.253.13): icmp_seq=1 ttl=251 time=630 ms

-- toradm.widgets.ca ping statistics --
3 packets transmitted, 2 packets received, 33% packet loss
round-trip min/avg/max = 610/620/630 ms
#
```

In this example, the interface being affected is a point-to-point protocol link, which is illustrated in the output of ifconfig. When the interface is marked down, packets will not be transmitted on that link, as shown using ping. When the interface is later marked up, traffic once again flows on that link.

The use of ifconfig to configure an interface is restricted to the super-user. Any user on the system, however, can use ifconfig to query the interface for its current operating statistics.

THE FINGER COMMAND

By default, finger lists the login name, full name, terminal name and terminal write status (as a "*" before the terminal name if write permission is denied), idle time, login time, office location, and phone number (if known) for each current user.

> Idle time is minutes if it is a single integer, hours and minutes if a colon (:) is present, or days and hours if a "d" is present.

N O T E

Longer format also exists and is used by finger whenever a list of names is given. (Account names as well as first and last names of users are accepted.) This is a multiline format; it includes all the information described earlier as well as the user's home directory, login shell, any plan the user has placed in the .plan file in her home directory, and the project on which she is working from the .project file that is also in her home directory. The output of finger is illustrated here:

```
$ finger chare
Login name: chare          (messages off)   In real life: Chris Hare
Directory: /u/chare                         Shell: /bin/ksh
On since Oct  8 22:06:31 on ttyp0
Project: Not assigned to one (yet).
Plan:
To complete the currently assigned tasks.
```

In the preceding code, the output from this finger command is for a user who is currently logged into the system. Notice the (messages off) text. This indicates that any attempts to contact this user with the write command will fail because the user does not allow writes to her terminal. When the user is not logged in, the output is different, as shown here:

```
$ finger andrewg
Login name: andrewg                         In real life: Andrew Goodier
Directory: /u/andrewg                       Shell: /bin/ksh
Last login Sun Sep 18 22:08
No Plan.
$
```

The following table lists the options that typically are available on the finger command.

TABLE 1.8
The Options for the finger Command

Option	Description
-b	Briefer output format
-f	Suppresses the printing of the header line (short format)
-i	Provides a quick list of users with idle times
-l	Forces long output format
-p	Suppresses printing of the .plan files
-q	Provides a quick list of users
-s	Forces short output format
-w	Forces narrow format list of specified users

It is important for you to recognize that the finger command allows the distribution of valuable user information, such as user names and home directories. For this reason, many sites choose to disable the finger daemon and remove the finger command entirely.

THE NETSTAT COMMAND

The netstat command is used to query the network subsystem regarding certain types of information. netstat, for example, can be used to print the routing tables, active connections, streams in use (on those systems that use streams), and more. netstat prints the information in a symbolic format that is easier for the user to understand. The options for netstat are listed in table 1.9.

TABLE 1.9
netstat Options

Option	Description
-A	Shows the addresses of any associated protocol control blocks. This option is primarily used for debugging only.
-a	Instructs netstat to show the status of all sockets. Normally, the sockets associated with server processes are not shown.
-i	Shows the state of the interfaces that have been auto-configured. Those interfaces that have been configured after the initial boot of the system are not shown in the output.

Option	Description
-m	Prints the network memory usage.
-n	Causes netstat to print the actual addresses instead of interpreting them and displaying a symbol such as a host or network name.
-r	Prints the routing tables.
-f address-family	Causes netstat to print only the statistics and control block information for the named address family. Currently, the only address family supported is inet.
-I interface	Shows the interface state for only the named interface.
-p protocol-name	Limits the statistics and protocol control block information to the named protocol.
-s	Causes netstat to show the per protocol statistics.
-t	Replaces the queue length information with timer information in the output displays.

The output from netstat in the following code illustrates the retrieval of interface statistics from the interfaces on the system.

```
$ netstat -i
Name Mtu   Net/Dest      Address        Ipkts     Ierrs Opkts    Oerrs Collis Queue
le0  1500  198.73.138.0  chelsea        2608027   26    1421823  1     2632   0
lo0  1536  loopback      127.0.0.1      765364    0     765364   0     0      0
$ netstat -in
Name Mtu   Net/Dest      Address        Ipkts     Ierrs Opkts    Oerrs Collis Queue
le0  1500  198.73.138.0  198.73.138.6   2608082   26    1421862  1     2632   0
lo0  1536  127.0.0.0     127.0.0.1      765364    0     765364   0     0      0
$
```

In the second invocation of netstat in the preceding code, the use of the -n option is employed. This causes netstat to print the address instead of the symbolic name that was printed in the first invocation of netstat. This information is dependent upon the link level driver for the interface. If that driver does not attach itself to the ifstats structure in the kernel, then the phrase No Statistics Available is printed.

In the output of netstat shown in the preceding example, columns of information are shown. These columns and their meanings are listed in table 1.10.

TABLE 1.10
netstat Column Headings

Column	Description
Name	The name of the configured interface
Mtu	The maximum transmission unit for the interface
Net/Dest	The network that this interface serves
Address	The IP Address of the interface
Ipkts	The number of received packets
Ierrs	The number of packets that have been mangled when received
Opkts	The number of transmitted packets
Oerrs	The number of packets that were damaged when transmitted
Collisions	The number of collisions recorded by this interface on the network

Keep in mind that the notion of errors is somewhat ill-defined according to many of the manual pages for netstat, calling into question the validity of the values in the error columns. In addition, with the tables always being updated, the information presented is, like the output of ps, only a snapshot of the status at any given interval.

One of the common uses of netstat is to find out if there are any network memory allocation problems. This is achieved using the command netstat -m, as shown here:

```
$ netstat -m
streams allocation:
                         config    alloc     free    total     max    fail
streams                     292       93      199    53882     112       0
queues                     1424      452      972   122783     552       0
mblks                      5067      279   478820190677     706       0
dblks                      4054      279   377515804030     706       0
class 0,    4 bytes         652       55      597   475300     277       0
class 1,   16 bytes         652        8      644  2404108      62       0
class 2,   64 bytes         768       22      746  9964817     232       0
class 3,  128 bytes         872      138      734  1223784     386       0
class 4,  256 bytes         548       34      514   230688      75       0
class 5,  512 bytes         324       12      312    92565      76       0
class 6, 1024 bytes         107        0      107  1226009      49       0
class 7, 2048 bytes          90        0       90   182978      67       0
class 8, 4096 bytes          41       10       31     3781      13       0
total configured streams memory: 1166.73KB
streams memory in use: 98.44KB
maximum streams memory used: 409.22KB
$
```

This output is from an SCO Unix 3.2 version 4.2 system. If there are any non-zero values in the fail column, then it is important to readjust the number configured. When the configured number of data blocks is reached, a failure is generated. This means that a TCP/IP application or service could not get the needed resources. The only way to correct this problem in the short term is to reboot the machine. Over the long run, the only way to prevent these failures is to adjust the values and relink the kernel. The output of netstat -m on a SunOS system is similar in content to the SCO systems.

The netstat command also can be used to list all the sockets that are on the system using the -a option. This option is illustrated here:

```
$ netstat -a
Active Internet connections (including servers)
Proto Recv-Q Send-Q  Local Address         Foreign Address        (state)
ip      0      0     *.*                    *.*
tcp     0    28672   oreo.20                topgun.4450            ESTABLISHED
tcp     0     286    oreo.telnet            topgun.4449            ESTABLISHED
tcp     0      0     oreo.ftp               topgun.4438            ESTABLISHED
tcp     0      0     oreo.1725              gateway.telnet         ESTABLISHED
tcp     0      0     *.printer              *.*                    LISTEN
tcp     0      0     *.pop                  *.*                    LISTEN
tcp     0      0     *.smtp                 *.*                    LISTEN
tcp     0      0     *.finger               *.*                    LISTEN
tcp     0      0     *.exec                 *.*                    LISTEN
tcp     0      0     *.login                *.*                    LISTEN
tcp     0      0     *.shell                *.*                    LISTEN
tcp     0      0     *.telnet               *.*                    LISTEN
tcp     0      0     *.ftp                  *.*                    LISTEN
udp     0      0     *.snmp                 *.*
udp     0      0     *.who                  *.*
$
```

This output shows the status of the currently connected sockets and to what they are connected. For the TCP sockets, the status of the socket is reported in the output. The state is one of the following listed in table 1.11.

TABLE 1.11
TCP Socket Explanations

State	Meaning
CLOSED	The socket is not being used.
LISTEN	The socket is listening for an incoming connection.
SYN_SENT	The socket is actively trying to establish a connection.
SYN_RECIEVED	The initial synchronization of the connection is underway.

continues

41

TABLE 1.11, CONTINUED
TCP Socket Explanations

State	Meaning
ESTABLISHED	The connection has been established.
CLOSE_WAIT	The remote has shut down: we are waiting for the socket to close.
FIN_WAIT_1	The socket is closed, and the connection is being shut down.
CLOSING	The socket is closed, and the remote is being shutdown. The acknowledgment of the close is pending.
LAST_ACK	The rmote has shut down and closed. They are waiting for us to acknowledge the close.
FIN_WAIT_2	The socket is closed, and we are waiting for the remote to shut down.
TIME_WAIT	The socket is waiting after the close for the remote shut down transmission.

With this information, it is easy to tell what state the connection is in and how to trace the connection through the various stages of operation.

THE TRACEROUTE COMMAND

The traceroute command is used to trace the route that a packet must take to reach the destination machine. This command works by utilizing the time-to-live (TTL) field in the IP packet to elicit an ICMP TIME_EXCEEDED response from each gateway along the path to the remote host. The following code uses the traceroute command.

```
# traceroute toradm.widgets.ca
traceroute to toradm.widgets.ca (142.77.253.13), 30 hops max, 40 byte packets
 1  gateway (198.73.138.50)  10 ms  10 ms  10 ms
 2  nb.ottawa.uunet.ca (142.77.17.1)  260 ms  300 ms  270 ms
 3  gw.ottawa.uunet.ca (142.77.16.3)  240 ms  240 ms  270 ms
 4  wf.toronto.uunet.ca (142.77.59.1)  280 ms  260 ms  310 ms
 5  alternet-gw.toronto.uunet.ca (142.77.1.202)  250 ms  260 ms  250 ms
 6  nb1.toronto.uunet.ca (142.77.1.201)  260 ms  250 ms  260 ms
 7  toradm (142.77.253.13)  880 ms  720 ms  490 ms
#
```

As in the preceding example, the traceroute command attempts to trace the route that an IP packet would follow to some Internet host. The command works by sending probes until the maximum number of probes has been sent, or the remote responds with an ICMP PORT UNREACHABLE message.

In the output of the traceroute command in the preceding example, the times following the host name are the round trip times for the probe. From this output, you can see that for a packet to travel from the originating host (oreo.widgets.ca), it must travel through seven hosts to reach the destination system, toradm.widgets.ca. The following illustrates another invocation of traceroute.

```
# traceroute gatekeeper.dec.com
traceroute to gatekeeper.dec.com (16.1.0.2), 30 hops max, 40 byte packets
 1  gateway (198.73.138.50)  10 ms  10 ms  10 ms
 2  nb.ottawa.uunet.ca (142.77.17.1)  250 ms  240 ms  240 ms
 3  gw.ottawa.uunet.ca (142.77.16.3)  270 ms  220 ms  240 ms
 4  wf.toronto.uunet.ca (142.77.59.1)  260 ms  270 ms  250 ms
 5  alternet-gw.toronto.uunet.ca (142.77.1.202)  250 ms  260 ms  260 ms
 6  Falls-Church1.VA.ALTER.NET (137.39.7.1)  470 ms  960 ms  810 ms
 7  Falls-Church4.VA.ALTER.NET (137.39.8.1)  760 ms  750 ms  830 ms
 8  Boone1.VA.ALTER.NET (137.39.43.66)  910 ms  810 ms  760 ms
 9  San-Jose3.CA.ALTER.NET (137.39.128.10)  930 ms  870 ms  850 ms
10  * * Palo-Alto1.CA.ALTER.NET (137.39.101.130)  930 ms
11  gatekeeper.dec.com (16.1.0.2)  830 ms  910 ms  830 ms
#
```

In this case, hop 10 did not report right away, but rather printed two asterisks before printing the gateway name and the round trip time. When traceroute does not receive a response within three seconds, it prints an asterisk. If no response from the gateway is received, then three asterisks are printed.

> Because of the apparent network load that traceroute can create, it should only be used for manual fault isolation or troubleshooting. This command should not be executed from cron or from within any automated test scripts.

N O T E

THE ARP COMMAND

The arp command displays and modifies the Internet-to-Ethernet address translation table, which normally is maintained by the address resolution protocol (ARP). When a host name is the only argument, arp displays the current ARP entry for that host. If the host is not in the current ARP table, then arp displays a message to that effect. The following illustrates using arp to find the Ethernet address for a specific host.

```
$ arp gateway
gateway (198.73.138.50) at 0:0:c0:11:57:4c
$ arp ovide
ovide (198.73.138.101) -- no entry
```

This illustrates the behavior of arp when no arguments are present. arp behaves a little differently, however, when options are combined. The available options for arp are defined in table 1.12.

TABLE 1.12
arp Command Line Options

Option	Description
-a	Lists all the entries on the current ARP table.
-d host	Deletes the corresponding entry for host from the ARP table.
-s host address [temp] [pub] [trail]	Creates an entry in the ARP table for the named host, using an Ethernet address. If the keyword [temp] is included, the entry is temporary. Otherwise, the entry is permanent. The [pub] keyword indicates that the ARP entry will be published. Use of the [trail] keyword implies that trailer encapsulation is to be used.
-f file	Instructs arp to read the named file and create ARP table entries for each of the named hosts in the file.

The most commonly used option with arp is -a, which prints the entire ARP table, and is illustrated here:

```
$ arp -a
ovide.widgets.ca (198.73.138.101) at 0:0:c0:c6:4f:71
gateway.widgets.ca (198.73.138.50) at 0:0:c0:11:57:4c
chelsea.widgets.ca (198.73.138.6) at 8:0:20:2:94:bf
fremen.widgets.ca (198.73.138.54) at 0:0:3b:80:2:e5
$
```

ARP is most commonly used to help debug and diagnose network connection problems. arp can help in that regard by assigning the Ethernet address for a given host. This is done by using the -s option, as shown here:

```
$ arp gateway
gateway (198.73.138.50) at 0:0:c0:11:57:4c
# arp -s ovide 0:0:c0:c6:4f:71
# arp -a
ovide.widgets.ca (198.73.138.101) at 0:0:c0:c6:4f:71 permanent
gateway.widgets.ca (198.73.138.50) at 0:0:c0:11:57:4c
#
```

This example illustrates adding an entry to the arp table. If you could not communicate with the remote host before the arp table entry was created, then you might have an addressing problem. If you still cannot communicate with the remote host after establishing the arp entry, then the problem is more likely to be hardware.

THE DIG COMMAND

The Domain Information Groper, dig, is a flexible command line tool that can be used to gather information from the Domain Name System servers. The dig tool can operate in simple interactive mode, where it satisfies a single query, and a batch mode, in which multiple requests are satisfied.

The dig tool requires a slightly modified version of the BIND resolver library to gather count and time statistics. Otherwise, it is a straightforward effort of parsing arguments and setting appropriate parameters. The output of dig can be rather convoluted, as shown here:

```
# dig gatekeeper.dec.com
; <<>> DiG 2.0 <<>> gatekeeper.dec.com
;; ->>HEADER<<- opcode: QUERY , status: NOERROR, id: 6
;; flags: qr rd ra ; Ques: 1, Ans: 1, Auth: 2, Addit: 2
;; QUESTIONS:
;;      gatekeeper.dec.com, type = A, class = IN

;; ANSWERS:
gatekeeper.dec.com.      150369   A        16.1.0.2

;; AUTHORITY RECORDS:
DEC.com.        166848   NS       GATEKEEPER.DEC.COM.
DEC.com.        166848   NS       CRL.DEC.COM.

;; ADDITIONAL RECORDS:
GATEKEEPER.DEC.COM.      150369   A        16.1.0.2
CRL.DEC.COM.    166848   A        192.58.206.2

;; Sent 1 pkts, answer found in time: 400 msec
;; FROM: oreo.widgets.ca to SERVER: default -- 192.139.234.50
;; WHEN: Mon Oct 10 15:07:41 1994
;; MSG SIZE  sent: 36  rcvd: 141

#
```

In the output shown here, the dig command searches the Domain Name Server records looking for gatekeeper.dec.com. A DNS record is found and reported to the user. Consequently, the dig command can be used to help resolve difficult name server problems.

USER COMMANDS

Just as there are a number of commands to assist the system administrator in the management of the system and network, there are a number of commands that are used by the users to get the information they want and to perform the tasks they need. While a user can execute some of the administration commands you have seen, the real work is done with commands you are about to examine: telnet, ftp, and the Berkeley r-commands.

THE BERKELEY R-COMMANDS

The first of the commands examined here fall into the set called the Berkeley r-commands. These are the rlogin, rcp, and rsh/rcmd commands. They are called the Berkeley r-commands because they all start with the letter r, and they originated from the University of California at Berkeley. The successful use of the command in this section is dependent upon user and host equivalency being properly configured. Most users have difficulty with these commands because their network administrators have not properly configured the host and user equivalency.

rlogin

The rlogin command connects your local session to a remote session on a different host. To initiate a remote terminal session, use the following command:

```
rlogin remote
```

This command starts a connection to the rlogind server on the remote host, as illustrated here:

```
$ rlogin gateway
Last    successful login for chare: Sun Oct 09 16:16:03 EDT 1994 on ttyp1
Last unsuccessful login for chare: Tue Sep 27 07:18:54 EDT 1994 on ttyp0
SCO UNIX System V/386 Release 3.2
Copyright (C) 1976-1989 UNIX System Laboratories, Inc.
Copyright (C) 1980-1989 Microsoft Corporation
Copyright (C) 1983-1992 The Santa Cruz Operation, Inc.
All Rights Reserved
gateway

Terminal type is dialup
$
```

The terminal type of the remote connection is the same as the terminal type that is in use for the current connections, unless modified by the user's shell startup files. All of the character echoing is done at the remote site, so except for delays, the use of the rlogin is transparent to the user. Termination of the connection is made either by logging out of the remote host, or through the termination character, which is ~. (tilde period).

rcp

The rcp, or remote copy, command enables the user to copy a file from one host to another. rcp copies files between two machines. Each file or directory argument is either a remote file name of the form "rhost:path", or a local file name (containing no ':' characters, or a '/' before any ':').

The syntax of the command is:

```
rcp [ -p ] file1 file2
    rcp [ -p ] [ -r ] file ... directory
```

The remote file must be specified using the syntax:

```
hostname:filename
```

The named file is copied to or from the remote system depending upon whether the source or destination file is remote. The following illustrates copying a file from the local host to the remote.

```
$ rcp test.new chelsea:test.new
$
```

When the file name, as illustrated in the preceding example, does not begin with a slash (/), the file is copied in a directory relative to your home directory on the remote system. The rcp command behaves like the cp command in that the file could be called by a different name on the remote system.

If the -r option is specified and any of the source files are directories, rcp copies each subtree rooted at that name; in this case, the destination must be a directory. By default, the mode and owner of file2 are preserved if the file already existed; otherwise, the mode of the source file modified by the umask on the destination host is used.

The -p option causes rcp to attempt to preserve (duplicate) in its copies the modification times and modes of the source files, ignoring the umask. The following illustrates using rcp with the -r option to copy a directory tree.

```
$ pwd
/u/chare
$ lc tmp
arp.ADMN      bootpd        dig.new       route.new
arp.new       bootpd.ADMN   rarpd.new     routed.new
$rcp -r chelsea:/tmp tmp
$ lf tmp
arp.ADMN      bootpd        dig.new       route.new     test.new
arp.new       bootpd.ADMN   rarpd.new     routed.new    tmp/
$
```

After executing the rcp command in the preceding example, a new directory is created called tmp in /u/chare/tmp. This directory contains the contents of the /tmp directory on host chelsea.

rsh, remsh, and rcmd

These three commands all perform a similar function, which is to execute a command on a remote system. Interactive commands are not good candidates for this type of execution.

The rsh implementation of remote execution is not to be confused with the restricted shell (rsh) that exists on System V Unix systems. Likewise, some System V Unixes use remsh instead of rsh also. Typically, the systems that use rsh for remote execution are BSD based Unix systems. rsh works by connecting to the specified host name and executing the specified command. rsh copies its standard input to the remote command, the standard output of the remote command to its standard output, and the standard error of the remote command to its standard error. Interrupt, quit, and terminate signals are propagated to the remote command; rsh normally terminates when the remote command does.

The command syntax of rsh is:

```
rsh [ -l username ] [ -n ] hostname [ command ]
rsh hostname [ -l username ] [ -n ] [ command ]
```

The execution of a command involves entering the name of the host where the command is to be executed and the name of the command. Running rsh with no command argument has the effect of logging you into the remote system by using rlogin. The following example illustrates using rsh to execute commands.

```
% rsh oreo date
Mon Oct 10 17:23:43 EDT 1994
% rsh oreo hostname
oreo.widgets.ca
%
```

There are only two options to rsh, as shown in table 1.13.

TABLE 1.13
rsh Command Line Options

Option	Description
-l username	Use username as the remote username instead of your local username. In the absence of this option, the remote username is the same as your local username.
-n	Redirect the input of rsh to /dev/null. You sometimes need this option to avoid unfortunate interactions between rsh and the shell that invokes it. If, for example, you are running rsh and start an rsh in the background without redirecting its input away from the terminal, it will block even if no reads are posted by the remote command. The -n option prevents this.

Virtually any command on the remote system can be executed. Commands that rely upon terminal characteristics or a level of user interaction, however, are not good candidates for the use of rsh.

The rcmd command is virtually identical to the rsh except that it typically is found on System V systems. Actually, the rcmd has the same options and operates the same fashion as the rsh command under BSD Unix . The following illustrates rcmd accessing a remote system by not specifying a command when starting rcmd.

```
$ rcmd chelsea
Last login: Mon Oct 10 17:18:10 from oreo.widgets.ca
SunOS Release 4.1 (GENERIC) #1: Wed Mar 7 10:59:35 PST 1990
%
```

The use of rsh/rcmd can be of value when you want to run a command on the remote system without having to log into that system. Some system administrators use it to see what processes are running on a remote system, as shown here:

```
$ rcmd gateway ps -ef ¦ more
    UID   PID  PPID  C    STIME  TTY       TIME COMMAND
   root     0     0  0   Sep 22  ?         0:00 sched
   root     1     0  0   Sep 22  ?        23:36 /etc/init -a
   root     2     0  0   Sep 22  ?         0:00 vhand
   root   221     1  0   Sep 22  ?         0:00 strerr
   root   150     1  0   Sep 22  ?         7:51 /etc/cron
   root   212     1  0   Sep 22  ?         0:35 cpd
   root   156     1  0   Sep 22  ?         3:21 /usr/lib/lpsched
   root   214     1  0   Sep 22  ?         0:00 slink
   root   317   315  0   Sep 22  ?         0:00 nfsd 4
   root   256     1  0   Sep 22  ?         0:00 /usr/lib/lpd start
 topgun  5740     1  0 10:30:51  2A        0:19/etc/pppd98.73.137.101log /u
sr/lib/ppp/ppp-users/topgun/log debug 2 nolqm
   root   306     1  0   Sep 22  ?         0:00 pcnfsd
   root 17008   234  0   Sep 29  ?         0:07 telnetd
   root 17009 17008  0   Sep 29  p0        0:02 -sh
   root   286     1  0   Sep 22  ?         0:05 snmpd
$
```

TERMINAL EMULATION USING TELNET

The rlogin command allows for a connection from one system to another. rlogin, however, requires the user to have an account on the remote machine and host equivalency to have been configured. telnet, on the other hand, does not need either of those things.

The telnet command uses the TELNET protocol to establish a connection from the client to a telnetd server on the remote system. Unlike rlogin, telnet has a host mode where it is connected to the remote system, and command mode where the user can enter commands and interact with the TELNET protocol to change how the connection is handled.

To create a telnet connection, the user enters the telnet command, with or without a host name. When telnet is started with a host name, a connection to the remote host is established. After the connection is established, the user must then provide a login name and password to access the remote system. This is illustrated in the following:

49

```
$ telnet chelsea
Trying 198.73.138.6...
Connected to chelsea.widgets.ca.
Escape character is '^]'.


SunOS Unix(chelsea.widgets.ca)

login: chare
Password:
Last login: Mon Oct 10 17:33:35 from oreo.widgets.ca
SunOS Release 4.1 (GENERIC) #1: Wed Mar 7 10:59:35 PST 1990
%
```

Command mode is entered either by starting telnet with no arguments, or by entering Control+], which is the telnet 'escape' key. This control key instructs telnet to enter command mode, as shown here:

```
chelsea.widgets.ca%
telnet> ?
Commands may be abbreviated. Commands are:

close           close current connection
logout          forcibly logout remote user and close the connection
display         display operating parameters
mode            try to enter line or character mode ('mode ?' for more)
open            connect to a site
quit            exit telnet
send            transmit special characters ('send ?' for more)
set             set operating parameters ('set ?' for more)
unset           unset operating parameters ('unset ?' for more)
status          print status information
toggle          toggle operating parameters ('toggle ?' for more)
slc             change state of special characters ('slc ?' for more)
z               suspend telnet
!               invoke a subshell
environ         change environment variables ('environ ?' for more)
?               print help information
telnet>
```

In the preceding example, the switch to command mode is performed and is indicated by the telnet> prompt. Once in command mode, there are a number of commands that can be used to alter or reconfigure the current session. The actual number of commands available in command mode is far too numerous to be discussed here.

telnet, however, has another useful feature. It is to allow the connection to a specific TCP port on a system, which may or may not be remote. The following example illustrates a connection to the SMTP port, port 25, on the local system.

```
$ telnet localhost 25
Trying 127.0.0.1...
Connected to localhost.widgets.ca.
Escape character is '^]'.
220 oreo.widgets.ca Server SMTP (Complaints/bugs to:  postmaster)
helo
250 oreo.widgets.ca - you are a charlatan
help
214-The following commands are accepted:
214-helo noop mail data rcpt help quit rset expn vrfy
214-
214 Send complaints/bugs to:  postmaster
quit
221 oreo.widgets.ca says goodbye to localhost.0.0.127.in-addr.arpa at Mon Oct
10
20:35:24.
Connection closed by foreign host.
$
```

While this is a useful feature to have when debugging connection problems, it also enables a user to forge e-mail by giving it directly to the SMTP or sendmail daemon. Actually, most TCP/IP daemons can be connected to by using telnet with the port number, which might allow for other security mechanisms to be breached, particularly with sendmail.

FILE TRANSFERS WITH FTP

FTP is the ARPANET File Transfer Program that uses the File Transfer Protocol to allow for the verified transfer of a file from one PC to another. To reduce the chance of confusion, ftp usually refers to the program, while FTP refers to the protocol that is used to transfer the files.

The client host that ftp is to communicate with is normally provided on the command line. If so, ftp will immediately try to connect with the ftp server on that system. If a connection is established, then the user must log in to access the system. Logging in can be achieved either by having a valid account on the system, or through accessing a server that allows anonymous ftp access. Accessing an ftp server through anonymous mode is illustrated in the following:

```
$ ftp ftp.widgets.ca
Connected to chelsea.widgets.ca.
220 chelsea.widgets.ca FTP server (SunOS 4.1) ready.
Name (ftp.widgets.ca:chare): anonymous
331 Guest login ok, send ident as password.
Password:
230 Guest login ok, access restrictions apply.
ftp> quit
221 Goodbye.
$
```

51

When configuring a server for anonymous ftp access, be sure to create the file /etc/ftpusers. This file contains a list of user names, one per line, who are not allowed to access the ftp server. On any ftp server that supports anonymous ftp, access to the server as the root user should not be permitted.

By not restricting access through certain accounts, anyone, once one machine is compromised, can gain access to the anonymous ftp server and complete the transaction shown the following example:

```
$ ftp ftp.widgets.ca
Connected to chelsea.widgets.ca.
220 chelsea.widgets.ca FTP server (SunOS 4.1) ready.
Name (ftp.widgets.ca:chare): root
331 Password required for root.
Password:
230 User root logged in.
ftp> cd /etc
250 CWD command successful.
ftp> lcd /tmp
Local directory now /tmp
ftp> get passwd passwd.ccca
local: passwd.ccca remote: passwd
200 PORT command successful.
150 ASCII data connection for passwd (198.73.138.2,1138) (736 bytes).
226 ASCII Transfer complete.
753 bytes received in 0.01 seconds (74 Kbytes/s)
ftp> quit
221 Goodbye.
$
```

The user who made this connection now has your password file. This type of connection can be prevented by creating the /etc/ftpusers file, as shown in the following:

```
# cd /etc
# s -l ftpusers
-rw-r--r--  1 root         10 Oct 10 20:53 ftpusers
# cat ftpusers
root
uucp
#
```

Now when a user tries to access the system by using the root account, he does not get the chance to enter a root password because ftp informs him that root access through ftp is not allowed, as shown in the following:

```
$ ftp ftp.widgets.ca
Connected to chelsea.widgets.ca.
220 chelsea.widgets.ca FTP server (SunOS 4.1) ready.
Name (ftp.widgets.ca:chare): root
```

```
530 User root access denied.
Login failed.
ftp> quit
221 Goodbye.
$
```

Another problem with ftp is the .netrc file that enables users to automate a file transfer. The reason this file is a problem is because users can insert login and password information in the file. The ftp client aborts the use of the file if it finds that it is readable by anyone other than the owner, but even that is not enough as the file can still leave security holes wide open.

The .netrc file resides in the user's home directory and can contain information for accessing more than one system. Consider the sample .netrc file shown here:

```
$ cat .netrc
machine yosemite.widgets.ca login chare password yippee
default login anonymous password chare@widgets.ca
```

The file format of the .netrc file is to include the information for each machine on a single line. The first entry of this file, for example, shows the connection to a machine called yosemite.widgets.ca. When this machine name is provided as an argument to ftp, the .netrc file is checked, and the login information here is used to access the system. The second entry is used as the default. If the system is not found explicitly, then use the anonymous entry to allow for anonymous access to the ftp site.

As mentioned, the ftp command does perform a security check on the .netrc. If the file is readable by anyone other than the owner, the connection is not established. This is illustrated in the following:

```
$ ftp yosemite.widgets.ca
Connected to yosemite.widgets.ca.
220 yosemite.widgets.ca FTP server (Version 5.60 #1) ready.
Error - .netrc file not correct mode.
Remove password or correct mode.
Remote system type is Unix.
Using binary mode to transfer files.
ftp> quit
221 Goodbye.
$ ls -l .netrc
-rw-r--r--   1 chare     group          103 Oct 10 21:16 .netrc
$
```

In the preceding example, the connection to yosemite is not made because the permissions on the .netrc file are incorrect. After the permissions are changed, the connection can be established without incident, as shown in the following:

```
$ ls -l .netrc
-rw-r--r--   1 chare     group          103 Oct 10 21:16 .netrc
$ chmod 600 .netrc
$ ls -l .netrc
-rw-------   1 chare     group          103 Oct 10 21:16 .netrc
```

53

```
149$ ftp gateway.widgets.ca
Connected to gateway.widgets.ca.
220 gateway.widgets.ca FTP server (Version 5.60 #1) ready.
331 Password required for chare.
230 User chare logged in.
Remote system type is Unix.
Using binary mode to transfer files.
ftp>
```

NOTE

It's a good idea to teach users who want to use the .netrc file about security. By improperly setting the permissions on the file, users can prevent themselves from accessing the remote machine using the auto-login features, but can still allow someone else access by giving that person their login name and password.

SUMMARY

This chapter has introduced TCP/IP, addressing, the TCP/IP daemons, and user level commands. It has examined some of the commands that are available to both the user and the system administrator, and outlined how TCP/IP can be used to access and manipulate information.

Like anything else, the ability to utilize information presented here comes from experimenting and examining your own system. Keep in mind that most System V systems use STREAMS as their transport layer, while BSD systems use SOCKETS. TCP/IP provides a wide array of protocols and services to allow users to transport data from one place to another.

## CHAPTER 2

SECURITY

Unless the computer you are trying to protect is in a locked room where access is controlled and no connections to this computer from outside the room exist, then your computer is at risk. Break-ins and security violations occur almost daily around the world. These violators are not just Internet vandals, they include the employee down the hall who steals computer time or services for his own personal or malicious use.

This chapter examines computer security in some detail. You learn what computer security is, how you can protect yourself, and what is available to help you perform these security tasks.

EXAMINING SECURITY LEVELS

According to the computer security standards developed by the United States Department of Defense, the Trusted Computer Standards Evaluation Criteria—the Orange Book, several levels of security are used to protect the hardware, software, and stored information from attack. These levels all describe different types of physical security, user authentication, trustedness of the operating system software, and user applications. These standards also impose limits on what types of other systems can be connected to your system.

LEVEL D1

Level D1 is the lowest form of security available. This standard states that the entire system is untrusted. No protection is available for the hardware; the operating system is easily compromised; and there is no authentication regarding users and their rights to access information stored on the computer. This level of security typically refers to operating systems like MS-DOS, MS-Windows, and the Apple Macintosh System 7.*x*.

These operating systems do not distinguish between users and have no defined method of determining who is typing at the keyboard. These operating systems also do not have any controls regarding what information can be accessed on the hard drives in the computer.

LEVEL C1

Level C has two sublevels of security—C1 and C2. *Level C1*, or the *Discretionary Security Protection system*, describes the security available on a typical Unix system. Some level of protection exists for the hardware because it cannot be as easily compromised, although it is still possible. Users must identify themselves to the system through a user login name and password. This combination is used to determine what access rights to programs and information each user has.

These access rights are the file and directory permissions. These *Discretionary Access Controls* enable the owner of the file or directory, or the system administrator, to prevent certain people, or groups of people, from accessing those programs or information. However, the system administration account is not prevented from performing any activity. Consequently, an unscrupulous system administrator can easily compromise the security of the system without anyone's knowledge.

In addition, many of the day-to-day system administration tasks only can be performed by the user login known as *root*. With the decentralization of computer systems today, it is not uncommon to enter an organization and find more than two or three people who know the root password. This itself is a problem because no way exists to distinguish between the changes Doug or Mary made to the system yesterday.

LEVEL C2

The second sub-level, *C2*, was meant to help address these issues. Along with the features of C1, level C2 includes additional security features that create a controlled-access environment. This environment has the capability to further restrict users from executing certain commands or accessing certain files based not only upon the permissions, but upon authorization levels. In addition, this level of security requires that the system be audited. This involves writing an audit record for each event that occurs on the system.

Auditing is used to keep records of all security-related events, such as those activities performed by the system administrator. Auditing requires additional authentication because without it, how can you be sure that the person who executes the command really is that person. The disadvantage to auditing is that it requires additional processor and disk subsystem resources.

With the use of additional authorizations, it is possible for users on a C2 system to have the authority to perform system management tasks without having the root password. This enables improved tracking of system administration-related tasks because the individual user performs the work and not the system administrator.

These additional authorizations are not to be confused with the SGID and SUID permissions that can be applied to a program. Rather, they are specific authorizations that allow a user to execute specific commands or access certain kernel tables. Users who do not have the proper authority to view the process table, for example, see only their processes when they execute the ps command.

LEVEL B1

B-level security contains three levels. The *B1 level*, or *Labeled Security Protection*, is the first level that supports multilevel security, such as secret and top secret. This level states that an object under mandatory access control cannot have its permissions changed by the owner of the file.

LEVEL B2

The *B2 level*, known as *Structured Protection*, requires that every object be labeled. Devices such as disks, tapes, or terminals might have a single or multiple level of security assigned to them. This is the first level that starts to address the problem of an object at a higher level of security communicating with another object at a lower level of security.

LEVEL B3

The *B3*, or *Security Domains level*, enforces the domain with the installation of hardware. For example, memory management hardware is used to protect the security domain from unauthorized access or modification from objects in different security domains. This level also requires that the user's terminal be connected to the system through a trusted path.

LEVEL A

Level A, or the *Verified Design level*, is currently the highest level of security validated through the Orange Book. It includes a stringent design, control, and verification process. For this level of security to be achieved, all the components of the lower levels must be included; the design must be mathematically verified; and an analysis of covert channels and trusted distribution must be performed. *Trusted distribution* means that the hardware and software have been protected during shipment to prevent tampering with the security systems.

EXAMINING LOCAL SECURITY ISSUES

Aside from the security products or regulations developed outside your organization, you must work to resolve security issues that may be local or restricted to your organization or to a subgroup within your organization. These local security issues include security policies and password controls.

SECURITY POLICIES

Two very major stances can be adopted when developing the policies that reflect security at your site. These major statements form the basis of all other security-related policies and regulate the procedures put into place to implement them.

That which is not expressly permitted is prohibited, is the first approach to security. This means that your organization provides a distinct and documented set of services, and anything else is prohibited. For example, if you decide to allow anonymous FTP transfers to and from a particular machine, but deny telnet services, then documenting support for FTP and not telnet illustrates this approach.

The alternative train of thought is *That which is not expressly prohibited is permitted.* This means that unless you expressly indicate that a service is not available, then all services are available. For example, if you do not expressly say that telnet sessions to a given host are prohibited, then they must be permitted. (You can still prevent the service, however, by not allowing a connection to the TCP/IP port.)

Regardless of which train of thought you follow, the reason behind defining a security policy is to determine what action should be taken in the event that the security of an organization is compromised. The policy is also intended to describe what actions will be tolerated and what will not.

THE PASSWORD FILE

The first line of defense against unauthorized access to the system is the /etc/password file. Unfortunately, it is also often the weakest link! The password file consists of lines or records in which each line is split into seven fields with a colon, as illustrated in the following example:

```
chare:u7mHuh5R4UmVo:105:100:Chris Hare:/u/chare:/bin/ksh
username:encrypted password:UID:GID:comment:home directory:login shell
```

Table 2.1 explains the contents and typical values for each file.

TABLE 2.1
The /etc/passwd File

Field Name	Description	Typical Values
username	This field identifies the user to the system. It is primarily for human benefit. They must be unique on a given machine and, ideally, unique within an organization.	chare rceh brb markd

continues

TABLE 2.1, CONTINUED
The /etc/passwd File

Field Name	Description	Typical Values
encrypted password	This field contains, or can contain, the encrypted password. How the passwords are encrypted is explained later in this chapter.	u7mHuh5R4UmVo x * NOLOGIN
UID	This is the numerical representation of the user on the system.	0–60,000
GID	This is the numerical representation of the login group to which the user belongs.	0–60,000
comment	This contains information regarding the user. It often lists a user's full name, phone number, or other information.	Chris Hare Ops Manager, x273
home directory	This is the directory where the user is placed upon login.	/u/chare /usr/lib/ppp/ppp-users
login shell	This is the login shell that is started for users to enable them to interact with the system. Remember, not all login shells are interactive.	/bin/sh /bin/csh /bin/ksh /bin/tcsh /usr/lib/uucp/uucico /usr/lib/ppp/ppd/

Table 2.1 provides some additional information worth mentioning. It is not necessary that the actual encrypted password be placed in the encrypted password field. This field can contain other values. For example, to prevent someone from logging in using a specific account, that password can be changed to a non-matchable value, such as NOLOGIN. This field, however, typically contains an x or an asterisk (*), indicating that the password is stored elsewhere.

In these situations, the password is stored either in the Trusted Computing Base (TCB), which is explained later in this chapter, or in the shadow password file.

The permissions on the password file are read only, which means that no one can edit the file. Similarly, the shadow password file and the files in the TCB are generally also read only.

The password information in these files are updated by the password command. The permissions on the password command include the SUID (Set User ID) bit, which makes the user executing the program look like the owner of the program, or in this case, root. Because of the application of the SUID bit, the user can change the password even though he does not have the authority to edit the file.

THE SHADOW PASSWORD FILE

The versions of Unix that do not include the advanced security options from SecureWare can support the shadow password file. When you see the character x in the password field, then the user's actual password is stored in the shadow password file, /etc/shadow. Unlike the /etc/passwd file, the shadow password file must be readable only by root, as illustrated in the following example:

```
# ls -l /etc/shadow
-r--------  1 root      auth          861 Oct 24 11:46 /etc/shadow
#
```

The format of the /etc/shadow file is identical to the /etc/passwd file in that it also has seven colon-delimited fields. However, the /etc/shadow file only contains the user name, encrypted password, and password aging information, as illustrated in the following example:

```
# cat /etc/shadow
root:DYQC9rXCioAuo:8887:0:0::
daemon:*::0:0::
mmdf:MZ74AeYMs4sn6:8842:0:0::
ftp:b80lug/92lMeY:8363::::
anyone::8418::::
chare:7xqmj9fj3bVw2:9009::::
pppdemo:4QYrWsJEHc8IA:9062::::
#
```

The /etc/shadow file is created by the command pwconv on both systems that support it. Only the superuser can create the shadow password file. On SCO systems, the information in the /etc/passwd and the protected password database are used to create the shadow password files. On SVR4 systems, the information from /etc/passwd is used.

The primary advantage to using the shadow password file is that it puts the encrypted passwords in a file not accessible by normal users, thereby decreasing the chances that a vandal will be able to steal the encrypted password information.

61

THE DIALUP PASSWORD FILE

The capability to install additional passwords on serial port lines is unfortunately not present in all versions of Unix. They have become most prominently found on SCO-based systems. The dialup password protection for these serial lines is controlled through two files: /etc/dialups and /etc/d_passwd. The /etc/dialups file contains of a list of the serial ports protected by a dialup password. The file is illustrated in the following example:

```
# cat dialups
/dev/tty2A
#
```

The file /etc/d_passwd is used to identify the login shell that a given password is for. Unlike the regular password that uses the user's login name, the dialup password is tied to the login shell that a given user is using. This means that every user who uses the Bourne shell has the same dialup password. The following example illustrates the typical dialup password.

```
# cat /etc/d_passwd
/bin/sh::
/usr/lib/uucp/uucico::
#
```

Each line or record in the file consists of two colon-delimited fields. The first field identifies the shell that the given password is for, and the second field lists the password. In the preceding example, neither shell has a password. This means that the user will not be prompted for a password when he logs in.

The dialup password is added through the use of the -m option on the passwd command. This option informs passwd that the password being collected is for a specific shell in the dialup passwords file. The syntax for this form of the command is as follows:

```
passwd -m shell_name
```

The execution of this command is illustrated in the following example:

```
# passwd -m /bin/s:
Setting modem password for login shell: /bin/sh
Please enter new password:
Modem password: testing
Re-enter password: testing
#
```

In the preceding example, the system administrator is adding a dialup password to the /bin/sh shell. This means that any users who log in to the system and have the Bourne shell as their login shell will be prompted for the dialup password. The password they must enter is shown in the preceding example as the system administrator would have typed it. Like the normal passwd command, the actual password is not displayed as it is typed. It is shown here only for illustration purposes. Note that only the system administrator can change the dialup password for a shell.

The passwd command modifies the contents of the d_passwd file to include the new password, as illustrated in the following example:

```
# cat d_passwd
/bin/sh:ORa691.Na1jjQ:
/usr/lib/uucp/uucico::
#
```

As shown in the preceding example, the Bourne shell users now have to provide the additional password when logging in on the terminal ports specified in the file /etc/dialups.

The following example illustrates the process that a user now experiences when he logs in with the dialup password.

```
gateway
gateway!login: chare
Password:
Dialup Password:
Last    successful login for chare: Fri Oct 28 22:52:02 EDT 1994 on tty2a
Last unsuccessful login for chare: Tue Oct 18 16:27:56 EDT 1994 on ttyp1
SCO Unix System V/386 Release 3.2
Copyright (C) 1976-1989 UNIX System Laboratories, Inc.
Copyright (C) 1980-1989 Microsoft Corporation
Copyright (C) 1983-1992 The Santa Cruz Operation, Inc.
All Rights Reserved
gateway
TERM = (ansi)
#
```

As illustrated, the user goes through the normal login procedure until he enters the user name and password. After these are validated, the dialup password control file, /etc/dialups, is checked. When the terminal on which the user is connecting is located in the file and the login shell is the Bourne shell, the user is prompted to enter the dialup password. If the dialup password is entered correctly, the user is granted access to the system, as illustrated in the preceding example. If the dialup password is incorrect, however, the login is aborted, and the user is forced to start over again. This is illustrated in the following example:

```
gateway
gateway!login: chare
Password:
Dialup Password:
Login incorrect
Wait for login retry: .
login: chare
```

```
Password:
Dialup Password:
Last    successful login for chare: Fri Oct 28 23:28:28 EDT 1994 on tty2a
    1 unsuccessful login for chare: Fri Oct 28 23:30:55 EDT 1994 on tty2a
SCO Unix System V/386 Release 3.2
Copyright (C) 1976-1989 UNIX System Laboratories, Inc.
Copyright (C) 1980-1989 Microsoft Corporation
Copyright (C) 1983-1992 The Santa Cruz Operation, Inc.
All Rights Reserved
gateway
TERM = (ansi)
$
```

THE GROUP FILE

The /etc/group file is used to control access to files not owned by the user. Recall how permissions work: If the user is not the owner of the file, then the group(s) to which the user belongs are checked to see if the user is a member of the group that owns the file. The group membership list is stored in /etc/group. The format of the file is shown in the following:

```
tech:*:103:andrewg,patc,chare,erict,lorrainel,lens
group name:password:GID:userlist
```

Table 2.2 explains each of the fields contained in the /etc/group file.

TABLE 2.2
The /etc/group File

Field Name	Description	Examples
group name	This is the name of the group. This name is primarily used for human purposes.	tech sales group
password	This is the password to use when switching to this group.	*
GID	This is the numerical group ID number stamped on all files.	0–30,000
userlist	This is a comma-separated list of users that are members of the group.	chare, andrewg

The password for the group file is not used, and no easy mechanisms are available to install a password in the file. If a user attempts to switch to a group that they are not a member of, then they are greeted by a prompt to enter a password, as illustrated in the following example:

```
$ newgrp tech
newgrp: Password
newgrp: Sorry
$ grep tech /etc/group
tech:*:103:andrewg,patc
$
```

If the user who executed this command had been a member of the group tech, then the newgrp command would have been successful. Many current versions of Unix, however, enable a user to be a member of more than one group at a time, thereby reducing or eliminating the need for the newgrp command.

It is important to consider that Berkeley Unix further protects the root account with the wheel group. Only the users who are also members of the wheel group can use the su command to become root.

WARNING

Be cautious of the users who are added to this group. As in some implementations of Unix, the members of the wheel group can provide their own password to achieve root, rather that the real root password.

PASSWORD AGING AND CONTROL

Many versions of Unix provide for *password aging*. This mechanism controls when users can change their passwords by inserting a value into the password file after the encrypted password. This value defines the minimum period of time that must pass before users can change their passwords, and the maximum period of time that can elapse before the password expires.

This explanation becomes clearer by thinking of a timeline, as shown in figure 2.1.

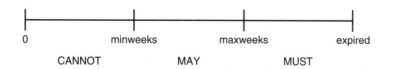

FIGURE 2.1

Password aging and lifetime.

The password aging control information is stored along with the encrypted password, as a series of printable characters. The controls are included after the password, preceded by a comma. Typically a number of characters after the comma represents the following information:

❖ The maximum number of weeks the password is valid

❖ The minimum number of weeks that must elapse before the user can change his or her password again

❖ When the password was most recently changed

The password aging values are defined in table 2.3.

TABLE 2.3
Password Aging Values

Character	Value in Weeks	Character	Value in Weeks
.	0	/	1
0	2	1	3
2	4	3	5
4	6	5	7
6	8	7	9
8	10	9	11
A	12	B	13
C	14	D	15
E	16	F	17
G	18	H	19
I	20	J	21
K	22	L	23
M	24	N	25
O	26	P	27
Q	28	R	29

Character	Value in Weeks	Character	Value in Weeks
S	30	T	31
U	32	V	33
W	34	X	35
Y	36	Z	37
a	38	b	39
c	40	d	41
e	42	f	43
g	44	h	45
i	46	j	47
k	48	l	49
m	50	n	51
o	52	p	53
q	54	r	55
s	56	t	57
u	58	v	59
w	60	x	61
y	62	z	63

Using this information and looking at a password that has password aging in place, you can decipher the meaning of the following example:

```
chare:2eLNss48eJ/GY,C2:215:100:Chris Hare:/usr1/chare:/bin/sh
```

In the preceding example, the password has been set to age using the value of "C" to define the maximum number of weeks before the password expires, and "2" to define the minimum number of weeks that must pass before the user can change the password again.

Two special conditions are recognized by the aging control mechanisms: One forces a user to change his password on the next login, and one prevents a user from being able to change it.

To force a user to change his password, such as for a new user, the password field for that user would be modified to include a comma, followed by two periods for the maximum and minimum time periods. In this case, the user is forced to change his password on the next login. Once changed, the "force" control information is removed from the password entry. An example of the forced entry in the password is shown in the following:

```
chare:2eLNss48eJ/GY,./:215:100:Chris Hare:/usr1/chare:/bin/sh
```

The second special case prohibits a user from being able to change his password. This condition is established by setting the maximum value to be less than the minimum value (that is, first < second). In this case, the user is informed that his password cannot be changed and is illustrated in the following example:

```
chare:,..:215:100:Chris Hare:/usr1/chare:/bin/sh
```

With newer, more secure versions of Unix currently on the market, you may hear the term *password lifetime.* This is a grace period after the maximum time period in which the user can still log in to his account using the expired password. When the lifetime has been reached, the account is disabled. When the user attempts to log in to a system using a disabled account, he is informed that the account has been disabled and to see the system administrator.

The password aging mechanism doesn't prevent a user from changing his password and then changing it back to the old one later. Only a few Unix system versions keep track of what passwords a user has used. The actual process of implementing password aging is version-dependent. To implement it on your system, consult your system documentation.

The program in Listing 2.1, pwexp.pl, is a PERL language program that advises users when their passwords are going to expire so that they can be prepared for the day when the system informs them that their passwords have expired. Note, however, that this version of the program is for standard System V Unix in which a shadow password file is not used.

PERL (Practical Extraction and Report Language) is a freely available and widely used programming language. It combines elements of many of the Unix commands into one neat package. Some of the features include pattern matching, arrays, conditional programming, and subroutines. PERL can be obtained from many anonymous FTP sites including uunet.uu.net and netlabs.com.

This program addresses the aging mechanism implemented in versions of Unix up to System V Release 3.2. At this level, some variations took place in the interest of increasing system security. The AT&T/USL versions moved to using the /etc/shadow file for storing the password information, whereas the SCO implementations moved to using the Trusted Computing Base facilities from SecureWare. In SCO's Unix 3.2v4 product, the aging control information may be in one of /etc/passwd, /etc/shadow, or the Trusted Computing Base files, depending upon which level of security you configure. It also is important to note in SCO, that both the Protected Password Database and the /etc/shadow database might be in use simultaneously.

VANDALS AND PASSWORDS

The term *hacker* did not always have such a negative connotation. Rather, it was a term denoting someone who was persistent, who tried to break things and figure out how they worked. As a result of this reputation, and because most of the people doing hacking were computer science wizards, the term hacker developed a negative connotation. However, for the purpose of this discussion, and because I know "good" hackers, the bad guys are referred to as *vandals*.

A vandal wants to get access to your system for one reason or another. Some of those reasons can include the following:

- ✦ Just for the fun of it

- ✦ To look around

- ✦ To steal computer resources like CPU time

- ✦ To steal trade secrets or other proprietary information

Note that not every attempt to access your system is intended to do harm. However, in most cases they should be treated that way. Regardless of the reasons behind the attack, the piece of information most wanted by a vandal is the /etc/passwd file. When the vandal has a list of valid user account names, it is trivial to create a program to simply guess passwords. However, many modern login programs include a time delay between login prompts that gets longer with each unsuccessful attempt. They also might include program code to disable the access port should too many unsuccessful attempts be recorded.

The primary source of protection is to use /etc/shadow or the Protected Password Database because these files and directories require root access to view them. This makes it harder for the vandal to obtain encrypted password information. However, recall that the password information in /etc/passwd is encrypted. How can the vandal even hope to gain access when he cannot decrypt the passwords as they are stored?

UNDERSTANDING HOW VANDALS BREAK PASSWORDS

It is correct to say that after the password is encrypted it cannot be decrypted. But this doesn't mean that the password is still safe. A password *cracker* is a program used by a vandal that attempts to "guess" the passwords in the /etc/passwd file by comparing them to words in a dictionary. The success of the cracker program is dependent upon the CPU resources, the quality of the dictionary, and the fact that the user has a copy of /etc/passwd.

Password crackers are fairly easy to write. A simple, although less-effective one, can be written in approximately 60 lines of C code or 40 lines of PERL code. That's it. In attempting to provide for better passwords on your system, a system administrator may well give consideration to writing one. Be warned, however, that you might be inviting disaster. If the program is efficient enough, or detects some deficiencies in the passwords on your system, you may have further defeated the security of your machine! An efficient cracker program may be stolen and subsequently used to gain access to other machines. Other ways to better protect the system are available using the logical security tools.

Furthermore, because of the possibility that your cracking program could be stolen, other legal issues could be involved should damage be a direct result of the use of the program. This issue is not to be taken lightly; it is a serious example of how successful these types of programs can be.

For example, a system administrator once had the unfortunate circumstance of not knowing the root password of a machine and no distribution media to reinstall. In this case, he was a friendly vandal in that he owned the machine. He retrieved the /etc/passwd file through anonymous UUCP (Unix to Unix Copy). (So much for security.) After he had the file, he sent it to a contact who tried his password cracking program on it. With no success, he sent it to another machine where a supercomputer chewed on the file for about 18 hours before finally cracking the root password. The ironic part about it was that the password was the name of the company he was working for at the time! Sometimes the simple practice is so effective.

Over the last few years, several password cracking, or guessing, programs have been posted to the Internet. This does not mean that you should run out to get one. In fact, it may the one program you do not want to have on your system. The authors of these programs clearly state in their documentation that they assume no responsibility for the use of these programs, yet they claim that the programs are highly efficient.

The moral of the story is to treat programs that try to guess passwords as dangerous and not worth the potential problems that they could be used to overcome.

C2 SECURITY AND THE TRUSTED COMPUTING BASE

The *Trusted Computing Base* (TCB) is part of the security system for C2-rated Unix systems. It adds a significant level of complexity to the operation of the system and to the administration of it. This system works by moving bits of the /etc/passwd file to other places, as well as adding additional information into the original information. The files that make up the databases for the trusted computing base are scattered in several different directory hierarchies. It is not a good idea to edit these files, however, because serious damage can result to your system.

On a system that uses the TCB, an asterisk is placed in the password field of /etc/passwd. This is because the actual user password is stored along with other user information in the Trusted Computing Base. Using the TCB doesn't change the operation of the system so much as how Unix provides the same services using TCB. On some versions of Unix, such as SCO Unix, even if you are not using C2 security, the Trusted Computing Base is still being used to provide the security services.

Table 2.4 shows the six components to the Trusted Computing Base.

TABLE 2.4
The Trusted Computing Base

Component	Description
/etc/passwd	The System Password File
/tcb/auth/files/	The Protected Password Database
/etc/auth/systems/ttys	The Terminal Control Database
/etc/auth/systems/files	The File Control Database
/etc/auth/subsystems/	The Protected Subsystem Database
/etc/auth/system/default	The System Defaults Database

When reference is made to the Trusted Computing Base, it points to all the components of table 2.4 collectively and not any single component.

The operation of a trusted system brings with it some concepts that must be understood to prevent putting the system in jeopardy.

The trusted computing base is comprised of a collection of software including the Unix kernel and the utilities that maintain the trusted computing base. These utilities include authck for verifying and correcting problems in the password database and integrity for verifying the accuracy of the system files. The trusted computing base implements the security policy on the system. This policy is a set of operating rules that governs the interaction between *subjects* such as processes, and *objects* such as files, devices, and interprocess communication objects.

Accountability for an action is defined only if the action can be traced back to a single person. On traditional Unix systems in which more than one person knows the root password, it is difficult, if not impossible, for the action to be traced to any single person. The pseudo-accounts like cron and lp run anonymously—their action can only be traced after the change of system information. This is corrected on a trusted Unix system because each account is associated with a real user, each action is audited, and every action is associated to a specific user.

Little *Identification and Authentication (I&A)* is performed on the traditional Unix system. On traditional Unix, the user logs in by providing a login name and password combination, which is validated by a search in the /etc/passwd file. If the login name and password are correct, then the user is allowed access to the system. In a trusted system, some additional rules are used to improve upon the standard I&A techniques. For example, new procedures for changing and generating passwords have been established, providing better protection for parts of the password database to prevent prying eyes from accessing it.

The following example illustrates a typical user entry in the trusted computing base on an SCO system that details the information for a specific user. This information should never be hand-edited because doing so could leave your system in a state of uselessness.

```
chare:u_name=chare:\         # Actual user name
    :u_id#1003:\             # User ID
    :u_pwd=MWUNe/9lrPqck:\   # Encrypted password
    :u_type=general:\        # User Type
    :u_succhg#746505937:\    # Last Successful Password Change
    :u_unsucchg#746506114:\  # Last Unsuccessful Password Change
    :u_pswduser=chare:\      #
    :u_suclog#747066756:\    # Last successful Login
    :u_suctty=tty02:\        # Last successful login on tty
    :u_unsuclog#747150039:\  # Last unsuccessful login
    :u_unsuctty=tty04:\      # Last unsuccessful login on tty
    :u_numunsuclog#1:\       # Number of unsuccessful logins
    :u_lock@:\               # Lock Status
    :chkent:                 #
```

The preceding example has been modified to insert the comments on the entry. The "# text" does NOT appear in the file. This example is included here to illustrate that in the TCB other information is, in fact, being tracked. This is not all of the information, but that which is contained in one file. For each user, a file named with the user name is stored and contains the information shown in the preceding example.

In the preceding illustration, the entry for u_succhg shows a value of 746505937. This is how Unix keeps track of time. The value is the number of seconds since January 1, 1970. The value can be given to a function in the Unix kernel that can convert it to the actual date and time.

Traditional Unix systems keep a limited amount of information regarding system activity, and in some cases, only when they have been configured to do so. In trusted Unix, *auditing* is a major element to ensure that the actions taken are associated with a specific user. The audit system writes a series of records for each action to generate an audit trail of the events that have occurred on a system. This trail consists of every action between a subject and an object that is either successful or unsuccessful in regards to object access, changes made to subject or object, and system characteristics. Consequently, the audit system provides the audit administrator with an extensive history of system actions. This helps the administrator determine what happened, who did it, and when it occurred.

UNDERSTANDING NETWORK EQUIVALENCY

The two primary types of network equivalency are trusted host access and trusted user access. Throughout this discussion, keep in mind that many network administrators prefer to use these facilities to deliver services throughout their organizations without understanding how they operate and what impact these facilities have on host and network security.

HOST EQUIVALENCY

Host equivalency, or *trusted access*, enables the users of a system to access their accounts on remote systems without having to use their login names and passwords. Through the use of the /etc/hosts.equiv file, the system administrator can list all the trusted systems. If no user names are identified for the machine entry, then all the users are trusted. Similarly, if the system administrator does not specify a particular machine for all users, each individual user can use the .rhosts file in their home directory to list machines to which they want trusted access.

Each entry in the hosts.equiv file is trusted. This means that users on the specified machine can access their equivalent accounts on the local machine without a password. This is not applicable for root because this would be a major security problem. For root, and for the user who wants to provide access to systems not included in the system-wide list, use of the .rhosts file in the user's home directory is required.

Consider the following sample /etc/hosts.equiv file:

```
# cat /etc/hosts.equiv
macintosh.mydomain.com
delicious.mydomain.com
#
```

In the preceding example, the entries enable any user on these machines to log in to the local system using the same account name without using a password. However, as the following example shows, it is possible to list account names in this file.

```
# cat /etc/hosts.equiv
macintosh.mydomain.com andrewg
delicious.mydomain.com
#
```

As the preceding example illustrates, the user andrewg on that system can log in using any account name other than root on the local system. Consequently, this creates the potential for problems because andrewg's account may be compromised, and then a vandal can access the local system from that machine. As a result, use of account names in the /etc/hosts.equiv and .rhosts files is discouraged.

The security issues regarding host equivalency include root equivalency and file permissions. It is very dangerous to allow root equivalency between systems. Although root equivalency makes the administration tasks easier to complete, it also makes vandalization of the network easier. If security is compromised on one node that has root equivalency with other nodes, it takes the vandal seconds to determine this and access the other machines. Consequently, it is the author's recommendation not to allow root equivalency in your network environment.

Another problem is the permissions on the network access files /etc/hosts.equiv and .rhosts. The /etc/hosts.equiv file must only be writable by root, although other users can read the file. The .rhosts file must only be writable by the owner of the file. Having the file *world writable*—and even world readable—can create problems such as enabling users to edit the file and add in other systems.

Some implementations of the Berkeley r-commands that use the .rhosts and /etc/host.equiv files check the permissions on them and refuse to use them if the permissions are set inappropriately. However, it wouldn't take too much effort to write a shell program to look for inappropriately authorized .rhosts files.

USER EQUIVALENCY

Trusted user access is much easier to configure but can be very difficult if it is being installed after a list of users has already been configured. User equivalence is a simple concept that is quite different from trusted host access. Trusted host access is not required for user equivalence to work. For NFS (Network File System) use, user equivalence becomes mandatory to prevent access problems.

User equivalence is configured by giving each user on your network, not just the machine, a unique user name and numerical UID (User ID). This means that on each machine, the user has an account with the same UID. If you do not want to allow a user to access a specific machine, then you do not have to provide an account. Another way to explain this is to say that all the /.etc/passwd and /etc/group files on the machines in the network will be the same.

As you will see, not using user equivalence in your networks can put your file systems and data at risk by allowing unauthorized access to them. Consider the following user list:

Username	UID
chare	003
janicec	1009
terrih	1009
andrewg	1004

The users in the preceding list each have a unique user name, but their UID numbers are not unique. In figure 2.2, you see that janicec has her account on macintosh.mydomain.com, and terrih has her account on delicious.mydomain.com.

FIGURE 2.2

A user equivalence example.

The file system on which terrih has her account is part of an exported file system to the users working on macintosh.mydomain.com. When janicec accesses the files in terrih's directory and lists them, the ls -l command lists janicec as the owner of the files because the UID numbers are the same. This means that janicec can erase or modify the information in those files as if she were the rightful owner. In this case, it does not matter that the user names are different. The key with NFS and user equivalence is the UID.

Another type of problem can occur when user equivalence is not properly configured. Consider the following user list:

Username	Home System
efudd (Elmer)	delicious
efudd (Elizabeth)	macintosh

In the preceding list, two users named efudd exist. The user efudd on the system named delicious is Elmer Fudd, whereas Elizabeth Fudd uses the account name efudd on the system known as macintosh. In an effort to make things easier, the system administrator on delicious has configured trusted host access, or host equivalency, for all the other systems in the network. One day Elizabeth uses the rlogin command to access macintosh and finds that she can log in without having to provide a password. She can see all the files that belong to Elmer, and she has access to all of them. That is because as far as macintosh is concerned, Elizabeth is really Elmer. In this situation, the user name is the determining factor—not the UID.

As you can see, both types of network equivalency, although creating a more productive and user-friendly environment, can actually create a list of security problems that are difficult to track down and correct.

Defining Users and Groups

As you saw in the preceding discussion on network equivalency, placing some forethought into how you will handle the addition of users in your network is essential to your defense. The comment that your /etc/passwd and /etc/group files will be the same across all the systems is an accurate one. However, a strategy for assigning UID numbers and ensuring their uniqueness is more the issue.

This can be done in many ways. You can assign them in sequential order, allocate number blocks to departments or categories of users, or allocate number blocks to offices. Regardless of the method, it is critical that it be the standard for adding users.

Understanding Permissions

The permissions that Unix uses on each file determine how access to the files and directories is controlled. Many situations can be prevented through the correct application of this simple, yet powerful mechanism. The next section reviews how permissions are handled in the Unix environment.

A Review of Standard Permissions

The permissions applied to a file are based upon the UID and GID (Group ID) stamped on the file and the UID or GID of the user trying to access the file. The three sets of permissions are as follows:

❖ Those applicable to the owner of the file

❖ The users who have the same GID as that on the file

❖ All other users

For each category of users, there are three permissions bits: read, write, and execute. This means that for each file or directory there are nine permission bits. These bits are represented in the following example:

```
$ ls -l output
-rw-r--r--  1 chare    users       236 Aug 24 20:13 output
$
```

In the output in the preceding example, the permissions are as follows:

```
-rw-r--r--
```

The first hyphen represents the file type, which can be one of the types listed in table 2.5, and the remaining characters represent the permissions.

Table 2.5
Unix File Types

Symbol	Description	Explanation
-	Regular file	A file that contains a program, data, or text
d	Directory	A special type of file that contains a list of files and the index to their location on the disk

continues

TABLE 2.5, CONTINUED
Unix File Types

Symbol	Description	Explanation
b	Block device file	A file that allows access to devices such as disk drives
c	Character device file	A file that allows access to devices such as terminals and modems
l	Symbolic link	A pointer to another file that can be on this or another filesystem
p	Named pipe	A method of communicating between two processes

In the permissions, the symbols, r, w, and x represent the read, write, and execute permissions respectively. Read permission means that the requesting user can view the contents of the file or directory. Write permission grants the user the authority to modify files or create new files in a directory. Finally, execute permission allows the file to be executed like a command. Table 2.6 summarizes these permissions and their impact on a file or directory.

TABLE 2.6
File and Directory Permissions

Permissions Symbol	Meaning	Impact on Files	Impact on Directories
r	read	View the file with cat or more	List the directory with ls
w	write	Modify the file with vi	Create or delete files
x	execute	Run the file as a command	Search the directory looking for a file; use the cd command

When the permissions on files or directories are not set appropriately, it creates pathways into the system for vandals and also offers the potential for any user to make a mistake and invite disaster. The following example shows some problems involving permissions.

This example illustrates a directory that has no write permission, thereby meaning that file cannot be removed with rm.

```
$ id
uid=1009(terrih)  gid=101(users)
$ ls -l
total 4
dr--r--r--  2 chare    users          48 Aug 24 21:09 a
dr-xr-xr-x  2 chare    users          48 Aug 24 21:12 a2
drwxr--xr--x  2 chare    users        32 Aug 24 21:08 micrc_light
$ ls -ld a2
dr-xr-xr-x  2 chare    users          48 Aug 24 21:12 a2
$ls a2
output
$ rm a2/output
rm: a2/output not removed. Permission denied
$ ls -l a2
total 1
-rw-rw-r--  1 chare    users         133 Aug 24 21:12 output
$ date > a2/output
$ ls -l a2
total 1
-rw-rw-r--  1 chare    users          29 Aug 24 21:14 output
```

As the user finds out, he cannot remove the file with the rm command because the directory does not have write permission. Remember, a directory is only a special type of file. As the user checks the permission on the file output itself, he sees that the file has its write permission turned on. This means that the contents of the file can be changed, as shown, by redirecting the output of the date command into the file.

What has not been mentioned yet is the fact that the user executing these commands is not the owner of the file. Here, through a common error, chare didn't protect his files from terrih because the contents of output could be erased even though he thought he had taken the needed precautions.

Such are the woes of the system administrator. Many attacks are successful not because the system administrator isn't doing his job, but because despite the best of intentions, the users leave these types of holes around. Some facilities, such as ftp and the r-commands, check the permissions on the files used by these commands and prevent their use if the file permissions are not correct.

The Set User ID (SUID) and Set Group ID (SGID) are a major part of the security on a Unix system. The SUID and SGID bits allow a user to assume another identity while executing the program. For example, the passwd command uses the SUID bit to allow users to become root in order to change the contents of the password file.

In the case of the SUID bit, the user who executes the program assumes the identity of the owner of the program. For SGID, the user who executes the program becomes a member of the same group that owns the program.

ROOT AND NFS

When you think about root, you think of uncontrolled access to the files, directories, programs, and devices on a system. However, when root attempts to access files on a remote system through NFS, the root user has little or no permission. This is due to the security features built into NFS. This security feature looks for a UID value of zero. When it finds that value, it knows that this is root, and it remaps the UID value to 65534, or -2. This means that over NFS, root falls into the other category of user.

The advantage here is that if you have no root equivalency between your network machines and one becomes compromised, it becomes harder for the vandal to propagate through your filesystems.

EXPLORING DATA ENCRYPTION METHODS

The opportunity to encrypt information to provide a higher level of security for your system and its data is of interest to users and system administrators everywhere. However, even encrypted data can be at risk without the proper monitoring and training for the users who want to use these facilities.

HOW PASSWORDS ARE ENCRYPTED

At one time, the passwords were stored in a plain text format, and only the administrator and system software had access to the file. However, numerous problems occurred when the password file (/etc/passwd) was being edited. Most editors create a temporary file, which is the file actually edited. At this point, the file would be world readable, giving away the passwords for all the accounts.

As a result, a method of encrypting the passwords using a one-way encryption algorithm was developed. The encrypted values were then stored instead of the clear text. However, the security of the system is only as good as the encryption method chosen.

When a user logs in to a Unix system, the getty program prompts the user for his user name and then executes the login program. The login program prompts for the password but does not decrypt it. In fact, the login program encrypts the password and then compares the newly encrypted value to the one stored in /etc/passwd. If they match, then the user supplied the correct one.

The Unix encryption method for password encryption is accessed through a kernel mechanism named *crypt(3)*. Because of United States Federal licensing issues, the crypt routines might not be available on your machine. The issue is that while the needed routines to encrypt information are available, those programs that decrypt information are not available outside the United States.

The actual password value stored in /etc/passwd is the result of using the user's password to encrypt a 64-bit block of zeroes using the crypt(3) call. The *clear text* is the user's password, which is the key to the encryption operation. The text being encrypted is 64 bits of zeroes, and the resulting *cipher text* is the encrypted password.

This crypt(3) algorithm is based upon the *Data Encryption Standard* (DES) developed by the National Institute of Standards and Technology or NIST. In normal operation according to the DES standard, a 56-bit key, such as eight 7-bit characters, is used to encrypt the original text, which is commonly called clear text. This clear text is typically 64 bits in length. The resulting cipher text cannot easily be decrypted without knowledge of the original key.

The Unix crypt(3) call uses a modified version of this method by stating that the clear text is encrypted in a block of zeroes. The process is complicated by taking the resulting cipher text and encrypting it again with the user's password as the key. This process in performed 25 times! When complete, the resulting 64 bits are split into 11 printable characters and then saved in the password file.

Despite the fact that the source for crypt can be obtained from many vendors, although the commercial distribution of this is limited outside the United States (you can find public versions of the code on the Internet), no known method is available to translate the cipher text or encrypted value back to its original clear text.

Robert Morris, Sr. and Ken Thompson, who originally implemented the Unix crypt(3) technology, were afraid that with the advent of hardware DES chips, the security of the Unix system could be easily bypassed. By using a "grain of salt," they managed to bypass this threat.

The "grain of salt," which has become known as salt, is a 12-bit number that is used to modify the result of the DES function. The value of this 12-bit number ranges from 0 to 4,095. So for each possible password, 4,096 ways exist that each password could be encrypted and stored in the password file. It is possible for multiple users on the same machine to use the same password, and no one, including the system manager, would be the wiser.

When a user runs the /bin/passwd program to establish a new password, the /bin/passwd program picks a salt based upon the time of day. This salt is used to modify the user's password.

The problem comes later in encrypting the password the next time the user logs in. It is possible, but unlikely, that the user will log in and the salt will be the same. For things to work correctly, Unix stores the salt in /etc/passwd as well. It, in fact, makes up the first two characters of the encrypted password. The following is a sample encrypted value.

```
2eLNss48eJ/GY
```

In the preceding example, the initial two characters—2e—are the salt for this password. When the user logs in to the system, the login program collects the salt from the stored password and uses it to encrypt the password provided by the user. If the newly encrypted password and the stored password match, then the password entered by the user is correct, and the user is logged in to the system. If the values do not match, then the user is greeted by a Login incorrect message, and the user must try to login again.

ENCRYPTING FILES

As you have seen, the encryption of passwords using a mechanism that is not easily decrypted provides a relatively secure method of preventing unauthorized users from having access to the system. But how can users prevent unauthorized access to their files? This can be accomplished through the use of the command crypt(1). This is a relatively unsecured method of encryption, however. Interestingly enough, some Unix commands support the direct manipulation of these encrypted files without having to decrypt them first.

Encrypting files using the crypt command is relatively simple. If no arguments are provided on the command line, crypt prompts for the key, reads the data to encrypt from standard input, and prints the encrypted information on standard output. Ideally however, the information to use is provided on the command line, as illustrated in the following example:

```
crypt key < clear > cipher
```

The preceding command reads from the file clear, encrypts the test using the password key, and saves the resulting encrypted text in the file cipher. Encrypted files can be viewed or decrypted by using a similar command line, as shown in the following:

```
crypt key < cipher > clear
crypt key < cipher ¦ pr ¦ lp
```

In the first command of the preceding example, the encrypted text in cipher is decrypted using key and saved in the file called clear. The second command-line example uses crypt to decrypt the text and sends the resulting clear text to pr for formatting and then to lp to be printed. The files generated by crypt can be edited by ed or vi, provided the version of ed or vi you have on your system supports editing encrypted files.

The exact mechanism used by crypt is well documented, and many versions of this command are publicly available on the Internet. crypt(1) does not use the same encryption routines as crypt(3), which is used for password encryption. The mechanism is a one-rotor encryption machine designed along the lines of the German Enigma, but using a 256-element rotor. Although the methods of attack on such types of encryption machines are known, the amount of work required may be large.

The encryption key used is the limiting factor to determine the level of effort to decrypt the data. The longer the password, the more complex the encryption pattern, and the longer it takes to transform the key to the internal settings used by the machine. For example, the transformation process is meant to take close to a second, but if the key is restricted to three lowercase letters, encrypted files can be read by expending only a substantial fraction of five minutes of real machine time!

Because the key given to crypt might be seen by prying eyes using ps, crypt destroys any record of the actual key immediately upon entry. Consequently, like any other security system, the password used to encrypt the data is the most critical component—and the most suspect.

This encryption mechanism is not unbreakable and can be figured out given enough time. One method of improving your chances of protecting your data is to compress the file prior to encrypting it.

EXAMINING KERBEROS AUTHENTICATION

The *Kerberos Authentication system* was developed by the Massachusetts Institute of Technology's Project Athena. Since that time, Kerberos has been adopted by other organizations for their own purposes. Many third-party application developers include support for the Kerberos Authentication system in their products.

UNDERSTANDING KERBEROS

Kerberos is an authentication system. Simply put, it is a system that validates a principal's identity. A *principal* can be either a user or a service. In either case, the principal is defined by the following three components:

- ✦ Primary name

- ✦ Instance

- ✦ Realm

In Kerberos terminology, this is called a *three-tuple* and is illustrated by the following example:

```
<primaryname, instance, realm>
```

The *primaryname,* in the case of a genuine person, is the login identifier. The *instance* is either null or contains particular information regarding the user. For a service, the primaryname is the name of the service, and the machine name is used as the instance, as in rlogin.mymachine. In either case, the *realm* is used to distinguish between different authentication domains. By using the realm, it is possible to have a different Kerberos server for each small unit within an organization instead of a single large one. The latter situation would be a prime target for vandals because it would have to be universally trusted throughout the organization. Consequently, it is not the best configuration choice.

Kerberos principals obtain tickets for services from a special server known as a *ticket-granting server.* Each ticket consists of assorted information identifying the principal that is encrypted in the private key for that service. Because only Kerberos and the service know the private key, it is considered to be authentic. The ticket granted by the ticket-granting server contains a new private session key that is known to the client as well. This key is often used to encrypt the transactions that occur during the session.

The major advantage to the Kerberos approach is that each ticket has a specific lifetime. After the lifetime is reached, a new ticket must be applied for and issued from the ticket-granting server.

DISADVANTAGES OF KERBEROS

As mentioned earlier, the Kerberos system was originally developed at MIT during the development of Project Athena. The disadvantage here is that the configuration of the environment at MIT is unlike any other organization. Simply speaking, Kerberos is designed to authenticate the *end user*—the human being sitting at the keyboard—to some number of servers. Kerberos is not a peer-to-peer system, nor was it meant for one computer system's daemons to contact another computer.

Several major issues concern the Kerberos authentication system. First and foremost, the majority of computer systems do not have a secure area in which to save the keys. Because a plain text key must be stored in the initial dialog to obtain a ticket-granting ticket, there must be a secure place to save this information. In the event that this plain text key is obtained by an unauthorized user, the Kerberos authentication server in that realm can be easily compromised.

The next problem is how Kerberos handles keys on multiuser computers. In this case, the cached keys can be obtained by other users logged in to the system. In a single-user workstation environment, only the current user has access to system resources, so there is little or no need to enable remote access to the workstation. However, if the workstation supports multiple users, then it is possible for another user on the system to obtain the keys.

Other weaknesses also exist in the Kerberos protocol, but these are difficult to discuss without a through understanding of how the protocol works and is implemented.

UNDERSTANDING IP SPOOFING

IP Spoofing is a potentially dangerous threat to any network connected to the Internet. On a network, a host allows other "trusted" hosts to communicate with it without requiring authentication. This is accomplished by setting up the .rhost and other files. Any communications coming from sources other than those defined as trusted must provide authentication before they are allowed to establish communication links.

With IP Spoofing, a host not connected to the network connects and makes it look as if they are one of the trusted hosts on the network. This is accomplished by changing their IP number to one of those on the network. In essence, the intruding host impersonates a local system's IP address and fools other hosts into not prompting for authentication.

Security measures to avoid being hit by IP Spoofing include avoiding any IP address based authentication. Require passwords every way you can, and implement encryption based authentication. Many firewalls are also capable of checking the IP source address against the physical location of origin and ascertaining whether or not the data is coming from a real host.

SUMMARY

This chapter examined some of the areas that both the user and system administrator must be concerned with to protect the system. It is vitally important that all users on a machine understand that the security of the machine is not up to the system administrator alone, but also to the users.

For example, the user of good-quality passwords helps to make the system less accessible. The fact of the matter is, though, that few users choose good passwords. Consequently, the system administrator can help achieve a higher level of security through the following mechanisms:

- ✤ Periodic examination of the system for common problems

- ✤ Use of a security probing tool like COPS (Computer Oracle and Password System) or TAMU (Texas A&M University)

- ✤ Education of system users that they each hold a key to the front door of the system

ACKNOWLEDGMENTS

Some of the text and examples in this chapter originally appeared in *Sys Admin Magazine,* Volume 1, No 1, "How Unix Password Controls Work" by Chris Hare; Volume 2, No 4, "More Network Security: Equivalency;" Volume 2, No. 6, "C2 Security: Is Big Brother Watching?". *Sys Admin Magazine* is published bimonthly by R&D Publications.

A SAMPLE PROGRAM

The sample program pwexp.pl reports the number of days until the user's current password expires. This program could be called from the /etc/profile file and if password aging is enabled for that user, it will report the number of days before the password expires.

LISTING 2.1—PWEXP.PL

```
#! perl
eval '(exit $?0)' && eval 'exec perl -S $0 ${1+"$@"}'
& eval 'exec perl -S $0 $argv:q'
if 0;
#
# pwexp.pl - PERL program to check for password expiration times
#
```

```
#
#
# get the passwd file entry for this account. $< is the numerical
# representation of our REAL UID
#
( $username, $passwd, $uid, $gid, $pwage,
  $comment, $gcos, $dir, $shell ) = getpwuid($<);
#
# If passwd aging value is defined
#
if ( $pwage ne "" )
   {
   #
   # extract the maxweeks value
   #
   $maxweeks = &a64l( substr( $pwage, 0, 1 ) );
   #
   # extract the minweeks value
   #
   $minweeks = &a64l( substr( $pwage, 1, 1 ) );
   #
   # extract the last changed value
   #
   $lastchange = &a64l( substr( $pwage, 2 ) );
   #
   # what is NOW?
   #
   $now = time / 604800;
   #
   # If maxweeks < minweeks, the user can't change his passwd
   #
   if ( $maxweeks < $minweeks )
        {
        printf "You cannot change your password. Ever. \n";
        }
   #
   # The special case where the password must be changed
   #
   elsif ( ( $minweeks == 0 ) && ( $maxweeks == 0 ) )
        {
        printf "You must change your password. Now.\n";
        }
   #
   # if lastchanged is > now, then expired
   # if now > lastchanged + maxweeks, then expired
   #
   elsif ( $lastchange > $now ||
                ( $now > $lastchange + $maxweeks ) &&
                ( $maxweeks > $minweeks ) )
        {
        printf "Your password has expired.\n";
        }
```

87

```perl
    #
    # tell the user when his password expires
    #
    else
        {
        printf "Your password expires in %d weeks.\n",
            $lastchange + $maxweeks - $now;
        printf "Please start thinking of a new one.\n";
        }
    }
else
  {
  printf "Password aging is not enabled.\n";
  }
exit(0);
#
# the a64l routine was written by Randall Schwartz after a call for help
# in the comp.lng.perl newsgroup. Thanks Randall!
#
sub a64l {
    local($_) = @_; # arg into $_
    die "a64l: illegal value: $_" unless m#^[./0-9A-Za-z]{0,6}$#;
    unless (defined %a64map) {
        @a64map{'.','/',0..9,'A'..'Z','a'..'z'} = 0..63;
    }
    local($result) = 0;
    for (reverse split(//)) {
        $result *= 64;
        $result += $a64map{$_};
    }
    $result;
}
```

CHAPTER 3

DESIGNING A NETWORK POLICY

Before building a firewall in preparation for connecting your network to the rest of the Internet, it is important to understand exactly what network resources and services you want to protect. The *Network Policy* is a document that describes an organization's network security concerns. This document becomes the first step in building effective firewalls.

This chapter discusses this first step of designing a Network Policy for your Internet. Among the issues explored are overall network security planning, site security policy, and risk analysis. This chapter discusses identification of resources and threats, network use and responsibilities, and action plans when the security policy is violated. It helps you monitor system use, mechanisms, and schedules; it also covers account and configuration management procedures and recovery procedures. Finally, this chapter discusses using encryption to protect the network, using authentication systems, and using Kerberos, mailing lists, newsgroups, and security response teams.

NETWORK SECURITY PLANNING

It is important to have a well-conceived and effective network security policy that can guard the investment and information resources of your company. A network security policy is worth implementing if the resources and information your organization has on its networks are worth protecting. Most organizations have sensitive information and competitive secrets on their networks; these should be protected against vandalism in the same manner as other valuable assets such as corporate property and office buildings.

Most network designers commonly begin implementing firewall solutions before a particular network security problem has been properly identified. Perhaps one reason for this is that coming up with an effective network security policy means asking some difficult questions about what types of Internetwork services and resources you are going to allow your users to access, and which ones you will have to restrict because of security risks.

If your users currently enjoy unrestricted access to the network, it can be difficult to enforce a policy that restricts their access. You should also keep in mind that the network policy that you should use is such that it will not impair the functioning of your organization. A network security policy that prevents network users from effectively implementing their tasks can have an unwanted consequence: network users may find means of bypassing your network policy, rendering it ineffective.

An effective network security policy is something that all network users and network administrators can accept and are willing to enforce.

SITE SECURITY POLICY

An organization can have multiple sites with each site having its own networks. If the organization is large, it is quite probable that the sites have differing network administrations with different goals and objectives. If these sites are not connected through an internal network, each of these sites may have their own network security policies. However, if the sites are connected through an internal network, the network policy should encompass the goals of all the interconnected sites.

In general a site is any part of an organization that owns computers and network-related resources. Such resources include, but are not restricted to, the following:

✤ Workstations

✤ Host computers and servers

✤ Interconnection devices: gateways, routers, bridges, repeaters

❖ Terminal servers

❖ Networking and applications software

❖ Network cables

❖ Information in files and databases

The site security policy should take into account the protection of these resources. Because the site is connected to other networks, the site security policy should consider the security needs and requirements of all of the interconnected networks. This is an important point because it is possible to come up with a network security policy that safeguards your interests but can be harmful to others. An example of this could be a deliberate use of IP addresses, behind the firewall gateway, that are already used by someone else. In this case, attacks made against your network by spoofing your network's IP addresses will be deflected to the organization whose IP addresses you are using. This situation should be avoided, because it is in your own interests to be a "good citizen" of the Internet.

RFC 1244 discusses site security policy in considerable detail. Many of the security policy issues in this chapter are based on the issues raised in this RFC.

N O T E

APPROACH TO SECURITY POLICY

Defining a network security policy means developing procedures and plans that safeguard your network resources against loss and damage. One possible approach to developing this policy is to examine the following:

❖ What resources are you are trying to protect?

❖ Which people do you need to protect the resources from?

❖ How likely are the threats?

❖ How important is the resource?

❖ What measures can you implement to protect your assets in a cost-effective manner and timely manner?

❖ Periodically examine your network security policy to see if your objectives and network circumstances have changed.

Figure 3.1 shows a worksheet that can be used to help you direct your thinking along these lines.

✤ The "Network Resources Number" column is an internal identification network number of the resources to be protected (if applicable).

✤ The "Network Resources Name" column is an English description of the resources. The importance of the resource can be on a numeric scale of 0 to 10, or in "fuzzy" natural-language expressions such as low, high, medium, very high, and so on.

✤ The "Type of users to protect resource from" column can have designations such as internal, external, guest, or group names such as accounting users, corporate assistants, and so on.

✤ The "Likelihood of a threat" column can be on a numeric scale of 0 to 10, or in "fuzzy" natural language expressions such as low, high, medium, very high, and so on.

✤ The "Measures to be implemented to protect network resource" column can have values such as "operating system permissions" for files and directories; "audit trail/alerts" for network services; "screening routers" and "firewall" for hosts and networking devices; or any other description of the type of security control.

In general, the cost of protecting your networks against a threat should be less than the cost of recovering should you be affected by the security threat. If you do not have sufficient knowledge of what you are protecting and the sources of the threat, reaching an acceptable level of security can be difficult. Don't hesitate to enlist the help of others with specialized knowledge concerning your network's assets and possible threats aginst it.

It is important to get the right type of people involved in the design of the network security policy. You might already have user groups who would consider implementation of a network security policy to be their specialty. These groups could include those that are involved with auditing/control, campus information systems groups, and organizations that deal with physical security. If you want universal support of the network security policy, it is important to involve these groups so that you can have their cooperation and acceptance of the network security policy.

Worksheet for Developing Security Approach

Network Resources		Type of users to protect resource from	Likelihood of a threat	Measures to be implemented to protect network resource
Number	Name, Importance of resource			

FIGURE 3.1 *A worksheet for developing a security approach.*

ENSURING RESPONSIBILITY FOR THE SECURITY POLICY

An important aspect of network security policy is ensuring that everyone knows their own responsibility for maintaining security. It is difficult for a network security policy to anticipate all possible threats. The policy can, however ensure that each type of problem does have someone who can deal with it in a responsible manner. There may be many levels of responsibility associated with a network security policy. Each network user, for example, should be responsible for guarding their password. A user who allows their account to be compromised increases the likelihood of compromising other accounts and resources. On the other hand, network administrators and system managers are responsible for maintaining the overall security of the network.

RISK ANALYSIS

When you create the network security policy, it is important to understand that the reason for creating a policy in the first place is to ensure that efforts spent on security are cost-effective. This means that you should understand which network resources are worth protecting, and that some resources are more important than others. You also should identify the threat source that you are protecting the network resource from. Despite the amount of publicity about external intruders breaking into a network, many surveys indicate that for most organizations, the actual loss from "insiders" is much greater.

Risk analysis involves determining the following:

- ✦ What you need to protect
- ✦ What you need to protect it from
- ✦ How to protect it

The risks should be ranked by the level of importance and severity of loss. You should not end up with a situation where you spend more to protect that which is of less value to you. Risk analysis involves determining the following two factors:

1. Estimating the risk of losing the resource *(Ri)*

2. Estimating the importance of the resource *(Wi)*

As a step towards quantifying the risk of losing a resource, a numeric value can be assigned. For example, the risk *(Ri)* of losing a resource can be assigned a value from 0 to 10, where 0 represents no risk, and 10 represents the highest risk. Similarly, the importance of a resource *(Wi)* can be assigned a value from 0 to 10, where 0 means no importance and 10 means highest importance. The overall weighted risk for the resource is then, the numeric product of the risk value and its importance (also, called the weight). This can be written as the following:

```
    WRi = Ri*Wi
WRi = Weighted risk of resource "i"
Ri = Risk of resource "i"
Wi = Weight (importance) of resource "i"
```

Consider figure 3.2, a simplified network with a router, a server, and a bridge. Assume that the network and system administrators have come up with the following estimates for the risk and importance of the network devices.

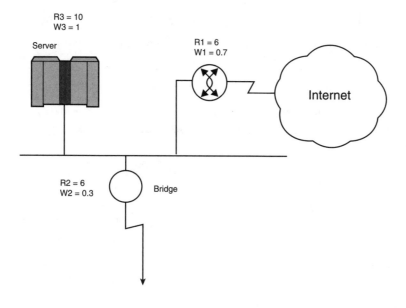

FIGURE 3.2

A simplified network layout with valued weights and risks.

Router:

$R1 = 6$

$W1 = .7$

Bridge:

$R2 = 6$

$W2 = .3$

Server:

> R3 = 10
>
> W3 = 1

The computation of the weighted risks of these devices is shown next:

Router:

> WR1 = R1 * W1 = 6 * 0.7 = 4.2

Bridge:

> WR2 = R2 * W2 = 6 * 0.3 = 1.8

Server:

> WR3 = R3 * W3 = 10 * 1 = 10

Figure 3.3 shows a worksheet that you can use for recording the previous calculations.

- ✦ The "Network Resources Number" column is an internal identification network number of the resource (if applicable).

- ✦ The "Network Resources Name" column is an English description of the resources.

- ✦ The "Risk to Network Resources (Ri)" column can be on a numeric scale of 0 to 10, or in "fuzzy" natural language expressions such as low, medium, high, very high, and so on.

- ✦ Similarly, the "Weight (Importance)of Resource (Wi)" column can be on a numeric scale of 0 to 10, or in "fuzzy" natural language expressions such as "low," "high," "medium," "very high," and so on. If you are using numerical values for the risk and weight columns, you can compute the value in the "Weighted Risk ($Ri * Wi$)" column as the product of the Risk and Weight values.

One can compute the overall risk of the resources on the network by using the following formula:

```
WR = (R1*W1 + R2*W2 + .... + Rn*Wn)/(W1 + W2 + ... + Wn)
```

For the network in figure 3.2, the overall network risk would be as follows:

```
WR = (R1*W1 + R2*W2 + R3*W3)/(W1 + W2 + W3)
   = (4.2 + 1.2 + 10)/(0.7 + 0.3 + 1)
   = 15.4/2
   = 7.7
```

Worksheet for Network Security Risk Analysis

Network Resources		Risk to Network Resources (Ri)	Weight (Importance) of Resource (Wi)	Weighted Risk (Ri * Wi)
Number	Name			

FIGURE 3.3 *A sample worksheet for a network security analysis.*

Other factors to consider in estimating the risk to a network resource are its availability, integrity, and confidentiality. Availability of a resource is a measure of how important it is to have the resource available all the time. Integrity of a resource is a measure of how important it is that the resource or the resource's data be consistent. This is particularly important for database resources. Confidentiality applies to resources such as data files to which you wish to restrict access.

IDENTIFYING RESOURCES

In performing a risk analysis, you should identify all the resources that are at risk of a possible security breach. Resources such as hardware are fairly obvious to list in this estimate, but resources such as the people who actually use the systems are often overlooked. It is important to identify *all* network resources that could be affected by a security problem.

RFC 1244 lists the following network resources that should be considered in estimating threats to overall security:

1. **HARDWARE:** processors, boards, keyboards, terminals, workstations, personal computers, printers, disk drives, communication lines, terminal servers, routers.

2. **SOFTWARE:** source programs, object programs, utilities, diagnostic programs, operating systems, communication programs.

3. **DATA:** during execution, stored on-line, archived off-line, backups, audit logs, databases, in transit over communication media.

4. **PEOPLE:** users, people needed to run systems.

5. **DOCUMENTATION:** on programs, hardware, systems, local administrative procedures.

6. **SUPPLIES:** paper, forms, ribbons, magnetic media.

IDENTIFYING THE THREATS

Once the network resources requiring protection are identified, you should identify the threats to these resources. The threats can then be examined to determine what potential for loss exists. You should also identify from what threats you are trying to protect your resources.

The following sections describe a few of the possible threats.

DEFINING UNAUTHORIZED ACCESS

Access to network resources should only be permitted to authorized users. This is called *authorized access*. A common threat that concerns many sites is unauthorized access to computing facilities. This access can take many forms, such as use of another user's account to gain access to the network and its resources. In general, the use of any network resource without prior permission is considered to be *unauthorized access*.

The seriousness of an unauthorized access depends on the site and the nature of the potential loss. For some sites, the mere act of granting access to an unauthorized user may cause irreparable harm by negative media coverage.

> Some sites, because of their size and visibility, may be more frequent targets than others. The Computer Emergency Response Team (CERT) has made the observation that in general, well-known universities, government sites, and military sites seem to attract more intruders.

RISK OF DISCLOSURE OF INFORMATION

Disclosure of information, whether it is voluntary or involuntary, is another type of threat. You should determine the value or sensitivity of the information stored on your computers. In the case of hardware and software vendors, source code, design details, diagrams, and product-specific information represent a competitive edge. Hospitals, insurance companies, and financial institutions maintain confidential information, the disclosure of which can be damaging to the clients and to the reputation of the company. Pharmaceutical labs may have patent applications and cannot risk loss due to theft.

At a systems level, disclosure of a password file on a Unix system may make you vulnerable to unauthorized access at a future date. For many organizations, a glimpse of a proposal or research project containing many years of research may give a competitor an unfair advantage.

> People often make the assumption that network and computer break-ins are made by individuals working independently. This is not always so. The dangers of systematic industrial and governmental espionage are unfortunate realities of life.

99

DENIAL OF SERVICE

Networks link valuable resources such as computers and databases, and provide services that an organization depends on. Most users on such networks rely on these services for performing their jobs efficiently. If these services are not available, there is a corresponding loss in productivity. A classic example of this was the Internet Worm incident that took place on November 2–3, 1988, where a large number of computers on the network were rendered unusable.

It is difficult to predict the form in which the denial of service may come. The following are some examples of how a denial of service can affect a network.

> ✤ A network may be rendered unusable by a rogue packet.

> ✤ A network may be rendered useless by traffic flooding.

> ✤ A network may be partitioned by disabling a critical network component such as a router joining the network segments.

> ✤ A virus might slow down or cripple a computer system by consuming system resources.

> ✤ The actual devices that protect the network may be subverted.

You should determine which services are absolutely essential, and for each of these services determine the effect of loss of this service. You should also have contingency policies on how you can recover from such losses.

NETWORK USE AND RESPONSIBILITIES

There are a number of issues that must be addressed when developing a security policy:

1. Who is allowed to use the resources?

2. What is the proper use of the resources?

3. Who is authorized to grant access and approve usage?

4. Who may have system administration privileges?

5. What are the user's rights and responsibilities?

6. What are the rights and responsibilities of the system administrator vs. those of the user?

7. What do you do with sensitive information?

These issues are discussed in the sections that follow.

IDENTIFYING WHO IS ALLOWED USE OF NETWORK RESOURCES

You must make a list of users who need access to network resources. It is not necessary to list every user on the network. Most network users fall into groups such as accounting users, corporate lawyers, engineers, and so on. You must also include a class of users called the external users. These are users who can access your network from elsewhere, such as stand-alone workstations or other networks. These external users can be users who are not employees, or who are employees accessing the network from their homes or while traveling.

IDENTIFYING THE PROPER USE OF A RESOURCE

After you determine which users are allowed access to network resources, you should provide guidelines for the acceptable use of these resources. The guidelines will depend on the class of user, such as software developers, students, faculty, external users, and so on. For each of these user classes, you should have separate guidelines. The policy should state what types of network usage are acceptable and unacceptable, and what type of usage is restricted. The policy that you develop is called the Acceptable Use Policy (AUP) for your network. If access to a network resource is restricted, you should consider the level of access the different user classes will have.

> Your AUP may clearly state that individual users are responsible for their actions. Each user's responsibility exists regardless of the security mechanisms that are in place. It makes no sense building expensive firewall security mechanisms if a user can disclose the information by copying files on disk or tape and making data available to unauthorized individuals.

NOTE

Though it may seem obvious, the AUP should clearly state that breaking into accounts or bypassing security is not permitted. This can help avoid legal issues raised by employees who bypass network security and later claim they were not properly informed or trained about network policy. The following is a guideline of issues that should be covered when developing an AUP:

✦ Is breaking into accounts permitted?

✦ Is cracking passwords permitted?

✦ Is disrupting service permitted?

✦ Should users assume that a file being world-readable grants them the authorization to read it?

✦ Should users be permitted to modify files that are not their own, even if they happen to have write permission?

✦ Should users share accounts?

Unless you have unusual requirements, the answer to most of these questions for most organizations will be *No*.

Additionally, you may want to incorporate a statement in your policies concerning copyrighted and licensed software. In general, your network usage procedures should be such that it should be difficult for employees to download unauthorized software from the network. Copying software illegally is punishable by law in most countries in the West. Large organizations often have very strict policies concerning licensing because of the risk of lawsuits and damage caused by publicity of incidents.

NOTE

> Many licensed software products for networks determine their usage and restrict the number of users that can access the network. However, some licensing agreements may require that you monitor the license usage so that the license agreement is not violated.

You may want to include information concerning copyrighted and/or licensed software in your AUP. Examples of the points that you may want to address are the following:

✦ Copyrighted and licensed software may not be duplicated unless it is explicitly stated.

✦ Indicate methods of conveying information on the copyright/licensed status of software.

✦ Err on the side of caution. When in doubt, do not copy.

An AUP that does not clearly state what is prohibited can make it difficult to prove that a user has violated the policy. Exemptions to your policy could be members of so-called *tiger teams,* charged with the responsibility of probing the security weakness of your networks. The users comprising these tiger teams must be clearly identified. On occasion you may have to deal with users who are self-appointed members of the tiger team and want to probe the security weakness for research purposes or to make a point. Your AUP should address the following issues about security probing:

❖ Is user-level hacking permitted at all?

❖ What type of security probing activities are permitted?

❖ What controls must be in place to ensure that the security probing does not get out of control?

❖ What controls must be in place to protect other network users from being victims of security probing activities?

❖ Who should have the permission to do security probing, and what is the process for obtaining permission to conduct these tests?

If you want to permit legitimate security probing, you should have separate network segments and hosts on your network for these tests. In general, it is very dangerous to test worms and viruses. If you must perform these tests, it would be foolish to conduct them on a live network. You should, instead, physically isolate the hosts and network segments that are used for the test, and do a complete and careful reload of all the software at the end of each test.

Assessing the security weaknesses and taking proper measures can be effective in repelling hacker attacks. Some organizations use outside consultants to evaluate the security of their services. As part of this evaluation, they may legitimately perform "hacking." Your policy should make allowances for these situations.

DETERMINING WHO IS AUTHORIZED TO GRANT ACCESS AND APPROVE USAGE

The network security policy should identify who is authorized to grant access to your services. You also should determine what type of access these individuals can grant. If you cannot control who is granted access to your system, it is difficult to control who is using your network. If you can identify the persons who are charged with granting access to the network, you can trace what type of access or control has been granted. This is helpful in identifying the cause of security holes as a result of users being granted excessive privileges.

You may want to consider the following factors in determining who will grant access to services on your networks:

✦ Will access to services be granted from a central point?

✦ What methods will you use for creating accounts and terminating access?

If the organization is large and decentralized, you may have several central points, one for each department, that is responsible for the security of its departmental network. In this case you must have global guidelines on what types of services are to be permitted for each class of user. In general, the more centralized the network administration is, the easier it is to maintain security. On the other hand, centralized administration can create problems when departments want greater control over their network resources. The correct amount of centralization or decentralization will depend on factors that are beyond the scope of this discussion.

The system administrators will, of course, need special access to the network, but other users may need certain privileges as well. The network security policy should address this issue. A universal policy restricting all special privileges, while being more secure, may prevent legitimate users from performing their work. A more balanced approach is needed.

The challenge is to balance restricted access to special privileges in order to make the network more secure, versus giving people who need these privileges access so that they can perform their tasks. In general you should grant only enough privilege to accomplish the necessary tasks.

Some system administrators take the easy way out and assign more privileges than the user needs, so the users will not bother them again. Also, the system administrator may not properly understand the fine points in assigning security and may err on the side of giving more privileges. Training and education can help avoid these types of problems.

People holding special privileges should be responsible and also accountable to some authority identified within the security policy. Some systems may have custom audit trails that can be used so that privileged users cannot abuse their trust.

If the people you grant privileges to are not accountable and responsible, you run the risk of creating security holes in the system and inconsistent granting of permissions to users. Such systems are invariably difficult to manage.

If there are a large number of network and system administrators, it is difficult to keep track of what permissions have been granted to network resources. A formalized way of granting requests can be used. After the user makes the request and the request is authorized by the user's supervisor, the system administrator must document the security restrictions or access the user has been granted.

Figure 3.4 shows a worksheet that can be used to keep a paper trail of what permissions have been granted to a user. The following is a description of the columns used in this worksheet.

- ❖ The network resource number column is an internal identification network number of each resource (if applicable).

- ❖ The resource name column is an English description of the resources.

- ❖ The type of access column can be used for a description of the resource, such as "read and execute access to directory."

- ❖ The operating system permissions column contains the operating system flags used to implement the security access. For Unix systems, these are the read(r), write(w), execute(x) flags. Other operating systems will use their own sets of flags.

You also should examine the procedure that you will be using to create user accounts and assign permissions. In the least restrictive case, the people who are authorized to grant access would be able to go into the system directly and create an account by hand or through vendor-supplied mechanisms. These mechanisms place a great deal of trust in the person running them, and the person running them usually has a large amount of privileges, such as the root user in Unix. Under these circumstances, you need to select someone who is trustworthy to perform this task.

You should develop specific procedures for the creation of accounts. Under Unix, there are several methods that can be used for creating accounts. Regardless of which procedure you decide to use, it should be well documented to prevent confusion and reduce mistakes.

Security vulnerabilities can easily occur as a result of mistakes made by the system administrator. If you have well-documented procedures, this will help ensure fewer mistakes.

Worksheet for Granting Access to System/Network Resources

Network Resources		Type of Access	Operating System Permission UNIX: rwx
Number	Name		

FIGURE 3.4 *A sample worksheet for granting access for system/network resources.*

These procedures also enable future system administrators to be easily trained on the peculiarities of a particular system. Another issue to consider is to select a user account creation procedure that is the simplest and most easily understood. This ensures that fewer mistakes will be made, and that the system administrators are most likely to follow them (as they normally should).

You also should have a policy on the selection of an initial password. The granting of an initial password is a vulnerable time for the user account. Policies such as the initial password being the same as the user name, or being left blank, can leave the accounts wide open. Also, avoid setting the initial password as a function of the user name, or part of the user name, or some algorithmically generated password that can easily be guessed. The selection of an initial password should not be obvious.

Some users do not use their account for a considerable period of time after their account is created; others never log in. In these circumstances, if the initial password is not secure, the account and the system are vulnerable. For this reason, you should have a policy for disabling accounts that have never been accessed for a period of time. The user is then forced into asking for enabling of their user account.

It is also a mistake to allow users to continue to use the initial password indefinitely. If the system permits, you should force users to change their password on their first login. Many systems have a password aging policy. This can be helpful in protecting the passwords. There are also Unix utilities such as password+ and npasswd that can be used to test the security of the password

---

CERT estimates that that 80 percent of all network security problems are created by insecure passwords.

N O T E

DETERMINING USER RESPONSIBILITIES

The network security policy should define the users rights and responsibilities for using the network resources and services. The following is a list of issues that you may want to address concerning user responsibilities:

✦ Guidelines regarding network resource usage such as whether users are restricted and what the restrictions are.

✦ What constitutes abuse in terms of using network resources and affecting system and network performance.

❖ Are users permitted to share accounts or let others use their accounts?

❖ Should users reveal their passwords on a temporary basis to allow others working on a project to access their accounts?

❖ User password policy—How frequently should users change their passwords and any other password restrictions or requirements?

❖ Are users responsible for providing backups of their data, or is this the system administrator's responsibilities?

❖ Consequences for users disclosing information that may be proprietary. What legal action or other punishment may be implemented?

❖ Statement on electronic mail privacy (Electronic Communications Privacy Act).

❖ A policy concerning controversial mailing or postings to mailing lists or discussion groups.

❖ A policy on electronic communications such as mail forging.

The Electronic Mail Association (EMA) recommends that every site have a policy on the protection of employee privacy. Organizations should establish privacy policies that are not limited to electronic mail, but which encompass other media such as disks, tapes, and paper documents. The EMA suggests five criteria for evaluating any policy:

1. Does the policy comply with law and with duties to third parties?

2. Does the policy unnecessarily compromise the interest of the employee, the employer, or third parties?

3. Is the policy workable as a practical matter and likely to be enforced?

4. Does the policy deal appropriately with all different forms of communications and record keeping with the office?

5. Has the policy been announced in advance and agreed to by all concerned?

DETERMINING THE RESPONSIBILITIES OF SYSTEM ADMINISTRATORS

The system administrator often needs to gather information from files in users' private directories to diagnose system problems. The users, on the other hand, have a right to maintain their privacy. There is, therefore, a tradeoff between a user's right to privacy and the needs of the system administrators. When threats to the network security occur, the system administrator may have greater need to gather information on files on the system, including the users' home directories.

The network security policy should specify the extent to which system administrators can examine users' private directories and files for diagnosing system problems and for investigating security violations. If the network security is at risk, the policy should allow a greater flexibility for the system administrators to correct the security problems. Other related questions that you should address are the following:

* Can the system administrator monitor or read a user's files for any reason?

* Do network administrators have the right to examine network or host traffic?

* What are the users', system administrators', and organization's liabilities for gaining unauthorized access to other people's private data?

WHAT TO DO WITH SENSITIVE INFORMATION

You must determine what types of sensitive data can be stored on a specific system. From a security standpoint, extremely sensitive data such as payroll and future plans should be restricted to few hosts and few system administrators. Before granting users access to a service on a host, you should consider what other services and information are provided that a user can gain access to. If the user has no need to deal with sensitive data, the user should not have an account on a system containing such material.

You also should consider if adequate security exists on the system to protect sensitive data. In general, you do not want users to store very sensitive information on a system that you do not plan to secure very well. On the other hand, securing a system can involve additional hardware, software, and system administration cost, and it might not be cost-effective to secure data on a host that is not very important to the organization or the users.

The policy also should take into account the fact that you need to tell users who might store sensitive information what services are appropriate for the storage of this sensitive information.

PLAN OF ACTION WHEN SECURITY POLICY IS VIOLATED

Each time the security policy is violated, the system is open to security threats. If no change to the network security occurs when the security policy is violated, then the security policy should be modified to remove those elements that do not have security.

A security policy and its implementation should be as non-obtrusive as possible. If the security policy is too restrictive, or improperly explained, it is quite likely to be violated.

Regardless of what type of policy is implemented, there is a tendency for some users to violate the security policy. Sometimes it is obvious when a security policy is broken; other times these infractions can go undetected. The security procedures that you implement should minimize the possibility of a security infraction going undetected.

When you detect a security policy violation, you should classify if the violation occurred due to an individual's negligence, an accident or mistake, ignorance about the current policy, or deliberate ignoring of the policy. In the latter case, the violation may be performed not by just one individual, but by a group of individuals who knowingly perform an act that is in direct violation of the security policy. In each of these circumstances, the security policy should provide guidelines on the immediate course of action.

An investigation should be performed to determine the circumstances surrounding the security violation, and how or why the violation occurred. The security policy should provide guidelines on the corrective action for a security breach. It is reasonable to expect that the type and severity of action will depend on the severity of the violation.

RESPONSE TO POLICY VIOLATIONS

When a violation takes place, the response can depend on the type of user responsible for the violation. Violations to policy may be committed by a wide variety of users. Some of these users may be local users and others may be external users. Local users are often called insiders and external users and called outsiders. The distinction between the two is usually based on network, administrative, legal, or political boundaries. The type of boundary determines what the response should be to the security violation. Examples of responses can range from a verbal reprimand or warning, a formal letter, or the pressing of legal charges.

You need to define actions based on the type of violation. These actions need to be clearly defined, based on the kind of user violating your computer security policy. The internal and external users of your network should be aware of your security policy. If you have outsiders who are using your computer network legally, it is your responsibility to verify that these individuals have a general awareness of the policies that you have set. This is particularly important if you need to take legal action against the offending parties. If a significant amount of loss was incurred, you may want to take more drastic action. If adverse publicity is involved, you may prefer to fix the security hole and not pursue legal action.

The security policy document also should include procedures for handling each security violation incident. A proper log of such security violations should be maintained, and should be periodically reviewed to observe trends and perhaps adjust security policy to take into account any new types of threats.

RESPONSE TO POLICY VIOLATIONS BY LOCAL USERS

You could have a security policy violation in which an internal user violates the security policy. This could occur in the following situations:

❖ A local user violates the local site security policy.

❖ A local user violates a remote site security policy.

In the first case, because your internal security policy is violated, you may have more control over the type of response to this security violation. In the second case, a local user has violated another organization's security policy. This could happen through a connection such as the Internet. This situation is complicated by the fact that another organization is involved, and any response you take will have to be discussed with the organization whose security policy your local user has violated. You also should consult your corporate attorneys or attorneys who specialize in computer legal security.

RESPONSE STRATEGIES

There are two types of response strategies to security incidents:

❖ Protect and Proceed

❖ Pursue and Prosecute

If the administrators of the security policy feel that the company is sufficiently vulnerable, they may choose the Protect and Proceed strategy. The goal of this policy is to immediately protect the network and restore it to its normal status so that the users can continue using the network. In order to do this, you may have to actively interfere with the intruder's actions and prevent further access. This should be followed with an analysis of the amount of damage done.

Sometimes it may not be possible to immediately restore the network to its normal operation; you may have to isolate network segments and shut down systems, with the objective of preventing further unauthorized access to the system. A disadvantage to this approach is that the intruders know that they have been detected and will take actions to avoid being traced. Also, the intruder could react to your protection strategy by attacking the site using a different strategy; at the very least, the intruder likely will live to pursue their hacking against another site.

The second approach—Pursue and Prosecute—adopts the strategy that the major goal is to allow the intruders to pursue their actions while monitoring their activities. This should be done as unobtrusively as possible so that the intruders are not aware of the fact that they are being monitored. The intruders' activities should be logged, so proof will be available in the Prosecute phase of the strategy. This approach is the one recommended by law enforcement agencies and prosecutors, because it yields proof these agencies can use in prosecuting the intruders. The disadvantage of this approach is that the intruder will continue stealing information or doing other damage, and you are still vulnerable to lawsuits resulting from damage to the system and loss of information.

One possible way of monitoring the intruders without causing damage to the system is to construct a "jail." A *jail*, in this case, defines a simulated environment for the intruders to use, so that their activities can be monitored. The simulated environment presents fake data, but the system is set up in such a way that the intruders' keystrokes and activities are monitored.

Figure 3.5 shows the general idea behind constructing a jail. To construct a jail, you need access to the source code for the operating system and in-house programming talent who can simulate this environment. It is safest to construct the jail using a sacrificial machine on an isolated network segment to minimize the risk of pollution of other network segments and systems by the intruders' activities. It is also possible to construct the jail using a software-simulated environment; however this approach is more difficult to set up.

On a Unix system the chroot mechanism can be very handy in setting up a jail. The chroot mechanism irrevocably confines a process to a single branch of the file system. For all practical purposes, the root of this branch of the file system appears as the root of the file system to the process. This mechanism prevents access to device files and the real password file (/etc/ passwd).

If you do not want other users logged into the sacrificial machine, you will have to periodically update the utmp file that contains a log of the users logged in so that the Jail looks realistic. You should also remove access to utilities that can reveal that the jail is a simulated environment. Examples of these utilities are netstat, ps, who, w. Alternatively, you can provide fake versions of these utilities to make the simulated environment appear like a real one.

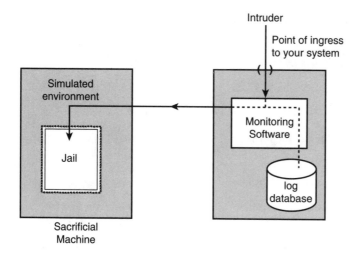

FIGURE 3.5

The general archi-tecture of a jail.

Once you have sufficient evidence against the intruder, you may want to prosecute. How-ever, prosecution is not always the best possible outcome. If the intruder is an internal user or a guest user such as a student, proper disciplinary actions can be equally effective without the additional cost of legal prosecution and the ensuing publicity. The network security policy should list these choices and provide guidelines on when they should be exercised.

> The following can be used as a guideline to help determine when the site should use a policy of Protect and Proceed or Pursue and Prosecute.

N O T E

The Protect and Proceed strategy can be used under the following conditions:

❖ If network resources are not well-protected against intruders.

❖ If continued intruder activity could result in great damage and financial risk.

❖ If the cost of prosecution is deemed too costly, or the possibility or willingness to prosecute is not present.

❖ If there is considerable risk to the existing users on the network.

❖ If the types of users for a large internal network are not known at the time of attack.

❖ If the site is vulnerable to lawsuits from users. This is true for insurance companies, banks, security forms, network providers, and so on.

The Pursue and Prosecute strategy can be used under the following conditions:

❖ If network resources and systems are well protected.

113

❖ If the risk to the network is outweighed by the disruption caused by present and potentially future intrusions.

❖ If this is a concentrated attack and has occurred before.

❖ If the site is highly visible and has been a target of past attacks.

❖ If not pursuing and prosecuting will invite further intrusions.

❖ If the site is willing to incur the risk to network resources by allowing the intruder to continue.

❖ If intruder access can be controlled.

❖ If the monitoring tools are sufficiently well-developed to create proper logs and gather evidence for prosecution.

❖ If you have in-house programming talent to construct specialized tools quickly.

❖ If the programmers, system and network administrators are sufficiently clever and knowledgeable about the operating system, system utilities, and systems to make the pursuit worthwhile.

❖ If there is willingness on the part of management to prosecute.

❖ If the system administrators know what kind of evidence would lead to prosecution, and can create proper logs of the intruders activities.

❖ If there is established contact with knowledgeable law enforcement.

❖ If there is a site representative versed in the relevant legal issues.

❖ If the site is prepared for possible legal action from its own users if their data or systems become compromised during the pursuit.

❖ If good backups are available.

DEFINING RESPONSIBILITIES OF BEING A GOOD CITIZEN ON THE INTERNET

The Internet is a cooperative venture, and the sites that have networks connected to it should be expected to follow rules of good behavior to other sites. This is similar to the workings of a successful modern society. Your security policy should include a statement that deliberate attempts at violating another site's networks is a violation of the company policy.

You should also define what types of information should be released. It may be more economical for you to publish documents about your organization on an FTP server. In this case, you should decide what type of information and how much should be released.

CONTACTS AND RESPONSIBILITIES TO EXTERNAL ORGANIZATIONS

The network security policy should define procedures for interacting with external organizations. External organizations could include law enforcement agencies, legal experts, other sites affected by the security violation incident, external response team organizations such as the CERT (Computer Emergency Response Team), CIAC (Computer Incident Advisory Capability), and if necessary, press agencies.

The people who are authorized to contact these organizations should be identified. You should identify more than one person for each area, to cover situations when the designated individuals may not be reachable. Issues that you should address can include the following:

✤ Identify "public relation types" who are versed in talking to the press.

✤ When should you contact local and federal law enforcement and investigative agencies?

✤ What type of information can be released?

INTERPRETING AND PUBLICIZING THE SECURITY POLICY

It is important to identify the individuals who will interpret the policy. It is usually not a good idea to have only one individual involved, in case that person would be unreachable at the time of crisis. One can identify a committee, but it is also not a good idea to have too many members of such a committee. From time to time, the security policy committee will be called upon to interpret, review, and revise the document.

Once the site security policy has been written and agreed upon, the site must ensure that the policy statement is widely disseminated and discussed. Mailing lists can be used. The new policy can also be reinforced by internal education such as training seminars, group briefings, workshops, one-on-one meetings with administrators, or all of these depending on the size of the institution and the needs at hand.

Implementing an effective security policy is a collective effort. Therefore, the network users should be allowed to comment on the policy for a period of time. You may want to hold meetings to elicit comments and to ensure that the policy is correctly understood. This also will help you in clarifying the language of the policy and avoid ambiguities and inconsistencies in the policy.

The meetings should be open to all network users and higher-level management who may be needed to make global decisions when important questions come up. User participation and interest further ensures that the policy will be better understood and more likely to be followed.

> If users perceive that the policy reduces their productivity, they should be allowed to respond. If necessary, additional resources may have to be added to the network to ensure that the users can continue performing their jobs without loss in productivity. To create an effective network policy, you need to find a fine balance between protection and productivity.

Sometimes new programs are met with enthusiasm initially, when everyone is aware of the policy. Over a period of time, though, there is a tendency to forget the contents of the policy. Users need periodic reminders. Also, as new users are added to the network, they need to understand the security policy.

Periodic reminders (properly timed) and continual education on the policy, will increase the chances that the users will follow the security policy. New users should have the policy included as part of their network user information packet. Some organizations require a signed statement from every network user that they have read and understood the policy. If users later require legal action for serious security violations, the signed statement can help you pursue the legal action successfully.

IDENTIFYING AND PREVENTING SECURITY PROBLEMS

The security policy defines what needs to be protected, but the policy may not explicitly spell out how the resources should be protected and the general approach to handling security problems. A separate section on the security policy should discuss the general procedures to be implemented to prevent security problems. The security policy may refer to the site's system administrator's guide for additional details on implementing the security procedures.

Before establishing the security procedures, you must assess the level of importance of network resources and their degree of security risk. The earlier discussion in the chapter on "Approach to Security Policy" and "Risk Analysis," and the worksheets in figures 3.1 and 3.3, can be used as a guide in focusing attention on the more important network resources.

> It is often tempting to start implementing procedures such as the following without first defining the network security policy:
>
> "Our site needs to provide users with telnet access to internal hosts and external hosts, prevent NFS access to internal hosts but deny this to external users, have smart cards for logging in from the outside, have dial-back modems ..."
>
> Without a proper understanding of the most important resources and those that are at the greatest risk, the previous approach could lead to some areas having more protection than they need, and other more important areas that do not have sufficient protection.

N O T E

Developing an effective security policy requires considerable effort. It takes a determined effort to consider all the issues and a willingness to set the policies in paper and do what it takes to see that the policy is properly understood by network users.

Besides performing a risk analysis of the network resources, you must identify other vulnerabilities. The following list is an attempt to describe some of the more common problem areas. This list can point you in the right direction, but is by no means complete, because your site is likely to have a few unique vulnerabilities.

- ❖ Access points
- ❖ Improperly configured systems
- ❖ Software bugs
- ❖ Insider threats
- ❖ Physical security

A discussion of these issues is next.

ACCESS POINTS

Access points are points of entry (also called *ingress*) by unauthorized users. Having many access points will increase the security risks to the network.

Figure 3.6 shows a simplified network for an organization in which there exists several points of ingress to the network. The access points are the terminal server and router on network segment A. The workstation on segment A has a private modem which is used for dial-out connections. Host B on network segment B is also an access point to this network segment. Because a router joins the two network segments, an intruder can use any of the access points on each network segment to reach the entire network.

FIGURE 3.6

Identifying access points in a network.

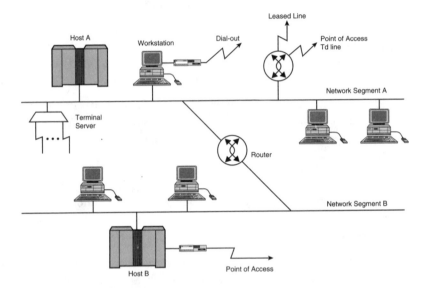

You may secure the listed access points in figure 3.6, but it is easy to forget the workstation on segment A which was going to be used for dial-out connections, perhaps to simple computer bulletin boards.

Consider the following situation: The user of the workstation on segment A may have an account with an Internet Access Provider. Suppose this user uses a SLIP (Serial Line Interface Protocol) or PPP connection to access this Internet Access Provider. If the TCP/IP software that the user is running on the workstation is also configured as a router, it is possible for an intruder to access the entire network. Also, if a routing protocol such as RIP (Routing Information Protocol) or OSPF (Open Shortest Path First) is enabled at the workstation, the workstation can expose the internal network to routing protocol-based attacks.

Note that the user may not deliberately enable the workstation as a router. The workstation operating system might be by default enabled as a router. This is true for many Unix systems as well as DOS/Windows TCP/IP packages. Even the workstation is properly configured by the networking staff, the user could plug in their laptop computer to the network and use a modem to dial out to the Internet Access Provider. If the user was using a dial-up (also called a shell account) where the user is running terminal emulation software at the workstation and not TCP/IP software, perhaps no harm can be done. However, if the user is using SLIP or PPP connection, the user has inadvertently created another access point which the network administration staff may not be aware of. This could represent a security risk to the entire network.

The situation in figure 3.6 can be prevented if the network security policy informs the user that private connections through individual workstations are prohibited. This situation also underscores the importance of having a network security policy that clearly delineates the AUP for the network.

If you want to connect to the Internet, you must have at least one network link to networks outside the organization. A network link can make available a large number of network services, both inside the network and outside the network, and each service has a potential to be compromised.

> Terminal servers can represent a security risk if not properly protected. Many terminal servers on the market do not require any kind of authentication. Check with your vendor about authentication capabilities of your terminal server. Intruders can use terminal servers to disguise their actions, dialing in to the terminal server and accessing your internal network.
>
> If the terminal server permits this, an intruder can access the internal network from the terminal server, and then use telnet to go out again, making it difficult to trace them. Also, if the intruder uses this to attack another network, it may appear that the attack originated from your network.

Dialup lines, depending on their configuration, may provide access merely to a login port of a single system. If connected to a terminal server, the dialup line may give access to the entire network. As mentioned in the discussion in figure 3.6, a dialup line at a workstation running TCP/IP software can give access to the entire network.

IMPROPERLY CONFIGURED SYSTEMS

If intruders penetrate the network, they usually try to subvert the hosts on the system. Hosts that act as telnet servers are popular targets. If the host is improperly configured, the system can be easily subverted. Misconfigured systems account for a large number of security problems on networks.

Modern operating systems and their associated software have become so complex that understanding how the system works is not only a full-time job, but often requires specialized knowledge. Vendors may also be responsible for misconfigured systems. Many vendors ship systems with wide-open security. Passwords to critical accounts may not be set, or they use easily guessable login name and password combinations. The book *The Cuckoo's Egg,* by Cliff Stoll, which tells the true story of the global hunt for a computer spy, mentions how an intruder obtained access to systems by using login name/password combinations such as "system/manager," "field/service," and so on.

SOFTWARE BUGS

As the complexity of software increases, so does the number and complexity of bugs in any given system. Perhaps software will never be bug free unless revolutionary ways of creating software are developed. Publicly known security bugs are common methods of unauthorized entry. If a system's implementation is open and widely known (such as with Unix), an intruder can use weaknesses in the software code that runs in a privileged mode to gain privileged access to the system.

The system administrators must be aware of security weaknesses in their operating systems and be responsible for obtaining updates and implementing fixes when these problems are discovered. You also should have a policy to report bugs (when found) to the vendor so that a solution to the problem can be implemented and distributed.

INSIDER THREATS

Insiders usually have more direct access to the computer and network software than to the actual hardware. If an insider decides to subvert the network, he can represent a considerable threat to the security of the network. If you have physical access to the components of a system, the system is easier to subvert. For example, many workstations easily can be manipulated to grant privileged access. One can easily run protocol decode and capture software to analyze protocol traffic. Most standard TCP/IP application services such as telnet, rlogin, and ftp have very weak authentication mechanisms where passwords are sent in the clear. Access to these services using privileged accounts should be avoided because it can easily compromise the passwords for these accounts.

PHYSICAL SECURITY

If the computer itself is not physically secure, software security mechanisms easily can be bypassed. In the case of DOS/Windows workstations, there is not even a password level of protection. If a Unix workstation is left unattended, its physical disks can be swapped out, or if the workstation is left in a privileged mode, the workstation is wide open. Alternatively, the intruder can halt the machine and bring it back up in privileged mode, and then plant Trojan-horse programs or take any number of actions that can leave the system wide open to future attacks.

All critical network resources such as backbones, communications links, hosts, important servers, and key machines should be located in physically secure areas. The Kerberos authentication mechanism, for example, requires that the Kerberos server be physically secure. *Physically secure* means that the machine is locked in a room or placed in such a manner that restricts physical access to the data on the machine.

Sometimes it is not always easy to physically secure machines. In this case care should be taken not to trust those machines too much. You should limit access from non-secure machines to more secure machines. In particular, you should not allow access to hosts using trusted access mechanisms such as the Berkeley-r* utilities (rsh, rlogin, rcp, rwho, ruptime, rexec).

Even when the machine is physically secure, care should be taken about who has access to these machines. Using electronic "smart" cards to access the room in which the machines are secured can limit the number of people with access and also provide a log of the identity and time-of-day individuals accessed the room. You should also have a policy for your employees that other persons cannot tag along when the door to the secure room is opened, even when the identity of the individual is known. If you allow people to tag along, you will not have a proper log of who entered the room and when.

> Also remember that maintenance and building staff may have access to the secure rooms. Make sure you take this into account when designing your system security.

N O T E

CONFIDENTIALITY

Confidentiality can be defined as the act of keeping things hidden or secret. This is an important consideration for many types of sensitive data.

Some of the situations in which information is vulnerable to disclosure are the following:

❖ When the information is stored on a computer system

❖ When the information is in transit to another system on the network

❖ When the information is stored on backup tapes

Access to information that is stored on a computer is controlled by file permissions, access control lists (ACLs), and other similar mechanisms. Information that is in transit can be protected by encryption or by firewall gateways. Encryption can be used to protect all three situations. Access to information stored on tapes can be controlled by physical security such as by locking them in a safe, or an inaccessible area.

IMPLEMENTING COST-EFFECTIVE POLICY CONTROLS

Controls and protection mechanisms should be selected so that they can adequately counter the threats found during risk assessment. These controls should be implemented in a cost-effective manner. It makes little sense to spend large sums of money, and over-protect and restrict the use of a resource if the risk of exposure is very small.

Common sense is often a very effective tool to use to establish your security policy. While elaborate security schemes and mechanisms are impressive, they can be quite expensive. Sometimes the costs of these implementations are hidden. For example, you might implement a freely available software security solution but not take into account the cost of administering such a system and keeping it updated. Also if the security solution is very elaborate, it may be difficult to implement and administer. If the administration is a one-time installation experience, the commands to administer such a system can be easily forgotten.

> You should also maintain a sense of perspective that no matter how elaborate is the solution, a weak password or stolen password can compromise the system.

The following are some guidelines for implementing cost-effective policy controls.

SELECTING THE POLICY CONTROL

The controls that you select are the first line of defense in the protection of your network. These controls should accurately represent what you intend to protect as outlined in the security policy. If a major threat to your system is external intrusions, it may not be cost-effective to use biometric devices to authenticate your internal users. If the major threat to your systems is unauthorized use of computing resources by internal users, you may want to establish good automated accounting procedures. If the major threat to your network is external users, you may want to build screening routers and firewall solutions.

Using Fallback Strategies

If the risk analysis indicates that protecting a resource is critical to the security of the network, you may want to use multiple strategies to protect your network. Using multiple strategies gives you the assurance that if one strategy fails or is subverted, another strategy can come into play and continue protecting the network resource.

It might be more cost-effective and simpler to use several simple-to-implement, but nevertheless effective, strategies rather than use a single elaborate and sophisticated strategy. The latter is an all-or-nothing approach. If the elaborate mechanism is circumvented, there is no fallback mechanism to protect the network resource.

> Examples of simpler controls are dial-back modems that can be used in conjunction with traditional logon mechanisms. These can be augmented with smart cards or one-time hand-held authenticators.

Detecting and Monitoring Unauthorized Activity

If a break-in or attempted break-in takes place, it should be detected as soon as possible. You can implement several simple procedures to detect unauthorized uses of a computer system. Some procedures rely on tools provided with the operating system by the vendor. There are also tools that are publicly available on the Internet.

Monitoring System Use

System monitoring can be done periodically by the system administrator. Alternatively, software written for the purposes of monitoring the system can be used. Monitoring a system involves looking at several parts of the system and searching for anything unusual. A few of the ways this can be done are outlined in this section.

Monitoring must be done on a regular basis. It is not sufficient to do this on a monthly or weekly basis, because this could leave a security breach undetected for a long time. Some security breaches may be detected a few hours after the fact by other means, in which case monitoring on a weekly or monthly basis will do little good. The goal of monitoring is to detect the security breach in a timely manner so that you can respond to it appropriately.

If you are using monitoring tools, you should regularly examine the output of these tools. If the logs are voluminous, you may want to use awk or perl scripts to analyze the output. These tools are also available for non-Unix systems.

Monitoring Mechanisms

Many operating systems store information about logins in special log files. The system administrator should examine these log files on a regular basis to detect unauthorized use of the system. The following is a list of methods that can be used at your site.

- ✦ You can compare lists of currently logged-in users with past login histories. Most network users have regular working hours and log in and log out at about the same time every day. An account that shows login activity outside the "normal" hours for the user should be closely monitored. Perhaps this account is in use by an intruder. Users can also be alerted to watch for the last login message that appears when they first log in. If they see some unusual times, they should alert the system administrator.

- ✦ Many operating systems can use accounting records for billing purposes. These records can also be examined for any unusual usage patterns for the system. Such unusual accounting records may indicate illegal penetration of the system.

- ✦ The operating system may have system logging facilities, such as the syslog used in Unix. The logs produced by such tools should be checked for unusual error messages from system software. For instance, a large number of failed login attempts in a short period of time may indicate someone trying to guess passwords. You should also monitor the number of attempts at logging into sensitive accounts such as root, sysadm, and so on.

- ✦ Many operating systems have commands, such as the ps command under Unix, to list currently executing processes. These can be used to detect users running programs they are not authorized to use, as well as to detect unauthorized programs which have been started by an intruder.

- ✦ Firewall gateways can be used to produce a log of the network access. These should be monitored regularly. Firewalls are discussed in detail later in the book.

❖ If you have special resources that you want to monitor, you can construct your own monitoring tools using standard operating system utilities. For example, you can combine the Unix ls and find commands in a shell script to check for privileged file ownerships and permission settings. You can store the output of your monitoring activity in lists that can be compared and analyzed using ordinary Unix tools such as diff, awk, or perl. Differences in file permissions of critical files can indicate unauthorized modifications to the system.

MONITORING SCHEDULE

Regular and frequent monitoring should be done by system administrators throughout the day. If the monitoring is done at fixed times, it can become very irksome, but monitoring commands can be run at any time of the day during idle moments, such as when you're conducting business over the phone.

By running monitoring commands frequently, you quickly will become aware of the normal output of the monitoring tools. This can help in detecting unusual monitoring outputs. One can try to automate this process by running search tools on the output, and one can look for certain set patterns, but it is generally difficult to anticipate all the unusual outputs caused by an intrusion into the system. The human brain is still better than most programs in detecting subtle differences in the monitor log.

If you run various monitoring commands at different times throughout the day, it is difficult for an intruder to predict your actions. The intruder cannot guess when a system administrator might run the monitor command to display logged in users, and thus runs a greater risk of detection. On the other hand, if the intruder knows that at 6:00 p.m. daily the system is checked to see that everyone has logged off, they will wait for the system check to be completed before logging in.

WARNING

Monitoring is useful, but the monitoring process can itself be subverted. Some intruders may be aware of the standard logging mechanisms in use on your system, and may attempt to disable these monitoring mechanisms. Regular monitoring can detect intruders, but does not provide any guarantee that your system is secure. It is not an infallible method of detecting intruders.

REPORTING PROCEDURES

In the event that unauthorized access is detected, you should have procedures on how this access will be reported and to whom it will be reported. In addition, your security policy should cover the following:

❖ Account management procedures

❖ Configuration management procedures

❖ Recovery procedures

❖ Problem reporting procedures for system administrators

ACCOUNT MANAGEMENT PROCEDURES

When creating user accounts, you must exercise care that you do not leave any security holes. If the operating system is being installed from the distribution media, the password file should be examined for privileged accounts that you do not need.

WARNING

> Some operating system vendors provide accounts for their field service and system services engineers. These accounts either have no password or they may be common knowledge. If you need these accounts, you should give them new passwords, or else disable or delete them. There is generally no good reason to allow accounts that do not have a password set.

Accounts without passwords are dangerous even if they do not execute a command interpreter, such as accounts that exist only to see who is logged in to the system. If these are not set up correctly, system security can be compromised. For example, if the anonymous user account used by FTP (File Transfer Protocol) is not set up correctly, you could allow any users to access your system to retrieve files. If mistakes are made in setting up this account and write access to the file system is inadvertently granted, an intruder can change the password file or destroy the system.

> Some operating systems such as Unix System V provide a special /etc/shadow password file that is used for storing passwords. This file is accessible only to privileged users. If your system supports this facility, you should use it.

The shadow password facility was first introduced with System V, but other Unix systems such as SunOS 4.0 and above, and 4.3BSD Unix Tahoe, provide this feature. The shadow password file permits the encrypted form of the passwords to be hidden from non-privileged users. The intruder, therefore, cannot copy the password file and attempt to guess passwords.

Your policy also should include procedures for keeping track of who has privileged user accounts, such as root on Unix, and MAINT under VMS. Under Unix, if you know the root password you can use the su command to assume root privileges. If the password is inadvertently discovered, the user can log in with his own personal accounts and assume root privileges. You must therefore implement a policy that forces change of passwords for privileged user accounts at periodic intervals.

WARNING

> Also, when a privileged user leaves the organization, you should be alerted and the passwords for the privileged accounts should be changed. In addition the user accounts for those who have left the company should be changed.

Network services should undergo a close scrutiny. Many vendors provide default network permission files which implies that all outside hosts are to be trusted. This is not the case when connected to a network such as the Internet.

Intruders themselves collect information on the vulnerabilities of particular system versions. Sometimes they circulate their findings in underground magazines such as the following:

2600 Magazine
Phrack
Computer Underground Digest

Some system administrators subscribe to these journals to keep abreast of the intruders.

Configuration Management Procedures

You should keep updated versions of the operating system and critical utilities. The security weaknesses of older systems are usually well known, and it is likely that the intruder is aware of the security problems. Unfortunately, new releases of software, while fixing old security problems, often introduce new ones. For this reason, it is important to weigh the risks of not upgrading to a new operating system release and leaving security holes unplugged, against the cost of upgrading to the new software.

Generally, most vendors can be trusted so that the new releases of software are more likely to fix old problems and not create bigger security problems. Another complication is that the new release may break existing application software that your users depend upon. You may have to coordinate your upgrade efforts with more than one vendor.

You also can receive fixes through network mailing lists. You must have competent personnel who can examine these bug fixes carefully and only implement them if they are safe.

As a rule, you should not install a bug fix unless you know the consequences of a fix. It is always possible that the authors of the fix may have non-obvious code to allow them unauthorized access to your system.

RECOVERY PROCEDURES

Whenever you install a new version of the operating system, you should not only take a backup of the binary image of the operating system kernel but also the files that are used to compile and configure the operating system. The same also applies to all other applications and networking software.

File system backups are like an insurance policy. They not only protect you in the event of disk or other hardware failures, but also against accidental deletions and as a fallback measure if your system has been penetrated. If you suspect your system has been broken into, you might have to restore the system from a backup to protect yourself against changes made by the intruder. If you cannot detect when the unauthorized changes took place, you have to examine several backups. If you do not have a good copy of your system software, it is hard to determine what your system data and files are supposed to be.

Daily backups, such as incremental backups, can be useful in providing a history of the intruder's activities. By examining older backups, you can determine when the system was first penetrated. Even though the intruder's files have been deleted, you can see them on the backup tapes.

When examining traces for intruders files, you should check for file names that normally would not show up in a directory listing. On Unix systems, some intruders like to save data in files beginning with a period (.), or files containing non-displayable characters. These files are harder to detect.

You must decide on a backup strategy. Backup strategies usually involve the combination of the following methods:

- ❖ Full backup

- ❖ Level 1 backup

- ❖ Level 2 backup

- ❖ Custom backup

In Unix systems a full backup is also called a level 0 backup. In Unix systems, a *level 1 backup* backs up all files that have been modified since the last level 0 backup. In general, a level *N* *backup* backs up all files modified since the last *N-1 backup*. In the case of backup utilities such as dump, a level *N backup* backs up all files modified since the last *N-1 backup* or lower.

One can use an arbitrary number of levels, but generally this does not make sense because it becomes difficult to keep track of the backups. The numeric backup levels are supported in BSD-style backup commands from levels 0 to 9, but the concept can be used on any system, and you may have to do some manual bookkeeping. On BSD Unix the backup program is dump, and the files that were backed up at a specific level are kept in the /etc/dumpdates file.

In *full backup* (level 0), all data is backed up, regardless of when it was last modified, or whether it has not been modified at all. An example of this is all directories and files in a file system. After the data is backed up, the archive bit is cleared for all files that are backed up.

> The full backup strategy is the most comprehensive of all backup strategies, because it backs up all files regardless of the fact that they have been modified since the last back up or not. Because of the large volume of data that may need to get backed up, however, it is the slowest of the backup strategies.

N O T E

A level 1 backup backs up all files that have been modified since the last full backup (level 0). This means that all files that were backed up in the first level 1 backup are also backed up in the second level 1 backup, together with any files that have been modified since the first level 1 backup. This process continues with each level 1 backup, and more files can be expected to be backed up with each level 1 backup.

There is an unfortunate confusion of terms to describe the level 1 backup. On Unix systems, the level 1 backup is called an *incremental* backup. On many non-Unix systems (DOS/ Windows/PC LAN operations systems), the level 1 backup is called a *differential* backup. The term incremental backup on many non-Unix systems means something entirely different. To avoid confusion, your policy must state which definition you are using.

To obtain a complete record of the most updated versions of the files, you would have to start with the most recent full backup (level 1), and add to it the files in the most recent level 1 backup. That is,

$$\text{Most Recent Backup} = \text{Last Full Backup} + \Delta d$$

where d is the most r ecent level 1 backup.

Because the last level 1 backup contains all files that have been modified since the last full backup, you can restore data with just two tape backup sets: the backup set for the full backup and the backup set for the last level 1 backup.

If the data on one of the last level 1 backups is corrupt, you have to fall back on the next-to-the-last differential backup. On the other hand, if any data in another level 1 backup tape is corrupt, it does not matter as long as the data in the most recent differential backup is good.

If a full backup has not been done for some time, and there have been many changes to the file, the size of the data that needs to be backed up tends to grow, with each level 1 backup. If all files have been modified, the level 1 backup session is the same as the full backup sessions. This tends not to be the case, because most file systems contain a mix of programs and data, and program files are not usually modified.

In many non-Unix systems the term *incremental backup* is used to describe a backup of all files that have been modified since the last backup (level 0 or level 1). This is like a level 2 backup on Unix systems. Files that have not been modified are not backed up. To obtain a complete record of the most update versions of the files, you would have to start with the most recent full backup and add all the incremental changes recorded in each incremental backup session. That is,

$$\text{Most Recent Backup} = \text{Last Full Backup} + 1 + 2 + n$$
$$= \text{Last Full Backup} + \quad i \ (i = 1 \text{ to } n)$$

where each i is an incr emental backup.

The incremental backup contains a sequential history of the files that have been modified. This means that to restore data, you need the last full backup and every incremental backup after it. If the data on one of the backup tapes is corrupt, you might not be able to restore data. The exception to this is situations in which later incremental backups have the files that were inaccessible on the corrupt tape. In this case, you could restore the data from a later tape.

Custom backup gives you complete control over what files to backup or not to backup. You can include or exclude parts of the directory structure to be backed up or select different type of data items to be backed up. Custom backups are useful if you want to selectively back up a few files and directories and not wait for a scheduled backup.

PROBLEM REPORTING PROCEDURES FOR SYSTEM ADMINISTRATORS

Earlier in this chapter, problem reporting procedures for users was discussed. System administrators should have a defined procedure for reporting security problems. In large network installations, this can be done by creating an electronic mailing list that contains the e-mail addresses of all system administrators in the organization. Some organizations set up a response team that provides a hotline service.

PROTECTING NETWORK CONNECTIONS

If the intruder attack is likely to take place through an externally connected network such as the Internet, you may want to protect your connections to the external network.

A firewall device can be used to provide a point of resistance to the entry of flames (intruders) into the network. Besides firewalls, screening routers can be used. These topics are the subject of discussion in the following chapters.

Some organizations' sites need to connect to other sites in the same organization and are prohibited from connecting to external networks. These networks are less susceptible to threats from outside the organizations' network. Unexpected intrusions can still occur through dial-up modems at users' desktop workstations.

An organization may require connections to their other sites through larger networks such as the Internet. If the protocols they are using are different from the Internet protocols, a technique called IP tunneling can be used. These sites are susceptible to external threats.

Many organizations require connections to the Internet because of the services it offers. The security risks of connecting to outside networks must be weighed against the benefits. You should limit the number of access points to the network. Moreover, you should connect to external networks through hosts that do not store sensitive material. Such hosts should also have removed software development tools and other privileged tools that could be used to probe your network. The idea is to provide a degree of isolation or a firewall between your network and the external network. Important services needed by the organization can be kept behind the isolated network segment.

You should seriously consider restricting the access to an external network through a single system. If all access to an external network is provided through a single host, this host acts as a firewall between you and the external network. The firewall system should be strictly controlled and password-protected. External users who need access to your internal network will have to pass through the firewall. The firewall host can properly screen the incoming calls.

> The firewall system is not a guarantee against a successful intruder attack. If the intruder succeeds in compromising the security of the firewall, the intruder can gain access to your internal network behind the firewall.

USING ENCRYPTION TO PROTECT THE NETWORK

Encryption can be used to protect data in transit as well as data in storage. Some vendors provide hardware encryption devices that can be used to encrypt and decrypt data on point-to-point connections.

Encryption can be defined as the process of taking information that exists in some readable form and converting it into a form so that it cannot be understood by others.

If the receiver of the encrypted data wants to read the original data, the receiver must convert it back to the original through a process called *decryption*. Decryption is the inverse of the encryption process. In order to perform the decryption, the receiver must be in possession of a special piece of data called the key. The key should be guarded and distributed carefully.

> The advantage of using encryption is that, even if other methods of protecting your data (Access Control Lists, file permissions, passwords, and so on) are overcome by an intruder, the data is still meaningless to the intruder.

There are several types of encryption packages in both hardware and software forms. The software encryption packages are available either commercially or as free software. Hardware encryption engines are usually built around dedicated processors and are much faster than the software equivalent. On the other hand, if the intruder has access to hardware, they can build hardware-based decryption schemes that can be used for a brute-force attack on your encrypted information.

Data in transit over a network may be vulnerable to interception. Some sites prefer to encrypt the entire file as a separate step before sending it. This is sometimes called end-to-end encryption. Others prefer encrypting the data dynamically as it reaches the network using hardware encryption engines creating a secure link.

If the entire packet is encrypted before being sent, as in the case of hardware encryption engines, the IP protocol routers that do not understand the encrypted packet will reject it. The Internet routers do not understand encrypted packets and will reject it. If you want to use encryption over the Internet, you must encrypt the data in a separate step and pass it to the application process.

The following is a brief discussion on the different types of encryption methods. In your network security policy, you must specify which, if any, of these encryption techniques should be used.

DATA ENCRYPTION STANDARD (DES)

DES is a very widely used data encryption mechanism. There are many hardware and software implementations of DES. DES transforms plain text information into encrypted data called *ciphertext* by means of a special algorithm and *seed* value called a key. If the key is known to the receiver, it can be used to convert from the ciphertext the original data.

A potential weakness of all encryption systems is the need to remember the key under which any data was encrypted. In this regard, it is similar to the problem of remembering the password. If the key is written and becomes known to an unauthorized party, they can read your original data. If the key is forgotten, then you are unable to recover the original data.

Many systems support a DES command, or utilities and code libraries that can be used for DES.

CRYPT

On Unix systems the crypt command also can be used to encrypt data. The algorithm used by crypt based on the World War II *Enigma* device and is very insecure. Files encrypted with crypt can be decrypted easily by brute-force approach in a matter of a few hours. For this reason, the crypt command should be avoided for sensitive data. It can be used for trivial encryption tasks. Chapter 2, "Security," discusses the use of the crypt command.

PRIVACY ENHANCED MAIL (PEM)

E-mail is usually sent on the Internet using SMTP (Simple Mail Transfer Protocol). This protocol is very simple and transmits data in the clear. Moreover, it can be used for transmitting ASCII text data only. If you want to send an encrypted message you have to use indirect means. You have to first encrypt the message. This converts the message into a binary file. Because SMTP cannot be used to transmit binary data—it transmits text data only—you have to encode the binary data as text.

A popular way of doing this on the Internet is to use a utility called uuencode. The recipient of the e-mail has to use a utility called uudecode to convert the text message back to the original encrypted binary form. If the recipient knows the key, he can decrypt the message. While it is possible to secure mail by using the method just outlined, it is cumbersome and laborious. Also, there is the problem of distributing the key to the recipients of the message. You should consider whether this should be done through the Internet, or by some other distribution methods.

Another approach that has attracted a great deal of interest is Privacy Enhanced Mail (PEM). PEM provides a means to automatically encrypt e-mail messages before sending. There are no separate procedures one has to invoke to encrypt the mail message. Therefore, even if the mail is intercepted at a mail distribution host, the interceptor cannot read the encrypted mail.

Origin Authentication

When an e-mail is received, the header of the e-mail indicates the originator of the message. Most users of Internet mail take it for granted that the header of the e-mail message truly indicates the sender of the message. It is possible, if one is clever enough, to forge the header so that it indicates a message sent from another e-mail address. This is called e-mail address *spoofing*. To prevent this type of forgery, a technique called origin authentication can be used.

Origin authentication provides a means to ascertain that the originator of a message is indeed who he claims to be. You might think of origin authentication as an electronic notary service similar to the human notary public who verifies signatures on legal documents. Origin authentication is commonly implemented by a public key cryptosystem.

A *cryptosystem* uses two keys. The keys are independent in the sense that one key cannot be derived from the other key using any mathematical or algorithmic procedures. One of the keys is a *public key*, which means that it can be easily found out by anyone and there is no attempt made to hide it. The other key is called a *private key* which means that this key is known only to the party who owns the key. The private key must be guarded very carefully.

In a public key cryptosystem, the originator uses a private key to encrypt the message. The recipient uses a public key obtained from the originator of the message to decrypt the message. The public key is used to authenticate that only the originator could have used their private key. There are several public cryptosystems that are available.

The most widely known implementation of the public key cryptosystem is the RSA (Rivest Shamir Adleman) system. The Internet standard for privacy enhanced mail makes use of the RSA system.

N O T E

INFORMATION INTEGRITY

When a file or document is sent on the network, you should have some means of verifying that the file or document has not been altered. This is called information integrity, and it refers to the process of verifying that the information that was sent is complete and unchanged from the last time it was verified. Information integrity is important for military, government, and financial institutions. It may also be important that classified information be undisclosed, whether it is modified or not modified. Information that is maliciously modified can create misunderstandings, confusion, and conflict.

If the information is sent in electronic form across the network, one way of ensuring that the information is not modified is to use *checksums*. Any form of encryption also provides information integrity, because an interceptor would have to first decrypt the message before modifying it.

USING CHECKSUMS

Checksums are a very simple and effective mechanism to verify the integrity of a file. A simple checksum procedure can be used to compute a value for a file and then compare it with the previous value. If the checksums match, the file is probably unchanged. If the checksums do not match, the file has been altered. Many compression and decompression utilities that can be used to conserve disk space and reduce transmission costs for files generate internal checksums to verify their compression/decompression algorithms.

Arithmetic checksums are simple to implement. They are formed by adding up 16-bit or 32-bit elements of a file to arrive at the checksum number. Though simple to implement, arithmetic checksums are weak from a security point of view. A determined attacker can modify and add data to the file so that the arithmetic checksum computes to the correct value.

The CRC (Cyclic Redundancy Checksum), also called the *polynomial checksum*, is more secure than the arithmetic checksum. Its implementation is fairly simple. However, like the arithmetic checksum, it too can be compromised by a determined interceptor.

> Checksums make it difficult for the interceptor to alter the information and be undetected. They cannot, however, guard against changes being made. You may want to use other mechanisms such as the operating system access controls and encryption. The operating system access controls can only guard the data when it is stored in a file system. It cannot protect data while it is being transmitted in a network.

Cryptographic checksums provide improvements over arithmetic checksums and CRC checksums. This type of checksum is discussed next.

CRYPTOGRAPHIC CHECKSUMS

In cryptographic checksums, also called *cryptosealing*, the data is divided into smaller sets and a CRC checksum is calculated for each data set. The CRCs of all the data sets are then added together.

This method makes it difficult to alter the data, because the interceptor does not know the sizes of the data sets that are used. The data set size can be variable and computed using pseudo-random techniques, thus making it extremely difficult for the interceptor to alter the data. A disadvantage of this mechanism is that it is sometimes computationally intensive.

Another method, called the *Manipulation Detection Code* (MDC) or one-way hash function, can be used to detect modifications to a file. The one-way hash function is so called because no two inputs can produce the same value. The data in the file is used as the input to the one-way hash function to produce a hash value. If the data in the file is modified, it will have a different hash value. One-way hash functions can be implemented quite efficiently and they make unbreakable integrity checks possible. Examples of a one-way hash function are the MD2 (Message Digest 2) and MD5 (Message Digest 5) functions, described in RFC 1319 and RFC 1321, respectively.

USING AUTHENTICATION SYSTEMS

Authentication can be defined as the process of proving a claimed identity to the satisfaction of some permission-granting authority.

On most systems, the user has to specify a password to their user account before they are allowed to log in. The purpose of the password is to verify that the user is who they claim to be. In other words, the password acts as a mechanism that authenticates the user. However, passwords can be stolen, and someone else can impersonate the user. Because adequate measures are not taken as often as they should be, stolen passwords are the cause of a large number of security breaches on the Internet.

Authentication systems are a combination of hardware, software, and procedural mechanisms that enable a user to obtain access to computing resources. Your site policy must state what type of authentication mechanism you should adopt. If users are to log in to their accounts from an external site, you should use stronger authentication mechanisms than passwords.

> Authentication mechanisms range from smart cards to biometric devices such as fingerprint readers, voice print readers, and retina scan devices.

NOTE

Authentication mechanisms can be augmented by challenge/response mechanisms. Challenge/response mechanisms ask the user to supply some piece of information shared by both the computer and the user, such as the user's mother's maiden name or some special information known to the user and the system.

USING SMART CARDS

A smart card is a hand-held portable (HHP) device that has a microprocessor, input-output ports, and a few kilobytes of non-volatile memory. The user must have one of these devices in their possession to be able to log on to the system. This authentication is based on "something you know." The host computer prompts the user for a value obtained from a smart card when asked for a password by the computer. Sometimes, the host machine gives the user some piece of information that the user has to enter into the smart card. The smart card then displays a response that must then be entered into the computer. If the response is accepted, the session will be established. Some smart cards display a number that changes over time, but is synchronized with the authentication software on the computer.

USING KERBEROS

Many systems can be modified to use the Kerberos authentication mechanism. Kerberos, named after the dog who in Greek mythology is said to stand at the gates of Hades, is a collection of software used in a large network to establish a user's claimed identity. Developed at the Massachusetts Institute of Technology (MIT), it uses a combination of encryption and distributed databases so that a user at a campus facility can log in and start a session from any computer located on the campus.

This mechanism was briefly discussed in Chapter 2.

KEEPING UP-TO-DATE

Your security policy, besides identifying the agencies with which you should establish contact in case of security incidents, should also designate individuals who should keep up-to-date with security issues and problems.

If your organization is connected to the Internet, you might want to join mailing lists or newsgroups that discuss security topics of interest to you.

Remember that it takes time to keep up with the information in mailing lists and newsgroups. Unless you identify the individuals who should keep up with this information, and make it part of their job description, your system administrators will probably not find any time to do so.

MAILING LISTS

Mailing lists are maintained by list servers on the Internet. When you join a mailing list, you can communicate with users in this mailing list through electronic mail. To send your response or views on a topic, you can send e-mail to the mailing list. Everyone who is on the mailing list will receive your message. The request to join a mailing list is sent to another e-mail address. This address is *different* from the list e-mail address. You should send your subscription request to the e-mail request address and not the e-mail address of the list. The members of a list, which may number in the thousands, will not appreciate receiving requests to join the mailing list! Some mailing list administrators complie a special list of Frequently Asked Questions (FAQs). FAQs are often a good place to begin finding more information.

Mailing lists can be moderated or unmoderated. In moderated mailing lists, the list owner usually acts as a moderator and screens out mail responses that are not in keeping with the objectives of the mailing list.

In unmoderated mailing lists, there is no screening process. Consequently, the signal-to-noise ratio can be very low. If you decide that the mailing list is not for you send an "unsubscribe" request to the e-mail request address for the mailing list (and not the mailing list itself!). This request should include the following in the mail body:

```
UNSUBSCRIBE  listname
```

The e-mail term *signal-to-noise ratio* borrows its meaning from the audio usage. *Signal* represents actual, relevant e-mail messages. *Noise* represents useless messages, such as subscribe and test messages, that hinder normal communications among others using the mailing list.

Unix Security Mailing Lists

The goal of the Unix security mailing list is to notify system administrators of security problems before they become common knowledge, and to provide information on security related topics. Because this kind of information can be damaging if it falls into the wrong hands, the Unix security mailing list is a restricted-access list. This list is open only to people who can be verified as being principal system administrators of a site.

In order to join this list, the requests must originate from the site contact listed in the Defense Data Network's Network Information Center's (DDN NIC) WHOIS database, or from the root account on one of the major site machines. You must include the destination e-mail address you want on the list. You should also indicate if you want to be on the mail reflector list or receive weekly digests. You should also include the e-mail address and voice mail telephone number of the site contact.

The e-mail address to send the subscription request is as follows:

```
security-request@cpd.com
```

The Risks Forum List

The Risks forum is a component of the ACM Committee on Computers and Public Policy. This is a moderated list and discusses risks to the public in computers and related systems. It also discusses security issues of topical interest, major international computer-related security incidents, problems in air and railroad traffic control systems, software engineering, and so on.

To join the mailing list, send an e-mail subscribe message to the following address:

```
risks-request@csl.sri.com
```

In the body of the list include the following line:

```
subscribe risks-request Firstname Lastname
```

If you want to receive a digest version, rather than individual e-mail responses, include the following line:

```
set risks-request digest
```

This Risks list is also available through the USENET newsgroup by the following name:

```
comp.risks
```

THE VIRUS-L LIST

The VIRUS-L list discusses computer virus experiences, protection software, and related topics. The list is open to the public and is implemented as a moderated digest. Most of the information is related to personal computers, although some of it may be applicable to larger systems. To subscribe, send e-mail to the following address:

```
listserv%lehiibm1.bitnet@mitvma.mit.edu
```

or

```
listserv@lehiibm1.bitnet
```

In the body of the list include the following line:

```
subscribe virus-L Firstname Lastname
```

If you want to receive a digest version, rather than individual e-mail responses, include the following line:

```
set virus-L digest
```

This list is also available through the USENET newsgroup by the following name:

```
comp.virus
```

THE BUGTRAQ LIST

The Bugtraq list discusses software bugs and security holes. This can be used to assess the security risk to your system. It also discusses how these security holes can be fixed, so that you can use this information to fix security holes in your system.

To subscribe, send e-mail to the following address:

```
bugtraq-request@crimelab.com
```

In the body of the list include the following line:

```
subscribe bugtraq-list Firstname Lastname
```

If you want to receive a digest version, rather than individual e-mail responses, include the following line:

```
set bugtraq-list digest
```

THE COMPUTER UNDERGROUND DIGEST

The Computer Underground Digest states its goal as "an open forum dedicated to sharing information among computerists and to the presentation and debate of diverse views."

This Computer Underground Digest contains discussions about privacy and other security-related topics.

To subscribe, send e-mail to the following address:

```
TK0JUT2%NIU.bitnet@mitvma.mit.edu
```

In the body of the list include the following line:

```
subscribe cud Firstname Lastname
```

You can mail your submissions to this list at the following address:

```
cud@chinacat.unicom.com
```

This list is also available through the USENET newsgroup by the following name:

```
alt.society.cu-digest
```

THE CERT MAILING LIST

The CERT (Computer Emergency Response Team) puts out advisories. CERT is discussed in this chapter in an earlier section on organizations you can contact for security-related help.

To subscribe, send e-mail to the following address:

```
cert-request@cert.sei.cmu.edu
```

In the body of the list include the following line:

```
subscribe cert Firstname Lastname
```

If you want to receive a digest version, rather than individual e-mail responses, include the following line:

```
set cert digest
```

THE CERT-TOOLS MAILING LIST

The CERT also maintains a CERT-TOOLS list for the purposes of exchanging of information on tools and techniques that increase the secure operation of Internet systems. The CERT/CC does not review or endorse the tools described on the list.

To subscribe, send e-mail to the following address:

```
cert-tools-request@cert.sei.cmu.edu
```

In the body of the list include the following line:

```
subscribe cert-tools Firstname Lastname
```

If you want to receive a digest version, rather than individual e-mail responses, include the following line:

```
set cert-tools digest
```

THE TCP/IP MAILING LIST

The TCP/IP mailing list is a discussion forum for developers and maintainers of implementations of the TCP/IP protocol suite. However, many of the questions that are received on the list are from users of various TCP/IP packages, or those seeking help on TCP/IP applications. This list also discusses network security problems.

To subscribe, send e-mail to the following address:

```
tcp-ip-request@nisc.sri.com
```

In the body of the list include the following line:

```
subscribe tcp-ip Firstname Lastname
```

If you want to receive a digest version, rather than individual e-mail responses, include the following line:

```
set tcp-ip digest
```

This list is also available through the USENET newsgroup by the following name:

```
comp.protocols.tcp-ip
```

THE SUN-NETS MAILING LIST

The SUN-NETS list discusses issues related to networking on SUN Microsystems workstation systems. The discussion centers around networking and security issues dealing with NFS, NIS, and name servers.

To subscribe, send e-mail to the following address:

`sun-nets-request@umiacs.umd.edu`

In the body of the list include the following line:

`subscribe sun-nets `*`Firstname Lastname`*

If you want to receive a digest version, rather than individual e-mail responses, include the following line:

`set sun-nets digest`

NEWSGROUPS

Newsgroups are discussion groups that exchange information through special news reader programs. To join a newsgroup, you must use a special news reader program. These are programs such as nn and tin for Unix systems. DOS/Windows systems have many commercial shareware/freeware packages. Using a news reader, you have greater flexibility in handling messages.

Like mailing lists, newsgroups can be moderated or unmoderated.

The USENET groups dealing with security-related issues are:

> misc.security
>
> alt.security
>
> comp.security.announce

The misc.security is a moderated group and also includes discussions of physical security and locks. The alt.security is unmoderated. The comp.security.announce newsgroup contains mailings sent to the CERT mailing list.

Some of the mailing lists are also available via newsgroups. These were mentioned in the section on mailing lists and are listed here for your reference.

> comp.risks
>
> comp.virus
>
> alt.society.cu-digest
>
> comp.protocols.tcp-ip

SECURITY RESPONSE TEAMS

Some organizations have formed a group of security experts that deal with computer security problems. These teams gather information about possible security holes in systems. They disseminate this information and report it to the appropriate people. They can help in tracking intruders, and provide help and guidance in recovering from security violations. The teams may have electronic mail distribution lists and special telephone numbers that you can call for information or to report a problem. Some of the teams are members of the CERT System.

COMPUTER EMERGENCY RESPONSE TEAM

The Computer Emergency Response Team/Coordination Center (CERT/CC) was established in December 1988 by the Defense Advanced Research Projects Agency (DARPA). The goal of this team was to address computer security concerns of research users of the Internet. The CERT is coordinated by the U.S. National Institute of Standards and Technology (NIST), and exists to facilitate exchange of information between the various teams.

> A major motivation for the promotion of the CERT/CC team was to prevent and handle incidents such as the Internet Worm. This incident was mentioned earlier in this chapter.

CERT is operated by the Software Engineering Institute (SEI) at Carnegie Mellon University (CMU). The CERT team has the ability to immediately confer with experts to diagnose and solve security problems. They can also assist in establishing and maintaining communications with your site and government authorities.

When not responding to emergencies, the CERT/CC serves as a clearinghouse for identifying and repairing security vulnerabilities in major operating systems. They can also provide informal assessments of existing systems and guide you in improving your emergency-response capability. Because of this, they can help you indirectly in formulating an effective network security policy. The team has also been known to work with vendors of software systems in order to coordinate the fixes for security problems.

CERT operates a 24-hour hotline that you can call to report security problems such as someone breaking into your system. You can also call this number to obtain current information about rumored security problems. This 24-hour hotline number for CERT is (412)268-7090.

The CERT/CC sends out security advisories to the CERT-ADVISORY mailing list whenever appropriate. To join the CERT-ADVISORY mailing list, send a message to:

```
cert-request@cert.sei.cmu.edu
```

Security information that is sent to this list also appears in the following USENET newsgroup:

```
comp.security.announce
```

Past security advisories are available for anonymous FTP from the host cert.sei.cmu.edu. The FTP server on the host cert.sei.cmu.edu maintains other useful information on security issues. The README file on this server can inform you on what is available. For more information, contact:

CERT
Software Engineering Institute
Carnegie Mellon University
Pittsburgh, PA 15213-3890
(412)268-7090
cert@cert.sei.cmu.edu.

DDN Security Coordination Center

For Defense Data Network (DDN) users, the Security Coordination Center (SCC) serves as a clearinghouse for host/user security problems and fixes, and works with the DDN Network Security Officer. In this regard, the DDN SCC provides a function similar to CERT.

The SCC publishes the DDN Security Bulletin. This bulletin discusses issues that relate to network and host security, security fixes, and concerns to security and management personnel at DDN facilities. The DDN Security Bulletin is available on-line, via Kermit downloads or anonymous FTP, from the host NIC.DDN.MIL. The security bulletins are in files with the following format:

```
SCC:DDN-SECURITY-yy-nn.TXT
```

The *yy* is the year and *nn* is the bulletin number.

The SCC provides assistance on DDN-related host security problems through the hotline number (800)235-3155 (6 a.m. to 5 p.m. Pacific Time).

To reach the SCC by e-mail, send a message to:

```
SCC@NIC.DDN.MIL.
```

For 24-hour coverage, you can call the MILNET Trouble Desk at (800)451-7413.

NIST COMPUTER SECURITY RESOURCE AND RESPONSE CENTER

The National Institute of Standards and Technology (NIST), besides dealing with standards issues, also has responsibility within the U.S. government for computer science and technology activities. The NIST has played a major role in organizing the CERT System, and serves as the CERT System Secretariat.

NIST operates a Computer Security Resource and Response Center (CSRC) that provides help and information regarding computer security events and incidents. They are also interested in raising awareness about computer security vulnerabilities. The CSRC team operates a 24-hour hotline at (301)975-5200.

The NIST provides on-line publications and computer security information that can be downloaded using anonymous FTP from the host csrc.ncsl.nist.gov.

In addition to the FTP server, NIST operates a personal computer bulletin board that contains information regarding computer viruses as well as other aspects of computer security. To access this bulletin board, use the following information:

Bulletin Board line: 301-948-5717

8 bits, no parity, 1 stop bit

When you first log in to the bulletin board, you must register your user name and address.

NIST also produces special publications related to computer security and computer viruses. These can be downloaded through the bulletin board or the FTP server. For additional information, you can contact NIST at the following address:

Computer Security Resource and Response Center
A-216 Technology
Gaithersburg, MD 20899
(301)975-3359
csrc@nist.gov

DOE COMPUTER INCIDENT ADVISORY CAPABILITY (CIAC)

The CIAC is the Department of Energy's Computer Incident Advisory Capability. CIAC was formed to provide a centralized response capability and technical assistance center for the DOE sites.

CIAC consists of a four-person team of computer scientists from Lawrence Livermore National Laboratory (LLNL). This group's primary responsibility is to assist DOE sites faced with computer security incidents such as intruder attacks, virus infections, worm attacks, and so on. CIAC keeps sites informed of current security-related events, and maintains liaisons with other response teams and agencies.

CIAC assists sites through direct technical assistance, by providing information, or referring inquiries to other technical experts. It also serves as a clearinghouse for information about security threats, known security incidents, and vulnerabilities. Additionally, it develops guidelines for security incident handling and develops software for responding to security incidents.

CIAC analyzes security events and trends, and conducts training and awareness activities to alert and advise sites about vulnerabilities and potential attacks.

The following are CIAC's business hours phone number and e-mail address:

(415)422-8193

ciac@tiger.llnl.gov

NASA AMES COMPUTER NETWORK SECURITY RESPONSE TEAM

The Computer Network Security Response Team (CNSRT) was formed by NASA Ames Research Center in August 1989. The team's primary goal is to provide help to Ames users, but it is also involved in assisting other NASA Centers and federal agencies.

The CNSRT is NASA's equivalent of CERT. The CNSRT maintains liaisons with the DOE's CIAC team and the DARPA CERT, and it is a charter member of the CERT System.

The CNSRT can be reached through 24-hour pager at (415)694-0571. CNSRT's e-mail address is:

cnsrt@ames.arc.nasa.gov

SUMMARY

This chapter discussed the factors and issues you need to take into account when designing a secure network. These factors are formalized into a Network Policy that helps you identify security threats, perform risk analysis, and determine how you are going to protect your network resources.

You need to formulate an effective network security policy before building a firewall for connecting your network to the rest of the Internet. It is important to understand exactly what resources and services that you want to protect on the network.

The Network Policy is a document that describes an organization's network security concerns. This document becomes the first step in building effective firewalls.

PART II

SCREENING ROUTERS AND FIREWALLS

## CHAPTER 4

AN INTRODUCTION TO SCREENING ROUTERS

Many commercial routers provide the capability to screen packets based on criteria such as the type of protocol, the source address and destination address fields for a particular type of protocol, and control fields that are part of the protocol. Such routers are called *screening routers*. Screening routers can provide a powerful mechanism to control the type of network traffic that can exist on any network segment. By controlling the type of network traffic that can exist on a network segment, the screening routers can control the type of services that can exist on a network segment. Services that can compromise the network security can therefore be restricted.

This chapter examines how devices such as screening routers can be used to improve network security.

CLARIFYING DEFINITIONS

Screening routers can discriminate between network traffic based on the protocol type and the values of the protocol fields in the packet. The router's capability to discriminate between packets and restrict packets on its ports based on protocol-specific criteria is called *packet filtering*. For this reason, screening routers also are called *packet filter routers*.

ZONES OF RISK

An example of a packet filtering service implemented by a screening router is shown in figure 4.1. This figure shows an enterprise network connected to the Internet through a router that performs packet filtering.

<table>
<tr><td>

FIGURE 4.1

A screening router forming a security perimeter.

</td><td>

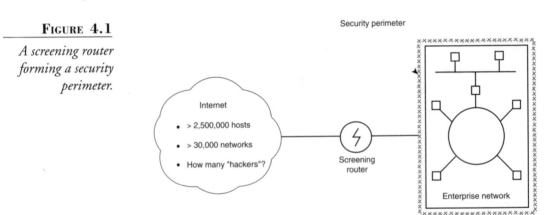

</td></tr>
</table>

The latest statistics on the Internet indicate that it consists of over 30,000 networks with a total of over 2.5 million hosts. With so many network users on the Internet, there is, unfortunately, a small segment of users who are malicious hackers. This situation is similar to moving to a large city that has its share of criminals. In this case, it is wise to protect your abode using locked doors. Prudence on your part also demands that if someone knocks on your door, you should have the ability to examine the person before allowing them entrance into your abode. Persons who appear to be harmful or look dangerous (high-security risks) should not be allowed entrance. In a similar manner, the screening router examines incoming packets to determine which of them could be potentially harmful.

In the network in figure 4.1, the enterprise network's boundary is called the *security perimeter*. Because malicious hackers abound on the Internet, it is useful to define a zone of risk. The *zone of risk* includes all TCP/IP-capable networks that are directly accessible through the Internet. *TCP/IP-capable* means that the host supports the TCP/IP protocol and its support protocols. *Directly accessible* means that there are no strong security measures (no "locked doors") between the Internet and hosts on your enterprise network.

From your point of view, the Internet's regional, national, and backbone networks represent a zone of risk. Hosts within the zone of risk are vulnerable to attacks. Placing your networks and hosts outside the zone of risk is highly desirable. However, without a device that can block attacks made against your network, the zone of risk will extend to your network. The screening router is one such device that can reduce the zone of risk so that it does not penetrate your network's security perimeter.

Not all hosts in your enterprise network may be TCP/IP-capable. Even so, these non-TCP/IP hosts can become vulnerable despite the fact that they are not technically part of the zone of risk. This can occur if the non-TCP/IP host is connected to the TCP/IP host. The intruder can use a protocol common to both the TCP/IP host and the non-TCP/IP host to access the non-TCP/IP host from the TCP/IP host (see fig. 4.2). If the hosts are on the same Ethernet segment, for example, the intruder can reach the non-TCP/IP host through the Ethernet protocol.

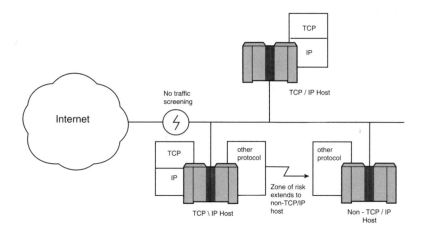

Figure 4.2

The zone of risk can extend to non-TCP/IP hosts.

Screening routers by themselves might not be able to eliminate the zone of risk. They can, however, be extremely effective in reducing the zone of risk.

The OSI Reference Model and Screening Routers

The term *router* in *screening router* implies a level of functionality dealing with routing issues. Understanding the overall role of the router in providing network communications helps you understand what types of filtering actions are provided by such routers. The preeminent

153

model for understanding communication functions is the OSI Reference Model. This model can be used to describe the functionality of a router, and it helps explain the extent of the packet filtering capability of a screening router and its limitations.

The OSI Reference Model was developed in 1978 by the International Organization of Standards (ISO) to specify a standard that could be used for the development of open systems and as a yardstick to compare different communication systems. Network systems designed according to OSI framework and specifications speak the same language; that is, they use similar or compatible methods of communication. This type of network system enables systems from different vendors to interoperate.

In the early days of computer networks (prior to the OSI model), the proprietary computer network architecture reigned supreme. In those days, an organization interested in installing a computer network examined the choices available from vendors such as IBM, DEC, HP, Honeywell, and Sperry and Burroughs (now UNISYS). Each of those choices had its own proprietary architecture; the capability to interconnect networks from different vendors was almost nonexistent.

Once committed to buying equipment from a specific vendor, the organization was virtually locked in. Updates or modifications to the system were provided by the vendor, and because the vendor had a closed proprietary architecture, no one could compete with that vendor in supplying equivalent services. Prices were determined based on what the customer could bear without complaining too much!

Today's users probably realize that in many areas of the computer industry, this picture has not changed much. Proprietary architecture history is still around, but the OSI model can, at the very least, provide you with a clearer picture of how the different components of a network relate to each other.

LAYERS OF THE OSI MODEL

The OSI model has seven layers, as shown in figure 4.3. The layers, working from the bottom up, are as follows:

Physical

Data link

Network

Transport

Session

Presentation

Application

The OSI Reference Model

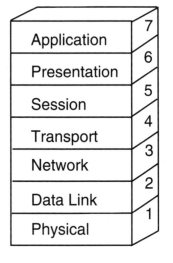

- Applications-specific services (API)
- Provides data representation
- Session services: checkpointing, activity management
- End-to-end data integrity
- Switches and router information
- Transmits information as groups of bits
- Transmits bit stream over physical medium

FIGURE 4.3

The OSI Reference Model (Graphic courtesy of Learning Tree International).

API = application program interface

The ISO applied five principles when structuring the layers of the model:

1. A layer should be created only when a different level of abstraction is needed.

2. Each layer should provide a well-defined function.

3. The function of each layer should define internationally standardized protocols.

4. The layer boundaries should minimize the information flow across layer interfaces.

5. Distinct functions should be defined in separate layers, but the number of layers should be small enough that the architecture does not become unwieldy.

The following is a summary of the functions of the seven layers.

PHYSICAL LAYER

The *physical layer* deals with the mechanical, electrical, and procedural interfaces over the physical medium. The physical layer transmits bits over a communication channel. The bits might represent database records or file transfers; the physical layer is oblivious to what those bits represent. The bits can be encoded as digital 1s and 0s or in analog form.

In the case of the enterprise network of figure 4.1, the physical layer represents the cabling, physical ports, and attachments of the enterprise network. The physical connection of the screening router to the Internet, such as a leased line of the T1-link, also is part of the physical layer.

DATA LINK LAYER

The *data link layer* builds on the transmission capability of the physical layer. The bits that are transmitted/received are grouped in logical units called a *frame*. In the context of LANs, a frame could be a token ring or Ethernet frame.

The bits in a frame have special meanings. The beginning and ending of a frame can be marked by special bit patterns. Additionally, the bits in a frame are divided into an address field, control field, data field, and error-control field. Figure 4.4 shows a typical data link frame.

FIGURE 4.4

A typical data link layer frame.

The *address field(s)* contains the sender and receiving node address. The *control field* is used to indicate the different types of data link frames, which include data frames and frames used for managing the data link channel. The *data field* contains the actual data being transmitted by the frame. The error control field usually detects errors in the data link frame. The data link layer also is the first layer in which you see error control concerns. The error control field usually is a hardware-generated checksum that is used to detect errors in the data link frame.

In figure 4.1, the screening router's Ethernet or token ring connection to the internal network is part of the data link layer. On the Internet port, the protocol used for the data link layer of the screening router could be SLIP, PPP, X.25, Frame Relay, and so on.

NETWORK LAYER

The *network layer* builds on the node-to-node connection provided by the data link layer by extending the node-to-node data link services across a network. An additional service provided by the network layer is how to route *packets* (units of information at the network layer) between nodes connected through an arbitrarily complex network.

Besides routing, the network layer helps eliminate congestion and regulate flow of data. The network layer also makes it possible for two networks to be interconnected by implementing a uniform addressing mechanism. Token ring or Ethernet LANs, for instance, have different types of data link addresses. To interconnect these two networks, you need a uniform addressing mechanism that can be understood by both token ring and Ethernet. For TCP/IP-based networks, this capability is provided by the Internet Protocol (IP).

The primary function of a router (including a screening router) resides in the network layer. When this router sees an IP packet, it examines the destination IP address in the packet. As discussed in Chapter 1, "Understanding TCP/IP," an IP address consists of a network number (also called netid) and a host number (also called hostid). The router examines the network number portion of the destination IP address in the IP packet and compares it to the entries in its routing table. If there is a match, the router forwards the IP packet as indicated in the routing table. If there is no match and there is no default route, the IP packet is rejected.

Screening routers can use criteria in addition to the routing table to forward the packet or reject it. The screening router can perform filtering at the network layer based upon the Source IP address, the Target IP address, and IP options (source routing or loose source routing). Figure 4.5 shows the fields within the IP packet on which the screening router can perform filtering, and figure 4.6 shows some of the IP options that can be used for filtering.

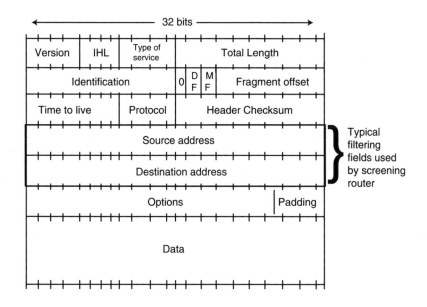

FIGURE 4.5

IP packet fields used by screening routers (Graphic courtesy of Learnimg Tree International).

157

FIGURE 4.6

IP options used by screening routers (Graphic courtesy of Learning Tree International).

IP Options Reference

Option Type	Option Length	Option Value
0	N/A	End of option list.
1	N/A	No operation.
2	11	Security. As required by DoD compartment, user group, handling restriction, label events.
3	variable	Loose source routing. Permits sender to specify *general* route followed by datagram.
4	variable	Timestamp. Permits a time trace of a datagram's route through the internet specified by sender.
7	variable	Record route. Traces path taken. Must *strictly* follow path.
8	4	Stream ID. Permits routers to handle collections of IP datagrams in a similar way. Provides a tailored virtual circuit service.
9	variable	Strict source routing. Packet must *strictly* follow path.

TRANSPORT LAYER

The *transport layer* provides enhancements to the services of the network layer. This layer helps ensure reliable data delivery and end-to-end data integrity. To ensure reliable delivery, the transport layer builds on the error-control mechanisms provided by the lower layers. If the lower layers do not do a good enough job, the transport layer has to work harder. For this reason, this layer is also called the "last chance for error recovery" layer. In fact, when it comes to providing error-free delivery, you could say "The buck stops here" at the transport layer.

The transport layer is the middle layer of the OSI model. The three lower layers constitute the network, and the three upper layers usually are implemented by networking software on the node. The transport layer usually is implemented on the node also; its job is to convert an unreliable subnet into a more reliable network.

The transport layer also can be responsible for creating several logical connections over the same network connection, a process called *multiplexing*. Multiplexing (or time sharing) occurs when a number of transport connections share the same network connection.

Because of multiplexing, several software elements (OSI terminology uses the term *protocol entity*) share the same network layer address. To uniquely identify the software elements within the transport layer, a more general form of addressing is necessary. These addresses, called *transport addresses,* usually are a combination of the network layer address and a transport Service Access Point (SAP) number. In TCP/IP, the term *port numbers* is used to identify transport addresses.

Routers normally do not perform processing at the transport layer. Screening routers, however, can examine port number fields in the TCP header. They can perform filtering decisions based on the port number values in the TCP header.

The source and destination port number fields used by screening routers are highlighted in the TCP header shown in figure 4.7. Many TCP/IP application services have standard port number values; for example, the FTP server uses port numbers 20 and 21. If you want to identify FTP sessions for the purposes of performing filtering, you can do so based on the port number values of 20 and 21. The source and destination port number are 16-bits, and can have values that range from 0 to 65535. The lower port numbers are assigned to Well Known Services (WKS) such as FTP, TELNET, and so on. The port numbers from 512 to 1024 usually are reserved for Unix-specific TCP/IP applications. Table 4.1 shows a few of the well-known port number assignments.

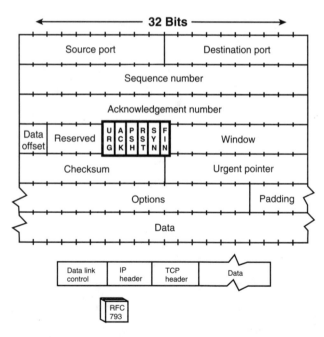

FIGURE 4.7

TCP fields used by screening routers (Graphic courtesy of Learning Tree International).

- **TCP characteristics**
  - Virtual circuits
  - Full duplex
  - Octet-stream orientation
  - Every octet numbered
  - Graceful close
  - Window flow control

159

TABLE 4.1
Some Well-Known TCP Port Numbers

Port Number	Description
0	Reserved
5	Remote Job Entry
7	Echo
9	Discard
11	Systat
13	Daytime
15	Netstat
17	Quotd (Quote of the day)
20	ftp_data
21	ftp (Control)
23	telnet
25	smtp (mail)
37	time
53	name server
70	Gopher protocol
79	Finger protocol
80	World Wide Web HTTP
88	Kerberos
102	ISO-TSAP
103	X.400
104	X.400 sending service
111	Sun RPC
123	Network Time Protocol (NTP)
139	NetBIOS session source
144	News

Port Number	Description
179	Border Gateway Protocol
512	exec
513	rlogin
514	rexec
515	lpd (line printer daemon)
517	talk
518	ntalk
2000	Open Windows (SUN)
X11	6000–6999

Besides port numbers, the screening routers are be able to filter packets based on the TCP flags. The TCP flags are used to indicate the type of TCP packet, such as the following:

✤ Open connection

✤ Acknowledgment of open connection

✤ Acknowledgment packet or data packet

The meanings of the TCP flags are shown in table 4.2. The most important TCP flags are the SYN and ACK flags. When the SYN flag is set to 1, it indicates that a TCP connection is being processed. This information is vital for designing proper filter rules for screening routers. If you want to prevent a TCP connection to an FTP service, for example, the screening router can reject packets to the FTP control port 21 that has the SYN flag set.

TABLE 4.2
TCP Flags

TCP Flags	Description
URG	This flag is used to send out-of-band data without waiting for the receiver to process octets already in the stream. When the URG flag is set, the urgent pointer field is valid. RFC 1122 states that the urgent pointer points to the sequence number of the LAST octet (not LAST+1) in a sequence of urgent data, and that RFC 793 describes it incorrectly as LAST + 1. A TCP implementation must support a sequence of urgent data of any length. A TCP layer must

continues

TABLE 4.2, CONTINUED
TCP Flags

TCP Flags	Description
	inform the application layer asynchronously whenever the TCP layer receives an Urgent pointer with no previous pending urgent data, or whenever the urgent pointer advances in the data stream. There must be a way for the application to learn how much urgent data remains to be read from the connection, or at least to determine whether more urgent data remains to be read. Although the urgent mechanism can be used for any application, it normally is used to send interrupt-type commands to a Telnet program. The asynchronous, or out-of-band, notification enables the application to go into urgent mode, reading data from the TCP connection. This enables control commands to be sent to an application whose normal input buffers are full of unprocessed data.
ACK	The ACK flag indicates that the acknowledgment number field is valid.
PSH	This flag tells TCP to deliver data for this message immediately to the upper-layer process. When an application issues a series of send calls without setting the PSH flag, the TCP may aggregate the data internally without sending it. Similarly, when a series of segments is received without the PSH bit, a TCP may queue the data internally without passing it to the receiving application. The PSH bit is not a record marker and is independent of segment boundaries. Some implementations incorrectly think of the PSH as a record marker, however. The transmitter should collapse successive PSH bits when it packetizes data to send the largest possible segment. TCP can implement PSH flags on send calls. If PSH flags are not implemented, then the sending TCP must not buffer data indefinitely and must set the PSH bit in the last buffered segment (for example, when no more queued data is to be sent). RFC-793 erroneously implies that a received PSH flag must be passed to the application layer. Passing a received PSH flag to the application layer is optional. An application program is logically required to set the PSH flag in a send call whenever it needs to force delivery of the data to avoid a communication deadlock. A TCP should send a maximum-size segment whenever possible to improve performance, however. This means that on the sender side, a PSH may not result in the segment

TCP Flags	Description
	being immediately transmitted. When the PSH flag is not implemented on send TCP calls (or when the application/TCP interface uses a pure streaming model), responsibility for aggregating any tiny data fragments to form reasonable-size segments is partially borne by the application layer. Generally, an interactive application protocol must set the PSH flag at least in the last send call in each command or response sequence. A bulk transfer protocol like FTP should set the PSH flag on the last segment of a file, or when necessary to prevent buffer deadlock. At the receiver, the PSH bit forces buffered data to be delivered to the application (even if less than a full buffer is received). Conversely, the lack of a PSH can be used to avoid unnecessary wake-up calls to the application process; this can be an important performance optimization for large time-sharing hosts.
RST	The RST bit resets the virtual circuit due to unrecoverable errors. The reason could be a host crash or delayed duplicate SYN packets.
SYN	This flag indicates the opening of a virtual-circuit connection. TCP connections are opened using the three-way handshake procedure.
FIN	The FIN flag terminates the connection. Connection termination in TCP is accomplished by using a graceful close mechanism. Both sides must agree to terminate by sending a FIN = 1 flag before connection termination can occur; doing this ensures that data is not unexpectedly lost by either side by an abrupt connection termination.

When the SYN flag is set to 1, the ACK flag can be set to either 0 or 1. The settings of the ACK flag indicate whether the TCP packet is a connection or connection acknowledgment packet. If the SYN flag is set to 1 and the ACK flag is set to 1, the TCP packet is a connection packet. You can see this in figure 4.8 where a connection is made by a client on the Internet to a server on a local network. The server has a passive open connection and is waiting for a connection packet on a specified port. When the TCP connection packet is received by the server, it sends an open connection acknowledgment packet. The open connection packet has the following flag settings:

SYN = 1

ACK = 0

The open connection acknowledgment packet has the following settings:

SYN = 1

ACK = 1

When the client receives the open connection acknowledgment packet, it acknowledges this packet, completing the three-way handshake. The acknowledgment of the open connection acknowledgment packet has the following TCP flag settings:

SYN = 0

ACK = 1

FIGURE 4.8

TCP open connection.

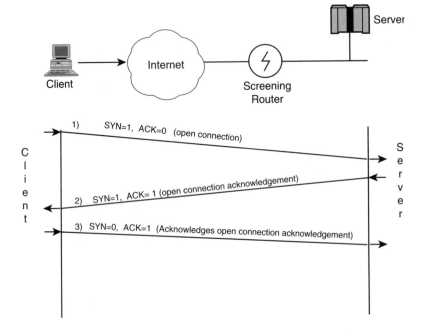

The three major combinations of SYN and ACK flag settings are summarized in table 4.3.

TABLE 4.3
SYN and ACK Flag Combinations

SYN Flag	ACK Flag	Meaning
1	0	Open connection TCP packet
1	1	Open connection acknowledgment
0	1	Acknowledgment packet or data packet

Figures 4.9 through 4.11 show a protocol decode of a TCP connection three-way handshake taken from a live TELNET connection. Figure 4.9 shows the open connection packet to the server, figure 4.10 shows the open connection acknowledgment, and figure 4.11 shows the acknowledgment to this open connection acknowledgment packet. Figure 4.11 shows that besides acknowledging the server connection acknowledgment, the client also sends application data that is part of the telnet protocol (option negotiation).

Thus, screening routers can perform packet filtering based upon the following:

❖ Source port number

❖ Destination port number

❖ TCP flags

Although screening routers can filter on any of the TCP flag settings, the flags that are most frequently used are the SYN and ACK flags.

Besides TCP, another transport protocol that can be used is UDP (User Datagram Protocol). The User Datagram Protocol is a simpler transport protocol than TCP. It is popular in many LAN-oriented applications and is a connectionless transport protocol, meaning that it does not use a preestablished connection to transmit data.

Whereas the TCP protocol is responsible for reliable, simultaneous, full-duplex connections, the UDP protocol provides unreliable connectionless transport services. The term *reliable* means that TCP takes care of transmission errors by resending the portion of data that was in error. Any application that uses TCP does not have to be concerned with reliability of data transmission because this is handled by TCP. TCP provides for simultaneous connections. This means that several TCP connections could be established at a host over which data could be sent simultaneously independent of data on other connections. TCP provides full-duplex connections, which means that data can be sent and received on a single connection.

On the other hand, the UDP protocol is not as robust as TCP and can be used by applications that do not require the reliability of TCP at the host-to-host layer. It is called an *unreliable protocol* because the protocol does not guarantee the reliable delivery of a packet. It makes the best efforts it can to deliver the packet. Although the UDP protocol does provide an optional checksum for data integrity, unlike TCP it does not guarantee the sequenced delivery of the packets. *Sequenced delivery* means that packets are received in the order in which they are sent. UDP cannot guarantee sequenced delivery because it has no provision for keeping track of sequence numbers for packets. UDP has less overhead compared to TCP. If additional reliability such as data being received in the order in which it was sent (sequenced delivery) is required, the application that uses UDP has to provide for it.

165

Figure 4.9

Three-way handshake: open connection TCP packet with SYN=1, ACK=0.

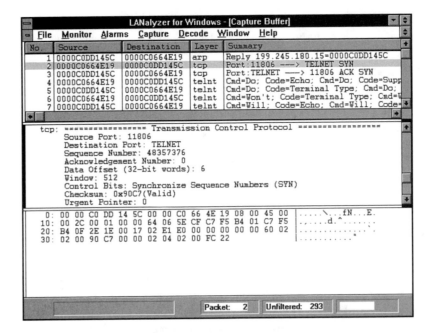

Figure 4.10

Three-way handshake: open connection acknowledgment TCP packet with SYN=1, ACK=1.

```
┌──────────────────────────────────────────────────────────────────────┬─┬─┐
│                 LANalyzer for Windows - [Capture Buffer]               │▼│▲│
├──────────────────────────────────────────────────────────────────────┼─┼─┤
│ □ File  Monitor  Alarms  Capture  Decode  Window  Help                │ │▲│
├────┬──────────────┬──────────────┬───────┬──────────────────────────┬─┤ │
│No. │ Source       │ Destination  │ Layer │ Summary                  │▲│ │
├────┼──────────────┼──────────────┼───────┼──────────────────────────┤ │ │
│  1 │0000C0DD145C  │0000C0664E19  │ arp   │Reply 199.245.180.15=0000C0DD145C│
│  2 │0000C0664E19  │0000C0DD145C  │ tcp   │Port:11806 ----> TELNET SYN│ │
│  3 │0000C0DD145C  │0000C0664E19  │ tcp   │Port:TELNET ----> 11806 ACK SYN│
│  4 │0000C0664E19  │0000C0DD145C  │ telnt │Cmd=Do; Code=Echo; Cmd=Do; Code=Supp│
│  5 │0000C0DD145C  │0000C0664E19  │ telnt │Cmd=Do; Code=Terminal Type; Cmd=Do;│
│  6 │0000C0664E19  │0000C0DD145C  │ telnt │Cmd=Won't; Code=Terminal Type; Cmd=W│
│  7 │0000C0DD145C  │0000C0664E19  │ telnt │Cmd=Will; Code=Echo; Cmd=Will; Code=│▼│
├─┼──────────────────────────────────────────────────────────────────┼─┤ │
│◄│                                                                   │► │
├────────────────────────────────────────────────────────────────────┴──┤ │
│ tcp: ================ Transmission Control Protocol ================  │▲│
│      Source Port: 11806                                               │ │
│      Destination Port: TELNET                                         │ │
│      Sequence Number: 48357377                                        │ │
│      Acknowledgement Number: 3825856002                               │ │
│      Data Offset (32-bit words): 5                                    │ │
│      Window: 512                                                      │ │
│      Control Bits: Acknowledgement Field is Valid (ACK)               │ │
│            Push Function Requested (PSH)                              │ │
│      Checksum: 0xD3A4(Valid)                                          │▼│
├────────────────────────────────────────────────────────────────────────┤
│  0: 00 00 C0 DD 14 5C 00 00 C0 66 4E 19 08 00 45 00 │.....\...fN...E. │
│ 10: 00 2E 00 02 00 00 64 06 5E CC C7 F5 B4 01 C7 F5 │......d.^....... │
│ 20: B4 0F 2E 1E 00 17 02 E1 E0 01 E4 09 EE 02 50 18 │..............P. │
│ 30: 02 00 D3 A4 00 00 FF FD 01 FF FD 03             │................ │
│                                                                        │
│                                                                        │
│                                                                        │
│                                                                        │
├────────────────────────────────────────────────────────────────────────┤
│            │ Packet:  4 │ Unfiltered:  293 │                           │
└────────────────────────────────────────────────────────────────────────┘
```

FIGURE 4.11

Three-way handshake: acknowledgment of open connection acknowledgment packet with SYN=0, ACK=1.

Figure 4.12 shows a UDP header. Notice that like the TCP packet in figure 4.7, the UDP header has source and port numbers. Because these port numbers refer to the UDP protocol that is distinct from the TCP protocol, these port numbers are in a different address space than the TCP port numbers. Some application services are available through both the TCP and UDP protocols, in which case they have port numbers defined for both TCP and UDP. Table 4.4 shows some of the examples for the UDP port numbers.

FIGURE 4.12

A UDP packet header (Graphic courtesy of Learning Tree International).

- **Notable points**
  - No sequence or acknowledgment numbers
  - No flow control
  - Messages can be duplicated or arrive out of order
  - Checksum includes pseudoheader

167

TABLE 4.4
Example UDP Port Numbers

UDP Port Number	Description
0	Reserved
2	Management Utility
3	Compression Process
5	Remote Job Entry
7	Echo
9	Discard
11	Active Users (systat)
13	Daytime
17	Quote of the Day (QUOTD)
35	Any private printer server
37	Time
39	Resource Location Protocol
42	Host name server (nameserver)
43	Who Is (nicname)
49	Login Host Protocol (login)
52	XNS Time Protocol
53	Domain Name Server (domain)
54	XNS clearing house
66	Oracle SQL*NET (sql*net)
67	Bootstrap Protocol Server (bootps)
68	Bootstrap Protocol Client (bootpc)
69	Trivial Transfer Protocol (tftp)
80	World Wide Web HTTP

UDP Port Number	Description
88	Kerberos
94	Trivoli Object Dispatcher (objcall)
95	SUPDUP
108	SNA Gateway Access Server (snagas)
110	Post Office Protocol - Version 3 (POP3)
111	Sun Remote Procedure Call (sunrpc)
119	Network News Transfer Protocol (NNTP)
123	Network Time Protocol (NTP)
134	INGRES-NET Service
137	NETBIOS Naming Service (netbios-ns)
138	NETBIOS Datagram Service (netbios-dgm)
139	NETBIOS Session Service (netbios-ssn)
142	Britton-Lee IDM
161	SNMP
162	SNMP Traps
191	Prospero
194	Internet Relay Chat Protocol (irc)
201	AppleTalk Routing Maintenance (at-rtmp)
202	AppleTalk Name Binding (at-nbp)
213	IPX (used for IP tunneling)
215	Insignia (Soft PC)
217	dBASE Unix
372	Unix Listserv
513	Maintains database on who is logged on to machines on a local net and the load average of the machine (who)
517	talk

continues

169

TABLE 4.4, CONTINUED
Example UDP Port Numbers

UDP Port Number	Description
518	ntalk
519	unixtime
525	Time Server (timed)
533	Emergency broadcasts (netwall)
556	RFS server (remoterfs)
565	Who Am I (whoami)
749	Kerberos Administration (kerberos-adm)
767	Phone (phonebook)
1025	Network Blackjack (blackjack)
1352	Lotus Notes (lotusnote)
2000	Open Windows
2049	Network File System (NFS)
6000 to 6999	X11
7000 to 7009	Used by Andrew File System (AFS)
17007	ISODE Directory User Agent (isode-dua)

The term *connectionless,* when applied to a protocol, means that the data can be sent without requiring that a data circuit be established. Each data unit is sent with complete source and destination IP addresses and port numbers that identify the application level processes that are involved in the data exchange. UDP is similar to ordinary postal services in that complete addressing information is sent with each UDP message.

A big advantage that UDP has over TCP is that UDP is more suited for applications that require broadcast data. A single datagram can be broadcast on the network by specifying a broadcast address on the destination address. UDP is popular in many LAN-based applications that are broadcast-based and do not require the complexity of TCP.

> Examples of applications that use UDP are NFS (Network File System), DNS (Domain Name System), SNMP (Simple Network Management Protocol), and TFTP (Trivial File Transfer Protocol). UDP also is used for IP tunneling.

N O T E

SESSION LAYER

The *session layer* of the OSI model makes use of the transport layer to provide enhanced session services. Examples of a session include a user being logged in to a host across a network, or a session being established for the purpose of transferring files.

The session layer can provide some of the following enhancements:

Dialog control

Token management

Activity management

A session, in general, enables two-way communications (full duplex) across a connection. Some applications might require alternate one-way communications (half duplex). The session layer has the option of providing two-way or one-way communications, an option called *dialog control*.

For some protocols, it is essential that only one side attempt a critical operation at a time. To prevent both sides from attempting the same operation, a control mechanism, such as the use of tokens, can be implemented. When using the token method, only the side holding a token is permitted to perform the operation. Determining which side has the token and how it is transferred between the two sides is known as *token management*.

> The use of the word *token* here should not be confused with token ring operation. Token management is a much higher level concept than token ring operation, residing at layer five of the OSI model. IBM's Token-Ring operation belongs to layers two and one of the OSI model.

N O T E

If you are performing a one-hour file transfer between two machines, and network crashes occur approximately every 30 minutes, you might never be able to complete the file transfer. After each transfer aborts, you have to start all over again. To avoid this problem, you can treat the entire file transfer as a single activity with checkpoints inserted into the datastream. That way, if a crash occurs the session layer can synchronize to a previous checkpoint. This operation of managing an entire activity is called *activity management*.

In the TCP/IP world, the RPC (Remote Procedure Call) protocol used by NFS (Network File System) can be considered an example of a session layer protocol.

PRESENTATION LAYER

The *presentation layer* manages the way data is represented. Many ways of representing data exist, such as ASCII and EBCDIC for text files, and 1s or 2s complement representation for numbers. If the two sides involved in communication use different data representations, they will not be able to understand each other. The presentation layer represents data with a common syntax and semantics. If all the nodes used and understood this common language, misunderstanding in data representation could be eliminated.

An example of this common language is Abstract Syntax Representation, Rev 1 (ASN.1), an OSI recommendation. In the TCP/IP world, the ASN.1 is used for encoding SNMP messages. Another example of a protocol that corresponds to this layer is the External Data Representation (XDR) protocol that is used in the NFS.

APPLICATION LAYER

The *application layer* contains the protocols and functions needed by user applications to perform communication tasks. Examples of common functions include the following:

❖ Protocols for providing remote file services, such as open, close, read, write, and shared access to files

❖ File transfer services and remote database access

❖ Message handling services for e-mail applications

❖ Global directory services to locate resources on a network

❖ A uniform way of handling a variety of system monitors and devices

❖ Remote job execution

Many of these services are called application programming interfaces (APIs). *APIs* are programming libraries that an application writer can use to write network applications.

> For TCP/IP, examples of application layer protocols are FTP, SMTP, TELNET, SNMP, NFS, and X-Windows.

N O T E

Firewalls used for protecting networks operate at the application layer of the OSI model. Because firewalls operate at the highest level of the OSI model, they have access to more information than screening routers and can be programmed to operate more intelligently than screening routers.

SCREENING ROUTERS AND FIREWALLS IN RELATIONSHIP TO THE OSI MODEL

Figure 4.13 compares screening routers and firewalls in relationship to the OSI model. This figure shows that the screening router functions correspond to the network (IP protocol) and transport (TCP protocol) layers of the OSI model. Firewalls often are described as gateways. Gateways can perform processing at all the seven layers of the OSI model. Typically, gateways perform processing at the seventh (application) layer of the OSI model. This is true for most firewall gateways.

FIGURE 4.13

Screening routers, firewalls, and the OSI model.

Figure 4.13 also shows that because firewalls cover the network and transport layers, they can perform packet filtering functions. Some vendors, for marketing reasons perhaps, blur the distinction between a screening router and a firewall, to the extent that they call their screening router products firewall products. For the sake of clarity, this book makes the distinction between screening routers and firewalls based on the OSI model.

Sometimes screening routers are also called packet filter *gateways*. Perhaps one justification of the use of the term gateway for the packet filter device is that filtering based on the TCP flags done at the transport layer is not a function of the router that operates at the network layer of the OSI model. Devices that operate above the network layer also are called gateways.

173

You will learn in Chapter 7, "Firewall Architecture and Theory," how screening routers and firewall gateways can be combined to provide robust network security.

UNDERSTANDING PACKET FILTERING

Screening routers can use packet filtering as a means to enhance network security. The screening function also can be performed by many commercial firewall products and by software-based products such as the Karlbridge PC-Based Filters. However, many commercial routers can be programmed to perform filtering. Router vendors such as Cisco, Wellfleet, 3COM, Digital, Newbridge, ACC, and many others provide routers that can be programmed to perform packet filtering functions.

PACKET FILTERING AND NETWORK POLICY

Packet filtering can be used to implement a wide variety of network security policies. As discussed in Chapter 3, the network security policy must clearly state the types of resources and services that are being protected, their level of importance, and the people from whom the services are being protected.

Generally the network security policy guidelines are focused more in keeping outsiders out, than trying to police insiders. For example, it is more important to prevent outsiders from breaking in and intentionally exposing sensitive data or disrupting services than preventing insiders from using external network services. This type of network security policy determines where screening routers should be placed and how they should be programmed to perform packet filtering. Good network security implementations also should make it difficult for insiders to harm the network security. This usually is not the major thrust of security efforts.

One of the goals of a network security policy is to provide a transparent mechanism so that the policy is not a hindrance to the users. Because packet filtering operates at the network and transport layers of the OSI model, and not at the application layer, this approach generally tends to be more transparent than the firewall approach. Recall that firewalls operate at the application layer of the OSI model, and security implementations at this layer tend not to be as transparent.

A SIMPLE MODEL FOR PACKET FILTERING

A packet filter usually is placed between one or more network segments, as shown in figure 4.14. The network segments are classified as either an external or internal network segment. *External network segments* connect your network to outside networks such as the Internet. *Internal network segments* are used to connect the enterprise's hosts and other network resources.

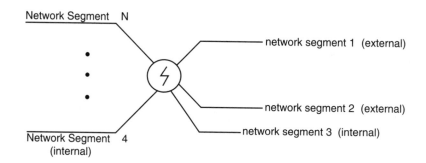

FIGURE 4.14

A packet filter placed between multiple segments.

Each of the ports of the packet filter device can be used to implement network policies that describe the type of network service that is accessible through the port. If the number of network segments that connect with the packet filter device is large, the policies that the packet filter device implements can become complex. In general, complex solutions to security problems should be avoided because of the following reasons:

❖ They are harder to maintain.

❖ It is easy to make mistakes in configuring packet filtering.

❖ They have an adverse effect on the performance of the device on which they are implemented.

In many instances, the simple model shown in figure 4.15 can be used to implement the network security policy. This model shows that the packet filter device has only two network segments connected to it. Typically, one of these network segments is an external network segment and the other is an internal network segment. Packet filtering is done to restrict the network traffic for the services that are to be denied. Because the network policy is written to favor insiders contacting external hosts, the filter on each side of the screening routers ports must behave differently. In other words, the filters are asymmetric.

FIGURE 4.15

A packet filter placed between two network segments.

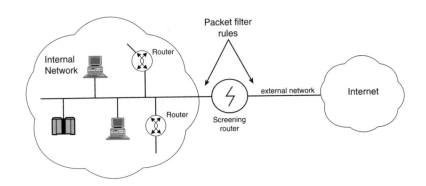

PACKET FILTER OPERATIONS

Almost all current packet filter devices (screening routers or packet filter gateways) operate in the following manner:

1. Packet filter criteria must be stored for the ports of the packet filter device. The packet filter criteria are called *packet filter rules.*

2. When the packet arrives at the port, the packet headers are parsed. Most packet filter devices examine the fields in only the IP, TCP, or UDP headers.

3. The packet filter rules are stored in a specific order. Each rule is applied to the packet in the order in which the packet filter rule is stored.

4. If a rule blocks the transmission or reception of a packet, the packet is not allowed.

5. If a rule allows the transmission or reception of a packet, the packet is allowed to proceed.

6. If a packet does not satisfy any rule, it is blocked.

These rules are expressed as a flowchart in figure 4.16.

From rules 4 and 5, you should realize that it is important to place the rules in the correct order. A common mistake in configuring packet filter rules is to place the rules in the wrong order. If the packet filter rules are placed in the wrong order, you might end up denying valid services, while permitting services that you wanted to deny.

Rule number 6 follows this philosophy:

That which is not expressly permitted is prohibited.

This is a fail-safe philosophy that you should follow when designing secure networks. It is the opposite of a permissive philosophy that says:

That which is not expressly prohibited is permitted.

If the latter philosophy were used for designing packet filters, you would have to think of every possible case not covered by the packet filter rules to make the network secure. And as new services are added, you easily can end up with situations in which no rule is matched. Rather than block this service and hear complaints from users if you have blocked a legitimate service (at which time you can unblock the service), you may end up allowing a service that can be a security risk to the network.

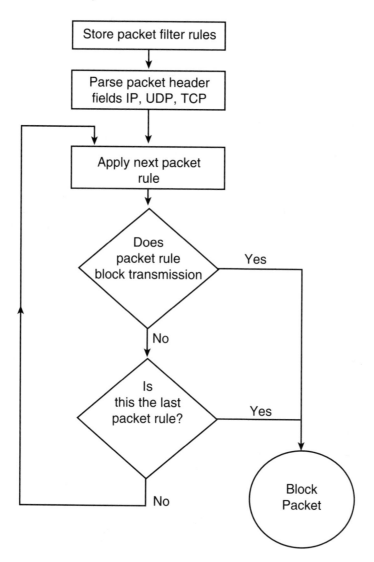

FIGURE 4.16

A Flowchart of packet filter operation.

PACKET FILTER DESIGN

Consider the network in figure 4.17 for which the screening router is used as the first line of defense between the internal protected network and an external untrusted network.

FIGURE 4.17

Sample network for packet filter design.

Assume that the network security policy requires that Internet mail be received from external hosts on a specific gateway, and you want to deny network traffic originating from the host named CREEPHOST that you do not trust. (Perhaps one reason for this could be that they have a tendency to send large messages that your mail cannot handle. Another could be that you suspect security threats originating from this host.)

In this example, the network security policy on SMTP use must be translated into packet filter rules. You could translate the network security rules into the following English language rules:

[Filter Rule 1]

We do not trust connections from host CREEPHOST.

[Filter Rule 2]

We wish to allow connections to our mail gateway.

These rules can be encoded into the table of rules shown in figure 4.18. The asterisk (*) symbol is used to match any values for that column.

For filter rule 1 (in figure 4.18) there is an entry for the External Host column, and all other columns have the asterisk symbol. The action is to block the connection. This translates to the following:

Block any connection from CREEPHOST originating from *any* (asterisk) of its ports to *any* (asterisk) of our ports on *any* (asterisk) of our hosts.

For filter rule 2 there is an entry for the Our Host and the Port on Our Host columns. All other columns have the asterisk symbol. The action is to allow the connection. This translates to the following:

> Allow any connection from *any* (asterisk) external host originating from *any* (asterisk) of its ports to port 25 of on our MAIL-GW host.

Port 25 is used because this TCP port is reserved for SMTP (refer to table 4.1).

Filter rule number	Action	Our Host	Port on Our Host	External Host	Port on External Router	Description
1	Block	*	*	CREEPHOST	*	Block traffic from CREEPHOST
2	Allow	Mail-GW	25	*	*	Allow connection to our MAIL gateway

Legend:　* = Matches all values

FIGURE 4.18

An attempt to encode packet filter rules.

The rules are applied in the order of their number in the table. If a packet does not match any of the rules, it is rejected.

A serious problem with the way the rules are specified in figure 4.18 is that it allows any external machine to originate a call from port 25. Port 25 should be reserved for SMTP, as per RFC 1700 (Assigned Numbers), but an external host could use this for other nefarious purposes. A better way to encode these rules is to permit internal hosts to make outgoing calls to an external hosts port 25. This enables the internal host to send mail to external sites. If the external site is not using port 25 for SMTP, the SMTP-sender process will not be able to send mail. This is equivalent to mail not being supported on the external host.

As mentioned before, a TCP connection is a full duplex connection and information flows in both directions. The packet filter rules in figure 4.18 do not explicitly specify in which direction the information in the packet is being sent: from our host to the external site, or from an external site to our host.

When a TCP packet is sent in any direction, it must be acknowledged by the receiver. The receiver sends the acknowledgment by setting the ACK flag. Figure 4.8 shows the use of the ACK flag in acknowledging the TCP open connection requests. However, ACK flags are used in normal TCP transmission as illustrated in figure 4.19. In this figure, the sender sends a TCP segment (data sent by TCP is called a *segment*) whose starting byte number (SEQ#) is 1001 and length is 100 bytes. The receiver sends back a TCP acknowledgment packet indicated by the ACK flag set to 1, and the acknowledgment number (ACK#) set to 1001+100 = 1101. The sender then sends two TCP segment numbers that are 200 bytes each. These are acknowledged by a single acknowledgment packet that has the ACK flag set to 1, and acknowledgment number indicating the starting byte number of the next TCP data segment (1101 + 200 + 200 = 1501).

179

FIGURE 4.19

Use of acknowledg-ments in TCP data transfer (Graphic courtesy of Learning Tree International).

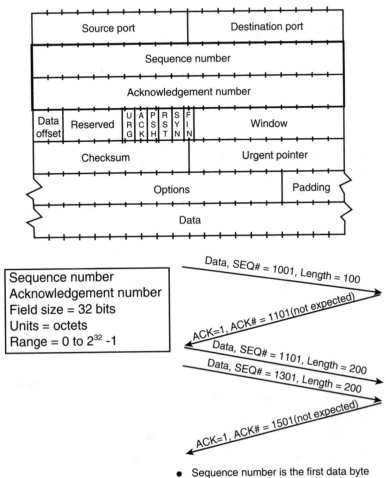

From figure 4.19, you can see that ACK packets will be sent on all TCP connections. When the ACK packet is sent, the sending direction is reversed, and the packet filter rules should take into account the ACK packets that are sent in response to control or data packets.

Based on the previous discussion, the modified set of packet rules can be written as indicated in figure 4.20.

180

Filter rule number	Action	Source Host	Source Host Port	Destination Host	Destination Host Port	TCP flags IP options	Description
1	Allow	199.245.19.0	*	*	25		Allow packet from network 199.245.180.0
2	Allow	*	25	199.245.180.0	*	ACK	Allow return acknowledgement

FIGURE 4.20

Packet filter rules for SMTP.

For filter rule 1 (in figure 4.20) there is an entry for the Source Host column of 199.245.180.0, and an entry in the Destination Host Port column of 25. All other columns have the asterisk symbol.

The action in filter rule 1 is to allow a connection. This translates to the following:

> Allow any connection from network 199.245.180.0 originating from *any* (asterisk) of its ports to *any* (asterisk) port on any (asterisk) destination host or network.

Note that because 199.245.180 is a class C network number (also called the *netid*), the 0 in the host number (also called *hostid*) field refers to any host on the class C network 199.245.180.

For filter rule 2 there is an entry for the Source Host Port column of 25, an entry in the Destination Host column, and a TCP ACK entry in the TCP flags/IP options column. All other columns have the asterisk symbol.

The action in filter rule 2 is to allow a connection. This translates to the following:

> Allow any connection from *any* network originating from port 25 and which has the TCP ACK flag set to *any* (asterisk) port on any (asterisk) host on our network (199.245.180.0).

The combined effects of filter rules 1 and 2 of figure 4.20 is to allow TCP packets between the network 199.245.180.0 to the SMTP port on any external host.

Because the packet filter examines only layers 2 and 3 in the OSI model, there is no way to absolutely guarantee that the return TCP acknowledgments are part of the same connection. In actual practice, the scheme works well because TCP connections maintain state information on each side. They know what sequence numbers and acknowledgments to expect. Also, the upper layer application services, such as TELNET and SMTP, can accept only those packets that follow the application protocol rules. It is very difficult (though theoretically possible) to forge return replies that contain the correct ACK packets. For a higher level of security, one can use application-level gateways such as firewalls.

PACKET FILTER RULES AND FULL-ASSOCIATIONS

Figure 4.21 shows a worksheet that can be used for designing packet filter rules. Screening routers, in general, can filter based upon any of the field values in the TCP or IP protocol headers. For most network security policies that can be implemented by screening routers, you need to specify only the TCP flags, IP options, and source and destination address values.

FIGURE 4.21

A worksheet for designing packet rules.

Filter rule number	Action	Source	Source Port	Destination	Dest. Port	Protocol Flags Options	Description
1							
2							
3							
4							
5							
6							
7							
8							

If you examine each row in the worksheet, you will notice that it completely describes the TCP connection. Formally, a complete description of a connection is called a *full association*.

When designing packet filter rules it is helpful to keep in mind the definitions of full association, half association, and endpoints. This helps you better understand the packet filtering rules.

A *full association* is illustrated in figure 4.22, which shows that a TCP connection between two hosts can be described by the following information:

✦ Protocol type

✦ Local IP address

✦ Local TCP port number

✦ Remote IP address

✦ Remote TCP port number

Process Addressing

FIGURE **4.22**

A full association (Graphic courtesy of Learning Tree International).

***Association* describes a connection in terms of**

- Protocol
- Local address
- Local port number
- Remote address
- Remote port number
- Example: (tcp, 199.21.32.2, 1400, 196.62.132.1, 21)

In figure 4.22, the protocol type is TCP, the local IP address is 199.21.32.2, the local TCP port number is 1400, the remote IP address is 196.62.132.1, and the remote TCP port number is port 21. The full association for this circuit is represented as a 5-tuple. In the example in figure 4.22, this 5-tuple is:

(TCP, 199.21.32.2, 1600, 196.62.132.1, 21)

Comparing this 5-tuple with the entries in worksheet 4.21, you can see that each worksheet describes the full association between hosts. The worksheet also contains the following additional information:

- ✤ Action

- ✤ TCP and IP options

- ✤ Order in which the rule should be executed

Each side of the connection can be described by a half association. A *half association* describes only one end of the connection and consists of the following:

✦ Protocol type

✦ IP address

✦ TCP port number

Thus, the two half associations that form the TCP connection of figure 4.22 are the following:

(TCP, 199.21.32.2, 1600)

(TCP, 196.62.132.1, 21)

The *endpoint,* also called the *transport address,* consists of the following:

✦ IP address

✦ TCP port number

The endpoints for the TCP connection in figure 4.22 are the following:

(199.21.32.2, 1600)

(196.62.132.1, 21)

Because each rule in the worksheet of figure 4.21 can have a range of values for any of the values in the fields that describe a full association, a number of different types of TCP circuits can be described by the packet filter rule. This enables a packet filter rule to implement a network security policy by describing a variety of different types of TCP connections.

SUMMARY

This chapter introduced the concepts necessary to understand screening routers and packet filtering. The role of the packet filter was described in reference to the OSI model. You also learned about the typical protocol flags on which routing decisions are made. The next chapter follows this logic and discusses how packet filter rules are implemented and applied.

## CHAPTER 5

PACKET FILTERS

THE LAST CHAPTER introduced packet filtering after explaining the information necessary to understand the process. This chapter continues that topic and discusses implementing packet filter rules, protocol-specific issues in packet filtering, and examples of screening router configurations.

To make the screening router configuration examples more practical, these discussions are done in the context of Cisco routers. These examples include defining access lists, using standard access lists, using extended access lists, filtering on incoming/outgoing calls, and IP security options for Cisco routers. You will learn about packet filter placement and filtering on input and output ports. This chapter discusses examples of filtering FTP network traffic and problems in filtering an FTP session.

IMPLEMENTING PACKET FILTER RULES

Once you have designed the packet filter rules and described them in the packet filter rule worksheet (shown in figure 4.21 of the preceding chapter), you have to implement them on the screening router or firewall (if it allows packet filter rules to be specified).

Each type of packet filter device has its own set of rules and syntax on how to program the packet filter rules. Therefore, one must read the packet filter device documentation and learn the peculiarities of the packet filter rules syntax for that device. If you change the vendor of the packet filter device, you will have to learn a different set of syntax rules.

NOTE

> One of the goals of this book is to give you practical advice on building Internet firewalls and improving network security. Because of this, the author believes that it is important to show some practical examples of how packet filter rules can be specified. This will be done in relationship to the screening routers from the router vendor Cisco, Inc.

A word or two about the selection of the vendor is perhaps in order. Selection of the Cisco routers in the packet filtering examples is by no means an endorsement of the product. The author would be equally happy discussing another router vendor's product. On the other hand, Cisco dominates the router market and implements many of the packet filter capabilities discussed in this book. The packet filter rules for other vendors' routers are similar in principle to the ones used by Cisco routers, but are syntactically different.

DEFINING ACCESS LISTS

Cisco routers define *access lists* as a sequential collection of permit-and-deny conditions that apply to Internet addresses. These access-list conditions are used to implement the packet filter rules.

When the screening router is programmed with access lists, it tests the packets against the conditions in the access list one by one. The first match determines if the router accepts or rejects the packet. Because the screening router stops testing conditions in the access lists after the first match, the order of the conditions is critical. If no conditions are matched, the packet is rejected.

The Cisco routers have two types of access lists:

❖ Standard access lists

❖ Extended access lists

The standard access lists have a single address for matching operations, and the extended access lists have two addresses with optional protocol-type information for matching operations. For many practical filtering operations, you need both the standard and extended access lists.

USING STANDARD ACCESS LISTS

The syntax for the standard access lists is as follows:

```
access-list list {permit ¦ deny} address wildcard-mask
no access-list list
```

The *list* is an integer ranging from 1 to 99 and is used to identify one or more permit/deny conditions. This integer value corresponds to the Filter rule number values described in figure 4.21 of the preceding chapter. Access list 0 is predefined; it permits any access that is the default access list for terminal lines.

The use of the keywords "permit" and "deny" corresponds to the words "allow" and "block" in the packet filter rules discussed earlier. Any IP destination address in the packet is compared to the *address* value specified in the access-list command. If the keyword "permit" is used, a match causes the packet to be accepted. If the keyword "deny" is used, a match causes the packet to be rejected.

The *address* and the *wildcard-mask* are 32-bit values and are written using the dotted-decimal notation. The *wildcard-mask* should not be confused with subnet masks that are used to subdivide an IP network number assignment. Address bits corresponding to a 1 in the *wildcard-mask* are ignored in the comparison. Address bits corresponding to a 0 in the *wildcard-mask* are used in the comparison. Consider the following example:

```
access-list 1 permit 199.245.180.0  0.0.0.255
access-list 1 permit 132.23.0.0  0.0.255.255
```

In this example, two address/wildcard-mask values are specified, and they both apply to the access-list number 1. The first access-list command permits access for hosts on the class C network 199.245.180.0, and the second access-list command permits access for hosts on the class B network 132.23.0.0.

187

If the wildcard-mask value is not specified, it is assumed to be 0.0.0.0; that is, all the bits in the address are compared. Thus, the following two access-list commands have an identical effect:

```
access-list 2 permit 132.23.1.3  0.0.0.0
access-list 2 permit 132.23.1.3
```

Both of the previous commands allow packets for the host with IP address 132.23.1.3 only. If the wildcard-mask value is non-zero, it can specify a range of IP addresses. Therefore, this should be done with care.

Perhaps another example of the use of standard access lists will clarify its use. Assume a class A network 67.0.0.0 connected to a screening router that is using a subnet mask of 255.255.0.0. Consider the following access-list commands:

```
access-list 3 permit 67.23.2.5  0.0.0.0
access-list 3 deny 67.23.0.0  0.0.255.255
access-list 3 permit 67.0.0.0  0.255.255.255
```

The first access list permits traffic for a single host with IP address 67.23.2.5 on subnet 23 of the class A network. The second access list blocks all traffic to subnet 23. Because this follows the rule that permits traffic to host 67.23.2.5, it does not affect traffic sent to that host. The third rule permits traffic sent to the entire class A 63.0.0.0 network. Therefore, the access lists implement the following network policy:

> "Block all traffic to subnet 0.23.0.0 for class A network 67.0.0.0, with the exception of allowing traffic to host 67.23.2.5 on this network. Allow traffic for all other subnets of 67.0.0.0."

You can use the "no access-list *list*" command to delete the entire access list. This is useful if you do not know if an access list for that number has been defined before, and you want to start with a clean slate.

USING EXTENDED ACCESS LISTS

The extended access lists enable you to filter interface traffic based on source and destination IP addresses and protocol information.

The syntax for the extended access lists is as follows:

```
access-list list {permit | deny} protocol source source-mask destination
destination-mask [operator operand]
```

The *list* is an integer ranging from 100 to 199 and is used to identify one or more extended permit/deny conditions. The numbers 100 to 199 are reserved for extended access lists and are outside the range of the numbers 1 to 99 used for standard access lists.

If the keyword "permit" is used, a match with the condition causes the packet to be accepted. This is equivalent to the "allow" rule used in packet filter design rules. If the keyword "deny" is used, a match causes the packet to be rejected. This is equivalent to the "block" rule used in packet filter design rules. The rest of the extended list is not processed after a match occurs.

The *protocol* can represent any of the following values corresponding to the IP, TCP, UDP, and ICMP protocols:

- ✤ ip
- ✤ tcp
- ✤ udp
- ✤ icmp

Because IP encapsulates TCP, UDP, and ICMP packets, it can be used to match any of these protocols.

The *source* and the *source-mask* are 32-bit values and are written using the dotted-decimal notation. These are used to identify the source IP address. The *source-mask* should not be confused with subnet masks that are used to subdivide an IP network number assignment. Address bits corresponding to a 1 in the *source-mask* are ignored in the comparison. Address bits corresponding to a 0 in the *source-mask* are used in the comparison.

The *destination* and *destination-mask* are used for matching the destination IP address. These also are written using the dotted-decimal notation, and the *destination-mask* is used in the same way as the *source-mask* for *source* addresses.

The *operator* and *operand* are used to compare port numbers, service access points, or contact names. These values are meaningful for the TCP and UDP protocols. For the tcp and udp protocol key values, the *operator* can be any of the following values:

- ✤ lt (less than)
- ✤ eq (equal to)
- ✤ gt (greater than)
- ✤ neq (not equal to)

The *operand* is the decimal value of the destination port for the specified protocol. The following are examples of the use of access-list commands.

EXAMPLE 1

Suppose network policy requires that you deny incoming SMTP connections from host 132.124.23.55 to your network 199.245.180.0. You can implement this policy by the following extended access list:

```
no access-list  101
access-list 101 deny  tcp 132.124.23.55 0.0.0.0 199.245.180.0 0.0.0.255 eq 25
```

The first command deletes any prior extended access-list 101. The second command denies a TCP packet coming from host 132.124.23.55 to network 199.245.180.0 with a destination port of 25 (SMTP).

EXAMPLE 2

In this example, the internal network is 133.34.0.0.

```
access-list 101 permit tcp 0.0.0.0 255.255.255.255 133.34.0.0 0.0.255.255 gt
➡1023
access-list 101 permit tcp 0.0.0.0 255.255.255.255 133.34.12.3 0.0.0.0 eq 25
access-list 101 permit icmp 0.0.0.0 255.255.255.255 133.34.0.0 255.255.255.255
interface ethernet 0
ip access-group 101
```

The first access-list command permits any incoming TCP connections with destination ports greater than 1023. The second access-list command permits incoming TCP connections to the SMTP port of host 133.34.12.3. The last access-list command permits incoming ICMP messages for error feedback.

Note that the extended access-list command must be used with the access-group interface command that can take an extended access list number (100 to 199) as an argument. The access-group command is used to apply the access-list definitions to the interface. The syntax of the access-group command is as follows:

```
ip access-group list
```

where *list* is a number from 1 to 199 and specifies the access list to be applied to the interface.

EXAMPLE 3

In this example, assume that you have a network (181.12.0.0) connected to the Internet. Your network security policy requires any host on the internal network to be able to form TCP connections to any host on the Internet. However, you do not want Internet hosts to be able to form TCP connections to hosts on the internal network, except to the mail (SMTP) port of a dedicated mail host (181.12.34.12).

The keyword "established" can be used for the TCP protocol to indicate an established connection. A match occurs if the TCP datagram has the ACK or RST bits set, which indicates that the packet belongs to an existing connection.

```
access-list 102 permit tcp 0.0.0.0 255.255.255.255 181.12.0.0 0.0.255.255
➡established
```

```
access-list 102 permit tcp 0.0.0.0 255.255.255.255 181.12.34.12 0.0.0.0 eq 25
interface ethernet 0
ip access-group 102
```

FILTERING ON INCOMING AND OUTGOING CALLS

To restrict incoming and outgoing connections between a line into the Cisco router and the addresses in an access list, you can use the access-class line configuration command.

```
access-class list {in | out}
```

The *list* is the number of the access list. Using the value "in" at the end of the command restricts incoming traffic between the Cisco device and the addresses in the access list. Using the value "out" at the end of the command restricts outgoing traffic between the Cisco device and the addresses in the access list. To remove access restrictions for a specified access list, use the following command:

```
no access-class access-list-number {in | out}
```

The following example defines an access list that permits only hosts on network 199.245.75.0 to connect to the virtual terminal ports 1 to 5 on the router:

```
access-list 18 permit 192.89.55.0 0.0.0.255
line 1 5
access-class 18 in
```

The following example blocks connections to networks other than network 156.233.0.0 on terminal lines 1 through 3:

```
access-list 19 permit 156.233.0.0 0.0.255.255
line 1 3
access-class 19 out
```

UNDERSTANDING THE IP SECURITY OPTION FOR CISCO ROUTERS

Cisco routers support both basic and extended security options. These are useful for those networks that implement IP security. The IP Security Option (IPSO) has the following abilities:

❖ Defines security level on a per-interface basis

❖ Defines single-level or multilevel interfaces

❖ Provides labeling of incoming datagrams

✥ Strips labels on a per-interface basis

✥ Reorders options to put any basic security options first

✥ Accepts or rejects messages with extended security options

EXAMINING PACKET FILTER PLACEMENT AND ADDRESS SPOOFING

When designing packet filter rules, you must specify whether to perform packet filtering on incoming or outgoing packets. A related issue is determining where to place a packet filter. Packet filter rules should also be written in a manner that prevents address spoofing. These issues are examined in the sections that follow.

PACKET FILTER PLACEMENT

Consider the screening router of figure 5.1. The router can examine packets at any one of its interfaces. In the case of figure 5.1, the router can examine the packet traffic at either the inside port or outside port. Another factor to consider is the fact that packets can be either incoming or outgoing at any of the router's interfaces. The packet filtering, therefore, can be done on either incoming packets, outgoing packets, or both. Until very recently, for example, Cisco routers performed filtering only on outgoing packets.

FIGURE 5.1

The placement of a packet filter.

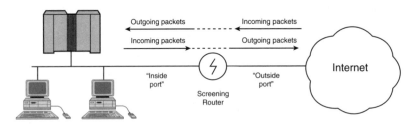

Many router vendors implement packet filtering on outgoing packets for efficiency reasons. For outgoing packets, the filter rules can be applied when the router consults its tables to determine the destination of the packet. If the packet is not routable, or there is no match of the filter rules, the packet is rejected, and an ICMP destination unreachable message is sent.

If routers filter packets at the time the packets are being sent out of a router port, some information is lost. The router does not know which interface the packet arrived on. This can leave your network vulnerable to a type of attack known as *address spoofing*.

Consider the network in figure 5.2. A class B network 135.12.0.0 is connected to the Internet using a screening router. This class B internal network is using subnetting. The subnet mask is 255.255.255.0 for both subnets 10 and 11. An outside TCP/IP host sends a packet claiming to originate from the IP address 135.12.10.201. This packet is received by the screening router in its outside port. If the router was filtering incoming packets, it could quickly catch this pretender packet because it knows that the network 135.12.10.0 is connected to a different(inside) port, and therefore the packet could not have originated on its outside port. However, if the packet filtering is done on outgoing packets, the router does not check to see that this packet that was received on an outside port could not have originated from the internal network.

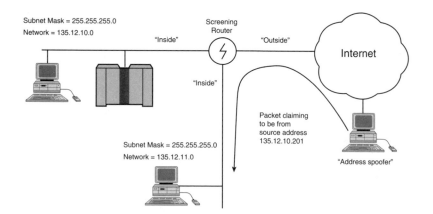

FIGURE 5.2

The placement of a packet filter.

Therefore, filtering on incoming packets can prevent a class of attack called address spoofing. In general, you should perform filtering as quickly as possible.

In figure 5.3, there are two inside ports and one outside port to the router. If all packets that are exchanged with the outside world are through this single access point, then the screening router can effectively act as a discriminating "choke" between the outside world (screening routers are also referred to as *chokes*) and the internal network.

Also in figure 5.3, if you wrote packet filter rules at the inside port for screening traffic between the internal network and the Internet, you would have to write a set of rules at each of the inside ports. This would additionally impact the router performance.

If the screening router has only two ports—one connecting to the external network and the other connecting to the internal network (see fig. 5.1)—then the packet filter rules are symmetric whether they are written for the inside or outside port. This is because the incoming packets on one port will appear, if not rejected by the router's routing table, as outgoing packets on the other port.

FILTERING ON INPUT AND OUTPUT PORTS

Not all routers can filter on both source and destination ports. Many routers filter on the destination port alone. The reason is that because TCP connections require data flow in both directions, the port on which you want to place the filter will appear as a destination port either when data is sent, or when the acknowledgment is received. However, because you are not able to supply source and destination ports simultaneously, this can cause problems.

Consider that your network security policy allows TCP connections for a custom application between an internal and external host. Assume that this custom service uses TCP port number 5555 on both sides. This situation is shown in figure 5.3. You can design the packet filter rule using the worksheet of figure 4.21 in the preceding chapter. This packet filter design table is shown in figure 5.4.

FIGURE 5.3

A custom application using port 5555.

FIGURE 5.4

The packet filter rule design for custom application when source and destination ports can be specified.

Filter Rule Number	Action	Source	Source Port	Destination	Dest. Port	Protocol Flags Options	Description
1	allow	199.245.180.1	5555	135.67.12.33	5555	TCP	Allow TCP session at port 5555 on specified hosts
2							
3							

This table shows that only one packet filter rule is needed. However, if the screening router permits only the destination port to be specified, the single filter rule in the table in figure 5.4 has to be written as two rules as shown in figure 5.5.

Filter Rule Number	Action	Source	Source Port	Destination	Dest. Port	Protocol Flags Options	Description
1	allow	199.245.180.1	*	135.67.12.33	5555	TCP	Allow TCP session to external host port 5555 from internal hosts
2	allow	135.67.12.33	*	199.245.180.1	5555	TCP	Allow TCP session to internal host port 5555 from external hosts
3							

Figure 5.5

The packet filter rule design for custom application when only destination port can be specified.

If you examine figure 5.6, you can see that although the new rules encompass the rule specified in figure 5.5, they are a lot more permissive. The new rules allow a set of full associations that includes the single full association specified in figure 5.4. This is because the rules allow the following types of connections:

1. Connection from any of the internal hosts' ports to port 5555 on the external host

2. Connection from *any port on the external host* to port 5555 on the internal host

Figure 5.6

A bogus program invading an internal machine as a consequence of rules specified in figure 5.5.

Rule 1 in figure 5.5 is probably not very damaging because you usually can trust an internal host. Rule 2 in figure 5.5, however, can be a breach in network security. Consider the situation in figure 5.6, where a bogus program on the host can connect to any port on the internal host. This type of connection was not intended in the network security policy but is allowed from rule 2 of figure 5.6.

Therefore, to write packet filter rules effectively, screening routers should allow both source and destination ports to be specified in a single matched rule.

EXAMINING PROTOCOL-SPECIFIC ISSUES IN PACKET FILTERING

When you design packet filter rules, you should understand the behavior of the application service that you are trying to filter. Some of the application services, such as FTP, require a call-back mechanism, in which an external host might need to initiate a connection to the internal host on a port that is not known at the time of specifying the packet filter rules.

The X11 protocol used in Unix X-Windows applications also requires an "incoming" call to an internal host from an external host. The internal hosts should be protected from these types of incoming calls. The sections that follow discuss the application services in relationship to packet filtering.

FILTERING FTP NETWORK TRAFFIC

The following section discusses the normal behavior of FTP and points out the problem this behavior poses for screening routers. Solutions to solve packet filtering for FTP sessions are discussed.

UNDERSTANDING THE FTP PROTOCOL

Figure 5.7 shows the FTP model. The FTP client makes a connection to the FTP server on the well-known Port 21 that is assigned to the FTP server. This connection is called the *control* connection. The control connection is used for sending FTP commands and receiving replies from the FTP server.

When a file is retrieved or stored on the FTP server, a separate data connection is established. This data connection is established on well-known Port 20 on the FTP server. The data connection exists only for the duration of the data transfer. It is destroyed at the end of the data transfer.

The different phases of an FTP transfer are discussed next for a live FTP session captured using a protocol analyzer. In this file transfer, the FTP client and FTP server have the following IP addresses:

FTP client: 199.245.180.1

FTP server: 199.245.180.15

FTP Model

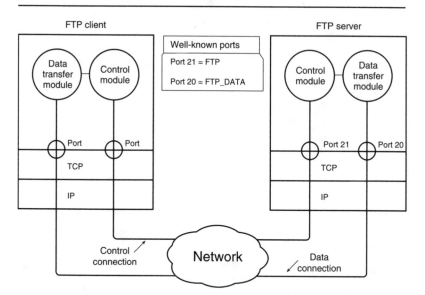

FIGURE 5.7

The FTP model (Graphic Courtesy of Learning Tree International).

- **Control connection**
  - Created when connection to FTP server is established
  - Used for FTP commands/replies only

- **Data transfer connection**
  - Created on demand for each data transfer
  - Destroyed on end of each data transfer

Figures 5.8 and 5.9 show that the FTP session had 43 packets. Figure 5.8 shows packets 1 through 27, and figure 5.9 shows packets 17 through 43. All references to packet numbers in the discussion that follows is to the first column in these figures.

Packets 1-3:

Packet 1 is the FTP client (199.245.180.1) doing an ARP broadcast announcing its hardware address and IP address association.

Packet 2 is the FTP client doing an ARP request broadcast to discover the FTP server's hardware address.

Packet 3 is the ARP reply from the FTP server. This ARP reply contains the server's hardware address (shown as 0000C0DD145C in figure 5.8).

Packets 4-6:

Packet 4 is the FTP client making an FTP control connection to the FTP server. The FTP client local-port number is 15676 and the FTP server port number is 21.

197

FIGURE 5.8

*The FTP
session packets
(screen 1 of 2).*

FIGURE 5.9

*The FTP
session packets
(screen 2 of 2).*

The protocol analyzer has translated this port number to the symbolic representation of "21" to "FTP" (see fig. 5.10). You can decode the hexadecimal dump of the packet, showing that the destination port has a value of 15(hex) or 21 decimal.

Packets 4 and 5 are useful when setting up packet filters. To detect an open FTP connection request, you can filter for the following conditions:

Destination port = 21.

TCP SYN flag is set.

TCP ACK flag is set in open-connection acknowledgment.

Packet 5 completes the three-way handshake. It is the acknowledgment packet that is sent in response to the open-connection acknowledgment packet.

FIGURE 5.10

An FTP Open Control connection packet.

Packets 7-8:

Packet 7 is the reply from the FTP server. The FTP commands are sent using a four-character ASCII text command followed by parameters. The FTP reply is a three-digit decimal status code followed by an optional text message.

The FTP command and FTP reply syntax are shown in figure 5.11. This figure also summarizes the FTP session activities that have taken place so far. Figure 5.12 shows

199

packet number 7 that contains the FTP reply code 220 that means "Service ready for new user." The text message that is sent for displaying at the FTP client console is ucs FTP server (Version 5.60) ready.

Packet 8 sent from the FTP client to the server acknowledges the server reply.

FIGURE **5.11**

The FTP command/reply actions (Graphic Courtesy of Learning Tree International).

Packets 9-11:

Packet 9 is an FTP command USER sent from the FTP client to the FTP server. Figure 5.13 shows the protocol decode for packet 9. This decode shows that the user requesting the FTP session is user1.

Packet 10 is the FTP server's reply to the FTP client's USER command. Figure 5.14 shows the protocol decode for packet 10. This decode shows that the reply code sent back is 331, which means that the user name is fine, but a password is needed.

Packet 11 sent from the FTP client to the server acknowledges the server's response.

FIGURE 5.12

An FTP server reply-ready packet.

FIGURE 5.13

The FTP USER command.

FIGURE 5.14

The FTP server's response to the USER command.

```
                          LANalyzer for Windows - [Capture Buffer]
  □  File  Monitor  Alarms  Capture  Decode  Window  Help
 ether: ===================== Ethernet Datalink Layer ====================
        Station: 00-00-C0-DD-14-5C -----> 68-01-14-2C-A2-01
        Type: 0x0800 (IP)
   ip:  ======================= Internet Protocol ======================
        Station:199.245.180.15 ---->199.245.180.1
        Protocol: TCP
        Version: 4
        Header Length (32 bit words): 5
        Precedence: Routine
                Low Delay, Normal Throughput, Normal Reliability
        Total length: 74
        Identification:  8196
        Fragmentation allowed, Last fragment
        Fragment Offset: 0
        Time to Live: 60  seconds
        Checksum: 0x669E(Valid)
   tcp: ================= Transmission Control Protocol =================
        Source Port: FTP
        Destination Port: 15676
        Sequence Number: 24602156
        Acknowledgement Number: 64208909
        Data Offset (32-bit words): 5
        Window: 4096
        Control Bits: Acknowledgement Field is Valid (ACK)
                      Push Function Requested (PSH)
        Checksum: 0x695C(Valid)
        Urgent Pointer: 0
   ftp: ===================== File Transfer Protocol ===================
        Reply: 331 (User name okay, need password.)
        Text:  Password required for user1.


                                   Packet:  10    Unfiltered:  44
```

Packets 12-14:

Packet 12 is an FTP command PASS sent from the FTP client to the FTP server. Figure 5.15 shows the protocol decode for packet 12. This decode shows that the user's password is user1pw.

Please note that the FTP command sends the password in the clear. Any protocol analyzer, such as the one used in this study, can be used to discover the FTP password. For this reason, a stronger authentication mechanism is needed if you want to access an FTP server using your user account over an untrusted network.

Packet 13 is the server's acknowledgment that it received the user password command.

Packet 14, sent from the client to the server, acknowledges this acknowledgment and sets the PSH flag, indicating that for the time being, there are no commands from the FTP client. Figure 5.16 summarizes the actions performed by packets 7 to 14.

Packets 15-16:

Packet 15 is the FTP server's reply to the user password. Figure 5.17 shows the protocol decode for packet 15. This decode shows that the user has logged in successfully.

Packet 16 sent from the FTP client to the server acknowledges the server's response.

FIGURE 5.15

The FTP PASS command.

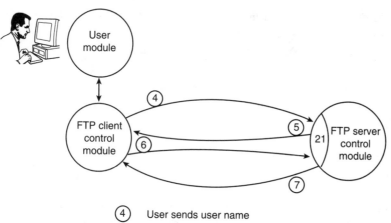

FIGURE 5.16

The FTP client user name authentication (Graphic Courtesy of Learning Tree International).

④ User sends user name

⑤ FTP server accepts

⑥ User sends password

⑦ FTP server authenticates password

At this point, the user has entered the following command from the FTP client console in order to retrieve the file "netstart."

```
get netstart
```

203

FIGURE 5.17

*An FTP server
response indicating a
successful user login.*

```
                    LANalyzer for Windows - [Capture Buffer]
  File   Monitor  Alarms  Capture  Decode  Window  Help
ether: =================== Ethernet Datalink Layer ====================
       Station: 00-00-C0-DD-14-5C ----> 68-01-14-2C-A2-01
       Type: 0x0800 (IP)
   ip: ===================== Internet Protocol =======================
       Station:199.245.180.15 ----->199.245.180.1
       Protocol: TCP
       Version: 4
       Header Length (32 bit words): 5
       Precedence: Routine
             Low Delay, Normal Throughput, Normal Reliability
       Total length: 67
       Identification:  8198
       Fragmentation allowed, Last fragment
       Fragment Offset: 0
       Time to Live: 60  seconds
       Checksum: 0x66A3(Valid)
  tcp: ================= Transmission Control Protocol =================
       Source Port: FTP
       Destination Port: 15676
       Sequence Number: 24602190
       Acknowledgement Number: 64208923
       Data Offset (32-bit words): 5
       Window: 4096
       Control Bits: Acknowledgement Field is Valid (ACK)
                     Push Function Requested (PSH)
       Checksum: 0x1E96(Valid)
       Urgent Pointer: 0
  ftp: ==================== File Transfer Protocol ====================
       Reply: 230 (User logged in, proceed.)
       Text:  User user1 logged in.

                              Packet:  15    Unfiltered:  44
```

As mentioned before, files are retrieved and stored using a separate data connection originating from the server's FTP port 20. However, the FTP server does not know the FTP client's local port to connect to. The FTP protocol solves this problem by having the FTP client send the local end-point address (IP address and port number) to the FTP server. The FTP server then knows the destination port number to open the connection. The FTP client sends its local port number using the PORT command.

Packets 17-18:

Packet 17 is the FTP command PORT sent by the FTP client to the server. Table 5.1 shows the FTP commands and their meanings. This table contains the definition of the PORT command. The last two numbers, p1 and p2, are the dotted decimal representation of the 16-bit port number. The FTP client selects a dynamic value (greater than 1024) that can be used by the server to make a data connection to the FTP client. Suppose the FTP selects the port number 55814, which is not in use. The PORT command sent by the FTP client with IP address 199.245.180.1 will be

PORT 199,245,180,1,218,6

The first four numbers represent the FTP client's IP address 199.245.180.1. The numbers 218 and 6 are the most significant and least significant bytes of the port number. If you were to convert this to a decimal port number, you could do so using the following calculations:

218*256 + 6

= 55808 + 6

= 55814

This value equals the port number that was selected by the FTP client.

Packet 18, sent from the FTP server to the client, acknowledges the client's PORT command.

TABLE 5.1
FTP Commands

FTP Command	Description
USER	Used to identify user for authentication.
PASS	Specifies user's password.
PORT	Specifies FTP client's Internet address and TCP port address as a series of 8-bit decimal numbers: PORT i1,i2,i3,i4,p1,p2. p1 and p2 represent the most significant and least significant bytes of the 16-bit port number.
TYPE	Data type used in file transfer: A = ASCII, E = EBCDIC, I = IMAGE, L = Logical byte size.
STRU	File structure of file to be transferred. F = Unstructured, R = Record, P = Page.
MODE	Transfer mode. S = Stream, B = Block, C = Compressed.
RETR	Gets a file from FTP server.
STOR	Stores a file on the FTP server.
QUIT	Logs user out.
PASV	Specifies that receiver should do a passive TCP open.
NOOP	No operation.

Packet 19:

Packet 19, sent from the FTP client to the FTP server, contains the RETR (Retrieve) command used to download this file. Figure 5.18 shows a protocol decode of this packet. This shows that the name of the file that is retrieved is netstart.

The events described by packets 17 to 19 are summarized in figure 5.19.

FIGURE 5.18

The FTP RETR command.

FIGURE 5.19

The use of the PORT and RETR commands (Graphic Courtesy of Learning Tree International).

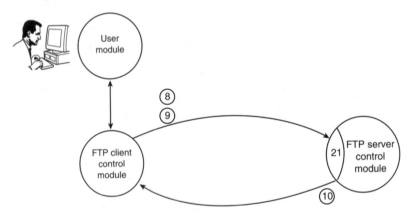

⑧ Client sends PORT command identifying the FTP_DATA connection. PORT command contains information on TCP half-association (IP address and port number)

⑨ File name is sent using RETR command

⑩ FTP server accepts

Packets 20-22:

In reply to the RETR command, the FTP server opens a data connection to the FTP client.

Packet 20 shows an incoming TCP connection request from the FTP server to the FTP client. The destination port in the connection request is the one that was specified by the FTP client in the PORT command. Figure 5.20 shows a protocol decode of packet 20. This shows that the source port is port number FTP_DATA (port 20), and the destination port is 55814, specified in the PORT command.

Packets 21 and 22 complete the open connection handshake.

Packets 20 to 22 are very important from a packet filtering standpoint. These packets represent an incoming call from the FTP server. If the FTP server resides on an untrusted network, you must place a filter to allow this connection. The problem is that one does not know beforehand what the port number used by the client is going to be. Because of this, it is difficult to set a proper filter for the incoming call.

FIGURE 5.20

An FTP data connection from FTP server to FTP client.

Packets 23-24:

In packet 23, the FTP server replies with a status on the file to be retrieved. Figure 5.21 shows a protocol decode of packet 23.

Packet 24 is sent from the FTP client to the FTP server to acknowledge the server's status of file reply. Figure 5.22 summarizes the events in packets 20-24.

FIGURE 5.21

The status of file reply sent by FTP server.

Packet 25:

Packet 25 commences the transfer of the data in the file to be retrieved. Figure 5.23 shows the data packet containing the contents of the file.

Packet 26:

The FTP server has sent the entire file as a TCP message segment for transmission to the TCP layer. The FTP server then server-announces its intention to break the data connection when file transfer is completed. Figure 5.24 shows a reply code of 226, which indicates that the data connection will close at end of file transfer.

Packets 27-32:

Data is transferred and acknowledged. This phase of the FTP session is illustrated by figure 5.25.

FIGURE 5.22

The FTP data connection creation (Graphic Courtesy of Learning Tree International).

⑪ FTP server creates data process

⑫ FTP client creates data process

⑬ FTP server data process opens connection with FTP client data process

⑭ FTP client data process acknowledges connection

Packet 33:

Packet 33 is the last data packet. The FIN flag is set in this packet indicating that the FTP server wants to close the connection (see fig. 5.26).

Packets 34-35:

TCP uses a graceful close mechanism, in which both sides have to agree to break the connection. Packet 34, sent from the FTP client to the FTP server with the FIN flag set, indicates that the FTP client agrees to close the connection (see fig. 5.27). Figure 5.28 summarizes the events described by packets 33 to 35.

Packet 35 is sent from the FTP server to the FTP client to acknowledge the client's agreement in the previous message to break the data connection.

FIGURE 5.23

An FTP data transfer packet.

FIGURE 5.24

The FTP server announces intention to break data connection.

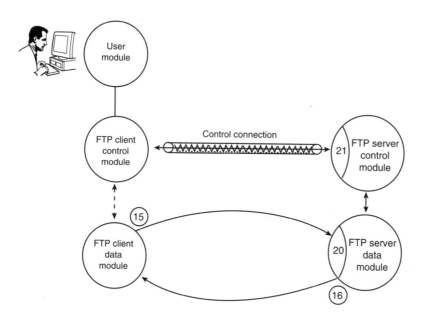

FIGURE 5.25

*The FTP data
transfer phase
(Graphic Courtesy
of Learning Tree
International).*

(15)   FTP server sends data segments

(16)   FTP acknowledges data segments

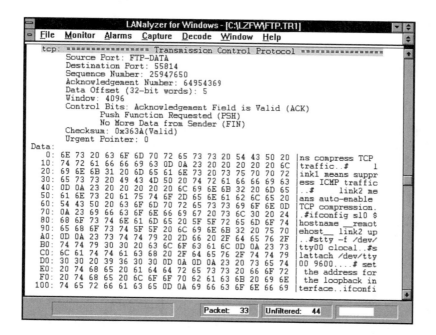

FIGURE 5.26

*The TCP layer in
FTP sends the FIN
flag to break data
connection.*

211

FIGURE 5.27

The TCP layer in FTP client sends a reciprocating FIN flag to break data connection.

Packets 36-37:

The user enters the QUIT or BYE command to end the FTP session. In packet 36, the FTP client issues the QUIT command to the FTP server (see fig. 5.29).

In packet 37, the FTP server replies that it is ready to close the connection (see fig. 5.30).

Packets 38-43:

The FTP server initiates a termination of the FTP connection with FIN flag set, and the FTP client agrees to it with FIN flag set. Additional packets are sent to acknowledge the termination, but the breaking of the control connection is similar to the breaking of the data connection, and therefore, protocol decodes are not shown.

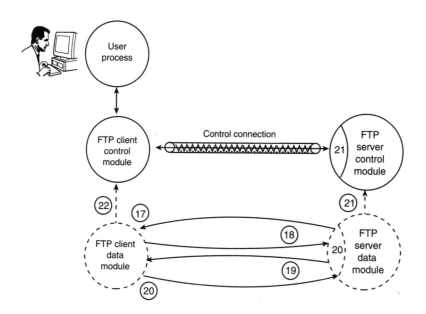

FIGURE 5.28

*The breaking of
the FTP data
connection
(Graphic Courtesy
of Learning Tree
International).*

(17)   FTP server sends last data segment

(18)   FTP client acknowledges last data segment

(19)   FTP server closes data connection

(20)   FTP client acknowledges close data connection request

(21)   FTP server data process terminates

(22)   FTP client data process terminates

PROBLEMS IN FILTERING AN FTP SESSION

The previous section showed the detailed behavior of an FTP session. Consider figure 5.31, in which a screening router is set up between an FTP client on an internal network and an FTP server on an external network. Assume that the network security policy allows internal hosts to initiate FTP sessions with external hosts. Figure 5.32 shows an attempt to set up packet filter rules to implement this policy. From figure 5.32, you can see that you do not know the destination port number for rule 2 because this is set dynamically by the FTP protocol. If you allow the host to call any one of the ports for the FTP "call back" from the server, a program written with evil intent can probe any of the internal network hosts if it originates a call from port 20. This is clearly undesirable.

FIGURE 5.31

An FTP session to an external host through a screening router.

Filter Rule Number	Action	Source	Source Port	Destination	Dest. Port	Protocol Flags Options	Description
1	allow	199.245.180.0	*	139.40.61.3	*	TCP	Permit outgoing TCP connection.
2	allow	1.39.40.61.3	20	199.245.180.0	?	TCP	Destination port not known.
3							

FIGURE 5.32

An attempt to set up an FTP connection filter.

FTP PACKET FILTERING USING PORT RANGE RULES AND TCP FLAGS

One way to solve the problem is to use the TCP ACK flag to identify legitimate incoming connections and to block connections to the internal host's standard service ports (usually less than 1024).

Figure 5.33 shows the redesigned packet filter rules for an FTP session. Filter rule 1 allows calls to the external host from any port from the internal network. Filter rule 2 blocks calls to ports less than 1024. This is safe for FTP operation because the local call-back port is greater than 1024 in standard FTP. Filter rule 3 only allows ACK packets from port 20 on the external host.

FIGURE 5.33

The redesigned packet filter rules using the ACK flag.

Filter Rule Number	Action	Source	Source Port	Destination	Dest. Port	Protocol Flags Options	Description
1	allow	199.245.180.0	*	139.40.61.3	21	TCP	Permit outgoing TCP connection
2	block	139.40.61.3	20	199.245.180.0	< 1024	TCP	Block connections to standard services
3	allow	139.40.61.3	20	199.245.180.0	*	TCP ACK=1	Allow ACK packets to any port on internal machine from port 20

A determined intruder could, however, still originate calls from port 20 and probe the port addresses above 1024. Some important services, such as X11, use high port numbers above 1024. These are susceptible to attack.

FTP PACKET FILTERING USING THE PASV COMMAND

RFC 1579 on "Firewall-Friendly FTP" proposed the use of an FTP command PASV (passive open) that does not require a modification to the FTP protocol, but a modification to the FTP clients. The FTP protocol says that, by default, all data transfers should be over a single data connection. The FTP server does an active open from TCP port 20 to a local dynamic port on the FTP client, which does a passive open on this local port.

Most current FTP clients do not behave that way; they assign a new local port for each transfer and announce this through the PORT command.

If the FTP client sends a PASV command to the FTP server, the server does a passive TCP open on a random port and informs the client of the port number. The client can initiate an active open to establish the connection using a random local port. This mechanism avoids the FTP server call-back to a service port on the FTP client. The FTP client initiates an active open to an external host, and this is usually not a problem with most organizations' network security policies.

216

If the FTP server does not implement the PASV command, this scheme does not work. PASV is required by STD 3 (RFC 1123); however, not all FTP servers implement it. You usually can detect this problem when you receive a reply code of 500 Command not understood.

When a PASV command is sent, the server can respond to it with the following:

> 227 Passive *i1,i2,i3,i4,p1,p2*

The *i1*, *i2*, *i3*, and *i4* are the decimal numbers of the server's IP address in dotted decimal notation. The *p1* and *p2* represent a random port assigned by the server. The FTP client can issue an active TCP open with destination port of 256*p1 + *p2* to the server FTP. This mechanism is shown in figure 5.34.

FIGURE 5.34

The use of PASV in Firewall-Friendly FTP.

FILTERING TELNET NETWORK TRAFFIC

TELNET traffic does not require any call-back mechanisms to an unprotected port on the TELNET client, so filtering TELNET sessions on standard port 23 is relatively straightforward.

TELNET can be used as a general mechanism to connect to any port using the following command:

```
telnet host [portnumber]
```

If *portnumber* is not specified, the default TELNET port of 23 is used. If your site security policy does not want internal users to contact services such as Gopher, WWW, or the Weather Underground, these actions are difficult to control if a non-standard port number is used.

TELNET also can be used by external users to probe what special services, if any, you are providing on TCP ports on your internal machines. You should protect all such services using screening routers or firewall gateway solutions.

FILTERING X-WINDOWS SESSIONS

The X11 protocol uses TCP. Like FTP, the X11 protocol requires an incoming call to the X11 server. The X-server here is the user's display (X-terminal or X-workstation). If internal users want to run an X11 application at an external site (see fig. 5.35), the X11 application needs to make an incoming call to the X11 server. The X11 servers usually use port numbers in the range 6000-6999. You should at a minimum protect the port range 6000-6100.

FIGURE 5.35

The X11 across a screening router.

Consider the network security policy specifying that X-access from the external site 128.23.0.0 should be allowed, but all other external access should be blocked. If the internal X11-servers use port numbers 6000-6100, you can use the filter design table in figure 5.36 as a start.

FIGURE 5.36

An example of X11 packet filter rules.

Filter Rule Number	Action	Source	Source Port	Destination	Dest. Port	Protocol Flags Options	Description
1	allow	199.245.180.0	*	*	*	TCP	Permit outgoing TCP connections
2	block	128.23.0.0	*	199.245.180.0	6000- 6100 6000- 6100	TCP	Block access to X11 services from 128.23.0.0
3	allow	*	*	199.245.180.0			Allow X11 access to all other sites

PACKET FILTERING AND THE UDP TRANSPORT PROTOCOL

The application services you have examined so far have used TCP. TCP is a connection-oriented protocol. It uses virtual circuits where each side maintains state information, such as sequence and acknowledgment numbers, to determine what data is expected next. This state information specifies a context in which the next packet should occur. This context information is very useful in packet filtering. You can use the TCP ACK flag, for example, to associate a packet as part of an existing TCP session. The ACK flag can be used to distinguish between an incoming or return packet, and the SYN flag can be used to indicate if the packet is part of an open-connection request.

UDP sessions are connectionless. UDP does not use virtual circuits, so it does not retain any state information. There are no sequence and acknowledgment numbers to determine the next packet. Because of this, one has to rely on filtering UDP based on port numbers.

Consider the situation (see fig. 5.37) where host 190.245.180.9 wants to poll an SNMP agent on an external machine at 157.23.13.44, and the network security policy permits such an operation. The SNMP agents use well-known UDP port number of 161. You could write this as a filter rule shown in figure 5.38. Filter rule 1 allows outgoing SNMP polls, and filter rule 2 allows incoming SNMP replies.

FIGURE 5.37

SNMP access.

219

FIGURE 5.38

The implemention of SNMP access security policy.

Filter Rule Number	Action	Source	Source Port	Destination	Dest. Port	Protocol Flags Options	Description
1	allow	190.245.180.9	157.23.13.44	157.23.13.44	161	UDP	Permit outgoing SNMP polls
2	allow		161	190.245.180.9	*	UDP	Allow SNMP replies
3							

Assume the local port used by the SNMP Manager is 1500. The SNMP poll packet consists of the following:

> Source IP address = 190.245.180.9
>
> Source port = 1500
>
> Destination IP address = 157.23.13.44
>
> Destination port = 161

The SNMP reply would be the following:

> Source IP address = 157.23.13.44
>
> Source port = 161
>
> Destination IP address = 190.245.180.9
>
> Destination port = 1500

What if the following reply was received?

> Source IP address = 157.23.13.44
>
> Source port = 161
>
> Destination IP address = 190.245.180.9
>
> Destination port = 1352

Because the source port is 161, by filter rule 2 in figure 5.38, you would allow this packet access. But what if someone has forged a UDP packet with a source port of 161? They could, then, use this to attack port 1352 on the local machine, which is assigned to Lotus Notes.

One way to solve this problem is to explicitly specify rules preventing access to Well-Known Services (WKS) running on internal hosts. The problem here is that it may be hard to keep the packet filter rules updated as new UDP services are added to the network.

Many of the UDP applications such as NFS, TFTP, and SNMP are LAN-oriented. There- fore, you may consider blocking these UDP services entirely. An exception to this is DNS, which uses UDP, and is definitely not confined to LANs. In this case, you might want to block all UDP traffic from external sites, except DNS. One possible set of filter rules for doing this is shown in figure 5.39. However, as explained earlier, someone can still do address spoofing by impersonating DNS port number 53, and packet filter rule 2 of figure 5.39 will permit this type of packet to reach the internal network 190.245.180.0.

Filter Rule Number	Action	Source	Source Port	Destination	Dest. Port	Protocol Flags Options	Description
1	allow	190.245.180.0	* *	*	*	UDP	Allow outgoing UDP packets
2	allow		*	190.245.180.0	53	UDP	Allow DNS queries
3							

FIGURE 5.39

Blocking UDP services with the exception of DNS.

PACKET FILTERING ICMP

The Internet Control Message Protocol (ICMP) is part of the Internet Layer and is described in RFC 792. ICMP must be implemented in all IP protocol modules. This means that all TCP/IP hosts have ICMP support.

ICMP is used to report errors on the IP datagrams. It does not make the IP protocol layer more reliable. It reports errors on the Internet layer, and it is up to an upper-layer protocol such as TCP to make the Internet layer more reliable. ICMP reports information on network parameters and errors on the network; it can also be used to diagnose the network. The following ICMP services are defined:

❖ Echo test—used to test the availability of a TCP/IP host (ping).

❖ Time stamp messages for measuring network delay.

❖ Time to Live expired messages.

❖ Destination network or host is unreachable messages.

❖ Errors in IP parameters in the IP header messages.

❖ Redirect messages for determining better routes.

❖ Determining subnet address mask of network to which host is attached.

❖ Source quench messages to inform source to slow down sending of packets. This is an attempt to provide flow control.

221

ICMP redirect messages generally are sent by routers to other devices, informing them about new routes. If ICMP redirect messages are allowed to filter into the internal network, an external site can send bogus ICMP redirect messages to internal hosts and cause havoc with the internal network's routing tables. This is an example of a "denial of service" attack because it disrupts normal operations. There generally is no good reason for an internal network to listen to ICMP redirect messages from an external network, especially if these originate from an untrusted network. For this reason, you might consider filtering out ICMP redirect packets coming from an external network.

Some hosts are susceptible to ICMP subnet reply messages, even when they have not made an ICMP subnet request. This is obviously a bug in the TCP/IP implementation, and should be identified and eliminated to prevent your network from responding to false ICMP subnet reply messages.

Although the ICMP echo service (popularly implemented by the ping utility) is useful for verifying connections, if you allow external sites to ping your internal network, they can obtain a logical map of your internal network. If this is an important security issue, you might consider denying ICMP requests to the internal network.

PACKET FILTERING **RIP**

RIP (Routing Information Protocol) is used by many internal networks. RIP exchanges "hop count" information about network and host destinations at periodic intervals (30 seconds). These RIP exchanges are based on trust between the routers. There is no authentication of RIP messages. If a router is mistaken about a route, this error can easily propagate to other routers, producing such ills as routing loops, inefficient routes, and unreachable destinations.

It does not take a great deal of imagination to see what can happen if false routing information is deliberately leaked to an internal network. Someone could change the default route information on hosts, for example, so that internal network traffic is diverted to an attacker's host.

You also should disable source routing at the screening router. An intruder can use source routing to force the sending and receiving of packets through the screening router. If you are using Cisco routers, for example, you can disable source routing by using the following command:

```
no ip source-route
```

EXAMPLE SCREENING ROUTER CONFIGURATIONS

This section discusses a few screen routing configuration scenarios to provide you with additional guidance on designing and implementing packet filter rules.

CASE STUDY 1

Figure 5.40 shows a network that has the following security policy:

1. All hosts on internal network 131.44.0.0 can access any TCP service on the Internet.

2. External hosts cannot connect to the internal network except through the mail gateway at 131.44.1.1 where they can access the SMTP mail service only.

3. ICMP messages to the Internet should be blocked.

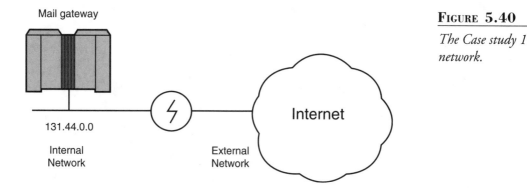

FIGURE 5.40

The Case study 1 network.

You can express this security policy as filter rules for the Internal (see fig. 5.41) and External port (see fig. 5.42) of the screening router.

Filter Rule Number	Action	Source	Source Port	Destination	Dest. Port	Protocol Flags Options	Description
1	allow	131.44.0.0 131.44.0.0	*	*	TCP	Allow outgoing TCP connections
2	block		NA	*	NA	ICMP	Block ICMP messages to external network
3							

NA = Not Applicable

FIGURE 5.41

Case study 1: Filter rules for external port.

FIGURE 5.42

*Case study 1:
Filter rules for
internal port.*

Filter Rule Number	Action	Source	Source Port	Destination	Dest. Port	Protocol Flags Options	Description
1	allow	* *	*	131.44.1.1	25 *	TCP	Allow incoming TCP connections to SMTP host
2	block		*	131.44.1.1		TCP	Block all other external TCP connections
3							

Using Cisco routers, the packet filter rules for the external port (see fig. 5.41) can be implemented as shown in the following.

Packet filter rule 1 for external port:

`access-list 101 permit tcp 131.44.0.0 0.0.255.255 0.0.0.0 255.255.255.255`

Packet filter rule 2 for external port:

`access-list 101 deny icmp 131.44.0.0 0.0.255.255 0.0.0.0 255.255.255.255`

Using Cisco routers, the packet filter rules for the internal port (see fig. 5.42) can be implemented as shown in the following.

Packet filter rule 1 for internal port:

`access-list 102 permit tcp 0.0.0.0 255.255.255.255 131.44.1.1  0.0.0.0 eq 25`

Packet filter rule 2 for internal port:

`access-list 102 deny tcp 0.0.0.0 255.255.255.255 131.44.0.0 0.0 0.0.255.255`

CASE STUDY 2

Figure 5.43 shows a network that has the following security policy:

1. Incoming e-mail and news are permitted to hosts 144.19.74.200, 144.19.74.201.

2. DNS access to gateway server 144.19.74.202 is allowed.

3. Access to NFS services on internal network is not allowed from external hosts.

4. Internal hosts are allowed all access to external networks, except to Gopher and WWW.

We can express this security policy as filter rules for the Internal (see fig. 5.44) and External port (see fig. 5.45) of the screening router.

Using Cisco routers, the packet filter rules for the external port (see fig. 5.44) can be implemented as shown in the following.

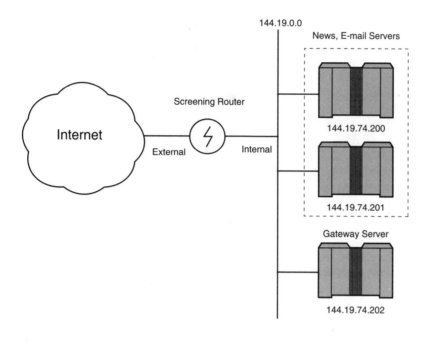

144.19.0.0

News, E-mail Servers

144.19.74.200

144.19.74.201

Screening Router

Internet

External   Internal

Gateway Server

144.19.74.202

FIGURE 5.43

The Case study 2 network.

Filter Rule Number	Action	Source	Source Port	Destination	Dest. Port	Protocol Flags Options	Description
1	block	144.19.0.0	*	*	70 80	* TCP	Block outgoing access to gopher
2	block	144.19.0.0	*	*		TCP TCP	Block outgoing access to WWW
3	allow	144.19.0.0	*	*			Allows all other TCP access

FIGURE 5.44

Case study 2: Filter rules for external port.

Filter Rule Number	Action	Source	Source Port	Destination	Dest. Port	Protocol Flags Options	Description
1	allow	*	*	144.19.0.0	* 25 25 119 119 53	TCP ACK=1 TCP RST=1	Permit incoming packets that are part of an established TCP connection
2	allow	*	*	144.19.74.200		TCP TCP ~~TCP~~	Allow E-mail access per security policy
3	allow	*	*	144.19.74.201		TCP	Allow E-mail access per security policy
4	allow	*	*	144.19.74.200		UDP	Allow NNTP access per security policy
5	allow	*	*	144.19.74.201			Allow NNTP access per security policy
6	allow	*	*	144.19.74.202			Allow DNS access per security policy

FIGURE 5.45

Case study 2: Filter rules for internal port.

Packet filter rule 1 for external port:

```
access-list 101 deny tcp 144.19.0.0 0.0.255.255 0.0.0.0 255.255.255.255 eq 70
```

Packet filter rule 2 for external port:

```
access-list 101 deny tcp 144.19.0.0 0.0.255.255 0.0.0.0 255.255.255.255 eq 80
```

Packet filter rule 3 for external port:

```
access-list 101 permit tcp 144.19.0.0 0.0.255.255 0.0.0.0 255.255.255.255
```

Using Cisco routers, the packet filter rules for the internal port (see fig. 5.45) can be implemented as shown in the following.

Packet filter rule 1 for internal port:

```
access-list 102 permit tcp 0.0.0.0 255.255.255.255 144.19.0.0  0.0.255.255
➡established
```

Packet filter rule 2 for internal port:

```
access-list 102 permit tcp 0.0.0.0 255.255.255.255 144.19.74.200 0.0.0.0  eq
➡25
```

Packet filter rule 3 for internal port:

```
access-list 102 permit tcp 0.0.0.0 255.255.255.255 144.19.74.201 0.0.0.0  eq
➡25
```

Packet filter rule 4 for internal port:

```
access-list 102 permit tcp 0.0.0.0 255.255.255.255 144.19.74.200 0.0.0.0  eq
➡119
```

Packet filter rule 5 for internal port:

```
access-list 102 permit tcp 0.0.0.0 255.255.255.255 144.19.74.201 0.0.0.0  eq
➡119
```

Packet filter rule 6 for internal port:

```
access-list 102 permit udp 0.0.0.0 255.255.255.255 144.19.74.202 0.0.0.0  eq
➡53
```

CASE STUDY 3

Figure 5.46 shows a network 144.19.0.0 that is using two subnets. The subnet 1 acts as a demilitarized zone (DMZ) between the internal and external networks. The DMZ is on subnet 15, and the internal protected network is on subnet 16. A firewall gateway, 144.19.15.1 exists in the DMZ. The mail router is on the subnet 16 and has an IP address of 144.19.16.1. The ports of the internal router connecting subnets 15 and 16 has IP address assignments of

144.19.15.81 and 144.19.16.82. The network has the following security policy for the internal router:

1. IP Source routing not permitted.

2. Services originating from subnet 16 are permitted to the firewall gateway on DMZ (subnet 15).

3. Allow all internal traffic to DMZ, except e-mail access to the DMZ (subnet 15).

4. Allow traffic from firewall gateway to internal network.

5. Allow connections from DMZ that show source ports in the range 1024 to 5000. The reason for this could be to allow FTP callbacks (another reason is to show you how to filter on port ranges).

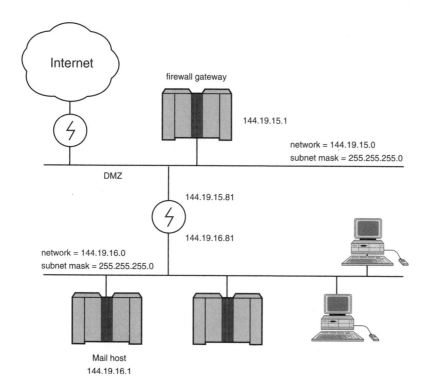

FIGURE 5.46

The Case study 3 network.

You can express this security policy as filter rules for Ethernet interface connections subnet 15 (see fig. 5.47) and subnet 16 (see fig. 5.48) of the router.

FIGURE 5.47

Case study 3: Filter rules for Ethernet interface on subnet "15".

Filter Rule Number	Action	Source	Source Port	Destination	Dest. Port	Protocol Flags Options	Description
1	allow	144.19.0.0	NA	*	NA 25 *	IP	Allow packets from internal network to firewall gateway
2	block	144.19.0.0	*	*		TCP TCP	Block E-mail access to DMZ per security policy
3	allow	144.19.0.0	*	*			Allow all other access to DMZ

NA = Not Applicable

FIGURE 5.48

Case study 3: Filter rules for Ethernet interface on subnet "16".

Filter rule number	Action	Source	Source Port	Destination	Dest. Port	Protocol Flags Options	Description
1	allow	144.19.15.1	NA	144.19.0.0	NA	IP	Allow traffic to internal network from firewall gateway
2	block	144.19.0.0	*	*	25	TCP	Block E-mail access to DMZ per security policy
3	allow	144.19.0.0	*	*	*	TCP	Allow all other access to DMZ

NA = Not Applicable

The following example shows a more complete procedure on configuring the router interfaces. To configure the router Ethernet interface on subnet 15, you can use the following:

```
no ip source-route      ! Disable source routing for router
interface ethernet 0    ! Identify physical interface
ip address 144.19.15.81 255.255.255.0 ! Assign IP address and subnet mask
ip group access 150     ! Extended access list 150 will apply to this
                          interface
```

To configure the router Ethernet interface on subnet 16, you can use the following:

```
! You do not need to disable source routing as it was done before
interface ethernet 1    ! Identify physical interface
ip address 144.19.16.81 255.255.255.0 ! Assign IP address and subnet mask
ip group access 160     ! Extended access list 160 will apply to this
                          interface
```

The packet filter rules for subnet 15 (see fig. 5.47) can be implemented as shown in the following.

Packet filter rule 1 for Ethernet 0 interface:

```
access-list 150 permit ip 144.19.0.0 0.0.255.255 144.19.15.1 0.0.0.0
```

Packet filter rule 2 for Ethernet 0 interface:

```
access-list 150 deny tcp 144.19.0.0 0.0.255.255  0.0.0.0 255.255.255.255 eq
➥25
```

Packet filter rule 3 for Ethernet 0 interface:

```
access-list 150 permit tcp 144.19.0.0 0.0.255.255  0.0.0.0 255.255.255.255
```

The packet filter rules for the Ethernet interface on subnet 16 (see fig. 5.48) can be implemented as shown in the following.

Packet filter rule 1 for Ethernet 1 interface:

```
access-list 160 permit ip 144.19.15.1 0.0.255.255 144.19.0.0 0.0.255.255
```

Packet filter rule 2 for Ethernet 1 interface:

```
access-list 150 deny tcp 0.0.0.0  255.255.255.255  144.19.0.0 0.0.255.255 lt
➥1024
access-list 150 deny tcp 0.0.0.0  255.255.255.255  144.19.0.0 0.0.255.255 gt
➥5000
access-list 150 permit tcp 0.0.0.0  255.255.255.255  0.0.0.0 255.255.255.255
➥lt 1025
```

SUMMARY

This chapter discussed the implementing of packet filter rules. The packet filter rules were implemented using examples of a commercially available router product. The problems of designing packet filter rules when a "call-back" connection is made from an external network were discussed. Call-back connections are required by most FTP and X11 implementations. Several case studies showing the design and implementation of packet filter rules were discussed.

## CHAPTER 6

PC PACKET FILTERING

PACKET FILTERING CAN BE applied to the PC world as well as to Unix towers and work-stations. PC-based products are popular because of their relatively low cost compared to RJSC-based Unix platforms or special router products. This chapter explores the ways in which that is possible—in particular, by carefully examining some popular PC-based products that serve as examples.

PC-BASED PACKET FILTER

Packet filtering software packages can be run on IBM-PCs. The IBM-PC, then, becomes a packet filter device. Two popular examples of such devices are:

❖ KarlBridge

❖ Drawbridge

THE KARLBRIDGE PACKET FILTER

The *KarlBridge* is a program written by Doug Karl of Ohio State University that runs on a 286/386/486 clone. The KarlBridge provides an inexpensive two-port Ethernet-to-Ethernet bridge that performs protocol filtering.

The KarlBridge filters packets based on any specified Ethernet protocol such as IP, XNS (Xerox Network System), DECNET (Digital Equipment Corporation Network), LAT (Local Area Transport), AppleTalk, NetBEUI (Net BIOS Extended User Interface), and Novell IPX (Internetwork Packet Exchange). As KarlBridge has evolved, some of its features resemble a firewall gateway more than a packet filter device.

KarlBridge can provide filtering of IP packets based upon IP address, network, and subnet combinations and port number values. Besides IP, it can also filter the following protocol types:

❖ DECNET packets based upon DECNET address, area, object number, and object name

❖ AppleTalk Phase 1 & 2 NBP packets based upon file server name, printer name, and/or zone name

❖ NetWare SAP packets based upon IPX network number, server name, and socket service number

The shareware working demo of KarlBridge V2.0 is available through anonymous ftp from the following host directory:

```
Host: 128.146.1.7
      nisca.acs.ohio-state.edu
      ftp.cis.ohio-state.edu
      teseo.unipg.it (/pub/msdos/tcpip/kbridge)
Directory: /pub/kbridge
```

The KarlBridge is also a commercial bridge or brouter product. The commercial products are based on the commercial version of the KarlBridge or KarlBRouter code. The Ethernet version of the commercial KarlBridge version comes with AUI/10BASE2 or AUI/10BASE-T connectors. It is implemented in a specially configured PC workstation with two Ethernet cards, a special boot ROM, and a floppy drive.

The KarlBridge Shareware/Demo is a limited-function, free version of the commercially available KarlBridge and KarlBRouter. Even though it is a demo version, it is very functional and, for many situations, has just the right features to be very useful.

REQUIREMENTS FOR KARLBRIDGE

To build your own KarlBridge, you need the following:

❖ 286, 386SX, 386DX, 486, or Pentium PC computer (Keyboard and monitor are optional.)

❖ Two SMC Elite 16 Ethernet cards 8013EPC

❖ KarlBridge software

The PC must be a good, reliable clone. The following lists typical hardware specifications for the KarlBridge:

❖ 16 MHz, 0 wait state 286 or 386SX motherboard or 386DX motherboard with AMI BIOS, 1 MB of RAM, floppy drive and controller; it must be able to boot with no monitor and no keyboard.

❖ The speaker connection must be modified to power a front panel LED that signifies LAN traffic. Different motherboards need different types of modification. Without this modification, the speaker clicks for each packet forwarded.

❖ The floppy drive must be capable of withstanding a dusty environment so that if the system is operating for months at a time and then a power failure causes a reboot, the floppy drive will still work. This usually requires a modification to the case so that the air does not flow through the floppy drive itself.

❖ For additional reliability, the entire system can be burned in for a minimum of two weeks with cycling temperature with full Ethernet load.

❖ Two SMC Elite 16 boards can be configured with either of the following configurations:

Configuration 1:

First board: IRQ 3 I/O Addr 280, Shared RAM D000 (Remote Port)

Second board: IRQ 5 I/O Addr 2A0, Shared RAM D400 (Local Port)

233

Configuration 2:

First board: IRQ 3 I/O Addr 280, Shared RAM E000 (Remote Port)

Second board: IRQ 5 I/O Addr 2A0, Shared RAM E400 (Local Port)

If you chose to construct your own PC clone, be aware that the designers of KarlBridge have not tested the program with hardware other than a 16 MHz, 0 wait state 286-16, 386SX-16, and 386DX40 with the I/O bus running at 8 MHz. The SMC cards may not function properly in some 486 machines.

The software is configured in a PC. The configuration produces a disk that contains properly configured software.

OVERVIEW OF SETTING UP KARLBRIDGE

After you obtain a copy of KarlBridge software, you must configure it on an MS-DOS PC. The current release is compressed ("zipped"), so you must use a tool such as PKUNZIP to extract the files. The distribution software comes with a program called KBRIDGE that you can use to configure the KarlBridge software. The KarlBridge distribution should contain the programs shown in table 6.1.

TABLE 6.1
KarlBridge Distribution Software

Program Name	Description
kbconfig.exe	KarlBridge configuration program
kbc.exe	KarlBridge configuration support program
kbc.sun4	Sun 4 Sparc version of kbc.exe program
kbconfig.cfg	File that contains IP address, mask, and so on
kbhelp.hlp	Help file for the KBCONFIG.EXE program
kbridge.exe	Executable image of KarlBridge for 2 SMC Elite 16 boards with the WD83C690 chip

The following is an outline of the steps to configure KarlBridge:

1. From the DOS prompt, change to the directory that has the KarlBridge software. Issue the following command on your PC:

```
KBCONFIG KBRIDGE.EXE
```

234

You should see the KarlBridge configuration program. Set up the KarlBridge configuration. The configuration procedure is quite lengthy and can be quite involved. Details of this procedure are presented in the next section.

2. The KBCONFIG program modifies the actual bridge program file KBRIDGE.EXE.

3. Create a bootable floppy. You can do this from the DOS prompt by issuing the following command:

   FORMAT A: /S

4. Create an AUTOEXEC.BAT file on the floppy disk that contains the following single command:

   KBRIDGE

5. Copy the KBRIDGE.EXE file and the AUTOEXEC.BAT to the bootable floppy:

   COPY KBRIDGE.EXE A:

6. You now have a bootable KarlBridge floppy.

7. After setting up the hardware for the KarlBridge, boot with this floppy.

KARLBRIDGE CONFIGURATION

The KarlBridge configuration is done by KBCONFIG.EXE. This is a menu-driven program that modifies the KBRIDGE.EXE program. The KarlBridge provides a great deal of flexibility. This section guides you in configuring the more important capabilities of KarlBridge. The shareware product is a bridge that can be configured to perform protocol filtering. If your network requires that the filter device be a router, you must purchase the router version of this product.

The term *remote* in the KBCONFIG program refers to machines connected to the bridge's Port 0. This is the SMC Ethernet board with the I/O address 280. The term *local* refers to machines connected to the bridge's Port 1. This is the SMC Ethernet board with the I/O address 2A0.

The rest of this section illustrates the different configuration options for KarlBridge. Start the configuration by issuing the following command:

KBCONFIG KBRIDGE.EXE

You should see the opening screen similar to figure 6.1. Select OK.

FIGURE 6.1

The KarlBridge opening screen.

Press Alt+S to invoke the setup menu. You should see a screen showing you the setup options (see fig. 6.2). Select the General Setup option (see fig. 6.3).

FIGURE 6.2

The KarlBridge Setup menu.

FIGURE 6.3

The KarlBridge General Setup screen.

The following options are enabled by default:

Enable Bridging

Enable Security Filters

Enable Watchdog Reboot Timer

Enable VGA real-time display

Select OK after making your selections. Use the spacebar to select/deselect. The meaning of the options in figure 6.3 are described next:

❖ **ENABLE BRIDGING.** The transparent bridging function will be enabled. The device acts as a bridge (examining the data-link layer addresses only), transferring packets between local and remote ports. If you want the Bridge/Router to perform the bridging function, then you must enable this. When bridging is enabled, the Bridge Menu can be used.

❖ **ENABLE IP ROUTING.** If you have purchased the IP Routing option with the KarlBridge, you can enable it with this button. The routing works properly only if the routes are set up in the IP Route menu.

❖ **ENABLE SECURITY FILTERS.** Enabling security filters causes the KarlBridge/KarlBRouter to analyze each of the network layer headers in a packet to determine if it should be passed or dropped. If the KarlBridge or KarlBRouter is to be used as a simple, standard transparent bridge or simple IP Router with no advanced filtering, then this feature should be disabled. If you want to use the advanced filtering, firewall, and security features, then you must enable security filters. Note that the default settings for UDP/TCP, Novell, AppleTalk, and DECNET is to drop the packets (*That which is not explicitly permitted is prohibited.*). After enabling security filters, you then must enable the appropriate protocol-specific security filter.

❖ **ENABLE DATA ENCRYPTION.** The Data Encryption option can be used either to encrypt tunneled data that flows between KarlBridge tunnel partners or to encrypt UDP/TCP packets that flow between KarlBridge/KarlBRouters. Because only the UDP/TCP data portion of the packet is encrypted, the packet is routed correctly by standard IP routers.

❖ **ENABLE REMOTE BRIDGING USING IP TUNNELS.** The KarlBridge/KarlBRouter supports a special feature that enables Ethernet packets of any protocol type to be encapsulated in IP and then sent to other KarlBridges for decapsulation. This tunneling behavior is described in RFCs 1226, 1234, and 1241. This method can be used to set up "virtual" Ethernet LANs between several points on an IP network.

❖ **ENABLE WATCHDOG REBOOT TIMER.** The KarlBridge/KarlBRouter contains a watch-dog timer reboot feature. If no packets are seen on the network for more than 10 minutes (a very rare occurrence), the KarlBridge/KarlBRouter reboots itself. After it reboots, the 10-minute reboot timer does not activate again until a packet is seen on one of the ports. This ensures that only one reboot occurs if the entire network is truly shut down.

❖ **ENABLE REAL-TIME DISPLAY.** Some KarlBridges and KarlBRouters contain a CGA, EGA, or VGA controller board and display. You can enable the displaying of real-time bridge/router statistics with this option. If you do not have a display, it is recommended that you disable this function.

The next step is to configure the network interfaces. For Ethernet, no special hardware setup is required because these settings are fixed in the hardware requirements discussed earlier. If Bridging is enabled, select Bridge Setup (press Alt+S to see the options). You should see a screen showing you the setup options (see fig. 6.4).

This is the main screen for configuring the bridge. The different configuration options are described next:

❖ **PROTOCOL TO BRIDGE/TUNNEL.** This menu specifies the Ethernet protocols to bridge, drop, or tunnel. Each protocol can be bridged or dropped by selecting the Bridge or Drop button.

All other protocols not specified in the menu are then either bridged or dropped depending upon the mode selected by radio buttons labeled Bridge all non-listed protocols or Drop all non-listed protocols.

It is recommended that you bridge only the protocols that you absolutely need and drop all non-listed protocols. This follows from implementing the security policy

That which is not explicitly permitted is prohibited. If you bridge IP, DECNET, Novell, or AppleTalk, you have the opportunity to set up additional filters under the Security Setup options. At this step, you can specify in more detail the types of services you want to allow or block in accordance with the security policy.

❖ **BRIDGE/DROP ALL NON-LISTED PROTOCOLS.** This setting determines whether the packets not listed in the Protocol to Bridge or Tunnel menu should be bridged or dropped.

❖ **PASS ETHERNET BROADCAST.** Standard Ethernet bridges always forward broadcast packets. Although many protocols do not use broadcasts, many do. For example, the IP, UDP, and ARP protocols use broadcasts. If you do not use IP or any other protocol that requires broadcasts, then you can drop them. Blocking broadcast packets reduces the traffic on your network and the number of interrupts that each computer connected to your network experiences. Networks with a high number of broadcasts slow down the processing of each attached computer even if it is not using the network.

❖ **PASS ETHERNET MULTICASTS.** Standard Ethernet bridges always forward multicast packets. Some protocols, such as IP and Novell IPX, do not use multicasts. Other protocols, such as OSPF, require multicasts. If you do not use protocols that use multicasts, then you can drop them by shutting off multicasts on the KarlBridge. Shutting off multicast packets reduces the traffic on your network as well as the number of interrupts that each computer connected to your network experiences.

❖ **PASS/DROP FOLLOWING ADDRESS PAIR.** This menu specifies the Ethernet addresses that should be either allowed or blocked. Both source and destination data-link address are checked against this filter. An entire 6-byte Ethernet address can be filtered or just portions of it. This menu can be used to inhibit or promote communication with several particular Ethernet addresses or groups of Ethernet addresses. Because the first 3-bytes of an Ethernet packet (or any IEEE LAN) represent the manufacturer's code, you can filter packets based on the make of the host's Ethernet board. This approach of specifying Ethernet addresses is similar to a standard bridge that supports Ethernet address filtering.

For example, if the menu is set to Drop following Pair and an address pair of 00-00-C0-00-1A-7B and 00-00-00-4F-XX-XX-XX is specified, then data packets from the address 00-00-C0-00-1A-7A to any addresses that start with 00-00-4F are dropped.

❖ **ADVANCED FEATURES.** This menu contains advanced bridging options. These options are described in figure 6.5.

FIGURE 6.5

*KarlBridge
Advanced Features
Bridging options.*

The advanced options are as follows:

✤ **ADVANCED FEATURES—PASS BAD ETHERNET SOURCE.** Most Ethernet bridges pass Ethernet packets with a broadcast or multicast address as their source (when the first bit is set to 1). The Ethernet specification for Non-Source Routing bridges does not allow these types of packets. These types of packets can be considered "bad" packets. A common failure mode of many Ethernet interfaces and networking software is to transmit packets that have broadcast or multicast addresses in their source address fields. If you do not need the KarlBridge to pass Source Routing packets, you can configure KarlBridge to drop these packets. The default is to pass bad packets.

✤ **ADVANCED FEATURES—PASS UNSEEN ETHERNET SOURCE.** Ethernet bridges always forward packets with destination addresses that have not been *learned* (addresses that have not been seen as a source address in a packet). This characteristic is essential for the proper operation of an Ethernet bridge. However, failure mode of many Ethernet interface cards is to send out erroneous packets with good CRCs but with random Ethernet destination and source addresses. Standard bridges pass these erroneous packets because they have not learned the random destination address, and they add this packet's random source address to their finite learned table. This situation can hinder the operation of standard bridges. If you chose to drop unlearned packets, the KarlBridge does not forward unicast packets to an Ethernet address that has not already been seen as a source address. This scheme works for most protocols because it relies on the characteristics of most upper-layer protocols to transmit ARP requests or Hello packets. The default is to pass packets with unseen source addresses.

✤ **ADVANCED FEATURES—ENABLE LEARNED TABLE LOCKDOWN.** A standard bridge watches the source addresses of each packet it receives on any of its ports. As new addresses are seen, entries are added in the bridge table. These entries contain the source address and the port number on which that address was received. If that source address is later seen on a different port, the bridge changes the port number in the

240

learned table entry. This condition could happen in a correctly functioning network if someone moved the computer to a different part of the network. This also could happen if someone was trying to capture network packets by spoofing the bridge. Enabling learned table lockdown prevents the port number from being changed after the source address has been seen.

A standard bridge also times-out the learned table records. If learned table lockdown is enabled, then these records are not be timed out; once a record is learned, it cannot be changed or deleted until either the bridge reboots or the learned table becomes completely filled and needs to be reset. A typical KarlBridge learned table can contain over 10,000 records. The default is for this option to be disabled.

✤ **ADVANCED FEATURES—ENABLE EXPANDED IP ARP SUPPORT.** Enabling this feature causes the bridge to also watch the IP/ARP packets that occur on the network. No action is taken in response to an IP/ARP packet because that is the role of an IP router. However, the bridge adds the IP address to its IP/ARP table. This feature is helpful on an IP network because it builds a database of MAC layer addresses to IP address pairs. An SNMP monitoring program such as KBCONFIG (Monitor menu) can be used to extract this information. Note that the IP/ARP table is never timed-out in this mode, and this feature is not available if the KarlBRouter is routing IP. The default is that this feature is disabled.

✤ **STORM THRESHOLDS.** One of the features of the KarlBridge/KarlBRouter is its capability to keep Broadcast and Multicast storms from spreading across a network. Network storms are common and can cause bridges, routers, workstations, servers, and PCs to slow down or crash. Storms occur if network equipment is configured incorrectly, network software is not functioning correctly, or programs, such as network games, are not designed correctly.

When you select the Storm Thresholds option in the Bridging Setup menu, you see something similar to figure 6.6.

FIGURE 6.6

KarlBridge Storm Thresholds options.

The options in this screen are explained next:

❖ **STORM THRESHOLDS—ADDRESS THRESHOLD—BROADCAST.** This is the number of broadcast packets that can occur in each one-second period before a storm condition is declared for a particular address (host). When a storm is declared, then any additional broadcast packets from that host address are dropped until the storm is determined to be over. The storm is determined to be over when 30 seconds has passed in which every one-second period has less than the stated threshold in broadcast packets.

❖ **STORM THRESHOLDS—ADDRESS THRESHOLD—MULTICAST.** This is the number of multicast packets that can occur in each one-second period before a storm condition is declared for a particular address. When a storm is declared, then any additional multicast packets from that host address are dropped until the storm is determined to be over. The storm is determined to be over when 30 seconds has passed in which every one-second period has less than the stated threshold in multicast packets.

❖ **STORM THRESHOLDS—PORT THRESHOLD—BROADCAST.** This is the number of broadcast packets that can occur in each one-second period before a storm condition is declared for a particular port. When a storm is declared, then any additional broadcast packets received on that port are dropped until the storm is determined to be over. The storm is determined to be over when a one-second period has occurred with no broadcast packets received on that port.

❖ **STORM THRESHOLDS—PORT THRESHOLD—MULTICAST.** This is the number of multicast packets that can occur in each one-second period before a storm condition is declared for a particular port. When a storm is declared, any additional multicast packets received on that port are dropped until the storm is determined to be over. The storm is determined to be over when a one-second period has occurred with no multicast packets received on that port.

❖ **STORM THRESHOLDS—PRESET.** This button sets the Broadcast and Multicast storm thresholds to the recommended values (see fig. 6.6). These values have been determined to offer good protection without interfering with the operation of the typical network. These values may need to be tuned for your particular network.

If in the General Setup menu the Remote Bridging using IP Tunnels is enabled, then tunnel partners can be set up. The Tunnel Partners menu specifies the IP addresses of each of the KarlBridges set up to participate in the tunnel group. Only specify the other bridges; do not specify the IP address of this bridge.

Some KarlBridges and KarlBRouters contain a special software encryption algorithm that is distinct from the optional WaveLAN DES encryption chip. If Data Encryption is enabled on the General Setup menu and if an Encryption Key is set up in the Data Encryption menu, then enabling encryption here causes all packets transmitted to tunnel partners to be encrypted and any packets received from tunnel partners to be decrypted.

Select IP Hosts Setup (press Alt+S to see the options). You should see a screen showing you the setup options (see fig. 6.7). This screen is used to set up the IP address of the KarlBridge.

FIGURE 6.7

IP Host settings.

The fields that you may need for bridges are described next:

✦ **OUR IP ADDRESS.** This is the IP address of the KarlBridge itself. If you want to configure or monitor your KarlBridge or if your network supports IP and you want to enable the Ping support and IP/SNMP support, set this to a valid IP address. Setting this address to 0.0.0.0 disables Ping and IP/SNMP support. The KarlBridge is not an IP router. It has only one IP address, and that address applies to both the remote and local networks (both sides of the bridge). Having two Ethernet interfaces with the same IP address is different from a standard IP host, but is appropriate for a transparent bridge.

✦ **OUR SUBNET MASK.** This is the subnet mask assigned to the IP address. The value is expressed as a hexadecimal pattern. Select a value that is compatible with your subnet.

If you want the KarlBridge to be monitored from an SNMP Manager station, select SNMP Setup (press Alt+S to see the options). You should see a screen showing the setup options (see fig. 6.8). This screen is used to set up the IP address of the KarlBridge.

FIGURE 6.8

SNMP Setup.

The fields that you may need for bridges are described next:

✦ **READ PASSWORD.** This is the read-only password used for SNMP I support. It is the SNMP password needed to read the MIB variables. The string *public* is the common password used by most SNMP monitors.

✦ **READ/WRITE PASSWORD.** This is the read/write password used for SNMP support. It is the SNMP password needed to write the MIB variables. The string should be set to a value known only by you. The factory default value for this variable is the string *public* and should be changed to a string known only to you.

✦ **SYSTEM CONTACT.** This defines the value of the MIB variable, *sysContact*, for system contact. This could be the name of a person or a telephone number.

✦ **SYSTEM NAME.** This defines the value of the MIB variable, *sysName*, for system name. This is a description of the system.

✦ **SYSTEM LOCATION.** This defines the value of the MIB variable, *sysLocation*, for system location. This is a description of the system.

✦ **TRAP HOST IP ADDRESS.** This is the address of the host to which the KarlBridge's trap messages are sent. The host must be set to run an SNMP trap logger that can log these traps. Typically, this is the IP address of the SNMP manager.

✦ **TRAP HOST PASSWORD.** Only hosts that have this password set for trap messages can receive this trap message. The string *public* is the common password used to receive SNMP trap receivers.

✦ **ENABLE SNMP COLD/WARM START TRAP.** When enabled, SNMP trap messages are sent for cold and warm boot of the SNMP agent in the KarlBridge. If you have an SNMP manager that can log these events, you should enable these messages in case an intruder causes a shutdown of the KarlBridge.

✦ **ENABLE SNMP AUTHENTICATION TRAPS.** If an SNMP manager uses an incorrect password when trying to poll the bridge, it could represent an intruder trying to probe the KarlBridge. In this case, an SNMP authentication failure trap message is sent if this option is enabled.

✦ **SNMP IP ACCESS LIST.** This identifies the SNMP managers that can poll the KarlBridge.

If you want the KarlBridge to be used as a screening router, select Security (Firewall) Setup (press Alt+S to see the options). You should see a screen showing the protocol options for which you set filters (see fig. 6.9). The protocol options are TCP/UDP, AppleTalk, DECNET, and Novell's IPX. If you select the TCP/UDP option, you should see a screen for programming the filter (see fig. 6.10).

FIGURE 6.9

Protocol options for setting filters.

FIGURE 6.10

Protocol configuration options.

These fields are described next:

✤ **REMOTE AND LOCAL SERVERS.** These menus specify up to 10 IP networks, subnets, host IP address combinations, and server port numbers (referred to as sockets in the interface) that are to be passed or dropped. These two menus must be used together and will be combined into one menu in a future release of the software (see fig. 6.11).

FIGURE 6.11

Remote and local servers.

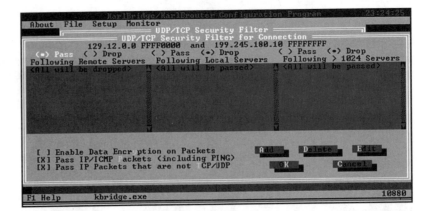

Each IP packet that passes through the bridge is checked against the filter entry consisting of an IP Address and an IP Mask. If a packet matches the Remote IP network then the corresponding entry in the Local menu is checked for a match. If a match is found in the Local IP network, the port number conditions set for this entry are matched.

Each IP packet source and destination address is checked against each entry in the list to determine if the packet is to be allowed or blocked. Blocked packets are dropped. Matching is performed on the first entry first and then goes down the list. When a match is found, the action specified on that line is performed immediately. A bit-wise AND operation is performed between the packet's IP addresses and the Mask values. The same is done for the addresses specified in the entry. The two results are then compared. If they are the same, a match has occurred.

Note that the KarlBridge is not an IP Router. This menu specifies the IP networks, IP subnets, and IP hosts on the remote network that hosts on the local network can communicate with.

The following examples can clarify the use of these filter specifications:

Example 1

IP Address	IP Mask	Action Performed
128.146.0.0	FFFF0000	Pass packets to Network 128.146.x.x
128.150.0.0	FFFF0000	Pass packets to Network 128.150.x.x
Drop All Others		Drop packets to all other networks

Example 2

IP Address	IP Mask	Action Performed
128.146.10.8	FFFFFFFF	Pass packets to 128.146.10.8
128.146.10.9	FFFFFFFF	Pass packets to 128.146.10.9
128.146.10.0	FFFFFF00	Drop packets to Subnet 128.146.10.x
128.150.25.0	FFFFFF00	Drop packets to Subnet 128.146.25.x
128.146.0.0	FFFF0000	Pass packets to Network 128.146.x.x
128.150.0.0	FFFF0000	Pass packets to Network 128.150.x.x
Drop All Others		Drop packets to all other networks

❖ **LOCAL IP ADDRESS/MASK MENU.** This menu specifies the local IP subnets and hosts that are to be allowed or blocked. Each entry consists of an IP address and an IP mask. A packet that matches is then either passed or dropped as indicated. Each IP packet's source or destination address is checked against each entry in the list to determine if the packet is to be passed or dropped. Matching is performed on the first entry first and then goes down the list. When a match is found, the action specified on that line is performed immediately. A bit-wise AND operation is performed between the packet's IP addresses and the Mask values. The same is done for the addresses specified in the entry. The two results are then compared. If they are the same, a match has occurred.

This option is similar in function to that configured in the Remote IP Address/Mask Menu discussed previously, with the exception that it applies to IP hosts, IP subnets, and IP network on the local network (connected to the local port of the KarlBridge).

✤ **PASS/DROP IP REMOTE SERVERS MENU.** This menu specifies the remote IP/UDP and IP/TCP server sockets to be passed or dropped. In this context, *server sockets* are sockets assigned numbers less than 1,024, such as the Telnet daemon, the FTP daemon, the SMTP daemon, and many others. *Remote server sockets* are servers located on the remote network. For example, if ftp and Telnet are passed and all other sockets are dropped in this menu, then machines on the local network can initiate an ftp or Telnet session to remote machines, but no other outgoing connections can be initiated.

If the Sockets button is selected (see fig. 6.12), you can specify the port numbers to be used for filtering.

FIGURE 6.12

Selecting service port numbers.

✤ **PASS/DROP IP LOCAL SERVERS MENU.** This menu specifies the local IP/UDP and IP/TCP server port numbers to be allowed or blocked. In this context, *server sockets* are sockets assigned numbers less than 1,024, such as the Telnet daemon, the FTP daemon, the SMTP daemon, and many others. *Local server sockets* are servers located on the local network. For example, if ftp and telnet are dropped and all other sockets are passed in this menu, then machines on the remote network cannot initiate an ftp or telnet session on local machines.

✤ **PASS/DROP IP SOCKETS > 1023 MENU.** This menu specifies the remote and local IP/UDP and IP/TCP sockets greater than 1,023 to be passed or dropped. X11, Multiuser Dungeons (MUD), NFS, and other nonprivileged sockets are in this range. No distinction is made between *local* and *remote* for this menu. You can drop MUD sockets, for example, either by specifying them individually or by setting the menu to pass nothing and Drop All Others. This causes the KarlBridge to drop all packets to or from server sockets > 1,023, which includes MUD, X11, NFS, and all other server port numbers in this range.

248

You can add a port filter specification by selecting the Add button. Figure 6.12 showed the flexibility available for adding port numbers.

When done setting up security filter, save your changes by pressing Alt+S and selecting Save. Exit the KBCONFIG program by pressing Alt+F and selecting Exit. The options that you have configured are stored in the KBRIDGE.EXE program.

KARLBRIDGE IMPLEMENTATION CONSIDERATIONS

The SMC Elite 16 Ethernet card-based KarlBridge is a general-purpose PC card and is not as fast at forwarding packets as some commercial bridges. At times, extra speed might be needed, such as in situations of network congestion or high network traffic. Commercial versions of KarlBridge are based upon special, ultra-fast Ethernet cards that boost the forwarding rate up to full Ethernet speed.

A commercial clone, such as 286/386/486/Pentium, provides adequate performance for most small networks. If additional performance and reliability are needed to withstand larger extremes of heat, dust, and restarting after power failures, you might want to use the commercial version of KarlBridge.

Currently, if you are using the shareware version of KarlBridge, you must use SMC Elite 16 cards with the 83C690 chip. The SMC Ultra card is expected to be supported in future versions of the shareware/demo KarlBridge.

Other enhancements planned for KarlBridge include the following:

❖ Drives for:

COM Port with 16650 UART (SLIP and PPP)

Aggregation of multiple ports, which means making multiple 56K/T1 or multiple V.Fast modem lines work together to provide faster remote Ethernet bridging and routing

CATV card for an Ethernet to CATV bridge/router

❖ Support for:

Additional wireless card to add to the existing WaveLAN support

FDDI support

Token Ring support

ATM card support

❖ Adding RIP to the IP router module of KarlBRouter

❖ Support for spanning tree and source routing

❖ Filter and firewall enhancements for IP and support for Windows NT server filters

USES OF THE KARLBRIDGE

The KarlBridge designers estimate that over 7,000 people worldwide use the shareware and commercial versions of the KarlBridge. The following paragraphs provide some examples that may benefit you in using KarlBridge.

A wireless KarlBridge with the CellWave algorithm was used at Interop, Las Vegas (Spring 1994) to provide a 2 Megabit/sec Internet connection from the Las Vegas Convention center to the MGM Grand hotel (2.5 miles away) and the Bally's hotel (2.0 miles away). Each location had over 25 diskless X terminals. The convention center was configured as a Wireless KarlBridge base station, and the hotels were satellite stations. The CellWave algorithm provides lossless connectivity and takes care of base station repeat and hidden node problems both normally associated with wireless networks.

The Ohio State University network uses over 150 KarlBridges. This network consists of an FDDI ring connecting five hub sites. Each hub has one or more Cisco 7000 Routers with an FDDI interface and several Ethernet interfaces. Each Ethernet network connects through fiber to one or more buildings. A KarlBridge is set up at the entrance to each building to filter out unwanted protocols and to provide firewall and broadcast storm protection and SNMP monitoring. Many of the university buildings have several departments, each with a KarlBridge that can be used to isolate unwanted network traffic between departments. The departments run a combination of AppleTalk, NetWare-based, and TCP/IP-based networks. Protocol problems characteristic for each type of network can be prevented from propagating to other networks. Thus traffic caused by zone name problems need not appear on NetWare networks, and network number collisions on NetWare networks can be prevented from appearing on other networks.

COMMERCIAL VERSION OF KARLBRIDGE

The commercial version of KarlBridge supports additional features, such as the following:

❖ Expanded firewall filters

❖ Logging of break-in attempts

❖ Broadcast storm detection and suppression

❖ Logging of all TCP establish packets

❖ A new SNMP management, monitoring, and configuration program

❖ Encryption

❖ IP Routing

❖ Supports for high-speed Ethernet cards that enable the KarlBridge/KarlBRouter to forward at full Ethernet speeds

❖ Support for WAN links such as a dual 56 KB/64 KB card with T1/E1 speeds, ATT/NCR/DEC WaveLAN wireless card, and standard 16550 UART and modem support for dial-up SLIP links

❖ PPP over the synchronous and asynchronous lines with support for channel aggregation

❖ RIP for the IP router module

❖ Intelligent firewall filters that enable the Karlbridge to function like an application level gateway

The commercial version of KarlBridge is also licensed to OEMs by KarlNet, Inc. KarlNet, Inc. is the main commercial supplier of the KarlBridge hardware and software in the United States. KarlBridges and KarlBrouters are manufactured and sold in the United Kingdom by Sherwood Data Systems, Ltd., and other resellers exist worldwide.

KarlNet, Inc. sells the Ethernet-to-Ethernet KarlBridge box for approximately $1,200 (prices vary). KarlBridge models that come with Flash ROM kits cost more.

KarlBridge/Brouter can be obtained with different networking options, such as the following:

❖ Ethernet-to-wireless bridging and routing using the ATT/NCR/DEC WaveLAN card

❖ Ethernet-to-56 KB/64 KB/T1/E1 bridging and routing, Ethernet-to-Async SLIP line

❖ A standard Hayes AT command set compatible modem (supports V.Fast modems, auto dial, dial on demand, and secure lines)

You can obtain additional information on KarlBridge from the following sources:

For the commercial version:

In the United States:

> KarlNet, Inc.
> 614-263-5275
> sales@KarlNet.com

In the United Kingdom:

> Sherwood Data Systems, Ltd. UK
> 44- (0) 494 464 264

For the shareware version:

> Doug Karl
> Senior Computer Specialist
> Networking Engineering Group
> Ohio State University
> kbridge@osu.edu

THE DRAWBRIDGE PACKET FILTER

The Texas AMU security tools include a package for implementing screening routers called *Drawbridge*. This package is available on the following FTP server:

```
FTP server: net.tamu.edu
Path:      /pub/security/TAMU
```

or

```
FTP server: sc.tamu.edu (128.194.3.57)
Path:            /pub/security/drawbridge
```

Version 1.1 of Drawbridge is available in drawbridge-1.1.tar.Z and drawbridge-1.1-des.tar.Z. The drawbridge-1.1.tar.Z package is the Drawbridge base package without DES support. The drawbridge-1.1-des.tar.Z package is a supplemental package that contains the DES support. This package is installed in addition to the drawbridge-1.1.tar.Z package; just extract it on top of the regular package. This adds a few source files and new makefiles to the filter and fm directories. Note that the DES package is not required to operate Drawbridge; it only allows you to manage Drawbridge in a secure manner.

Because of United States export restrictions, only U.S. domestic sites can download the DES package. The package can function without any encryption package, but with reduced security on filter updates across the network.

Drawbridge is a copyrighted but freely distributed bridging filter. It uses a PC with two Ethernet cards to perform the filtering. It is composed of the following three tools:

❖ Filter

❖ Filter Compiler

❖ Filter Manager

Drawbridge was designed and programmed by David K. Hess, Douglas Lee Schales, and David R. Safford of Texas A&M University. You can send comments and suggestions about their package to drawbridge@sc.tamu.edu

OVERVIEW OF DRAWBRIDGE

Drawbridge is a bridging filter that has filtering at the center of the design. It uses custom, table-driven software called the Filter that can run on a dedicated PC. The authors recommend a 33-MHz 486 or better PC. The PC requires two Ethernet cards. Only 16-bit SMC cards are currently supported. The Filter Manager and Filter Compiler both run on Sun workstations.

The Filter Manager communicates and manages Filter (running on a PC) using SUN's NIT support. The Filter Compiler generates filtering tables that are loaded into Filter through the Filter Manager.

The Filter program filters TCP/IP on an incoming and outgoing basis and UDP/IP on an incoming basis. All other protocols are transparently bridged.

EXTRACTING THE DRAWBRIDGE SOFTWARE

The file is a Unix "GNU zipped" tar file. After you download this file, you must use the Unix gunzip and tar utilities on the downloaded file. The following commands are listed as a guideline to performing these steps:

```
mkdir  /usr/tamu        # Create a working directory
#Retrieve archive into this directory. The following
#commands assume that the name of the archive is
#drawbridge.tar.Z
gunzip drawbridge.tar.Z              # This unzips the file
tar -xvBf drawbridge.tar             # On BSD UNIX. Your UNIX command
                                     # may differ.
```

The following subdirectories and files are created relative to your working directory:

```
drawbridge-1.1/
drawbridge-1.1/drawbridge.README
drawbridge-1.1/fm/
drawbridge-1.1/fm/Makefile
drawbridge-1.1/fm/comm.c
drawbridge-1.1/fm/crypt.c
drawbridge-1.1/fm/fm.8
drawbridge-1.1/fm/fm.c
drawbridge-1.1/fm/fm.h
drawbridge-1.1/fm/lex.h
drawbridge-1.1/fm/lex.l
drawbridge-1.1/fm/nit.c
```

253

```
drawbridge-1.1/fm/util.c
drawbridge-1.1/doc/
drawbridge-1.1/doc/OVERVIEW
drawbridge-1.1/doc/MANAGER
drawbridge-1.1/doc/FILTER
drawbridge-1.1/doc/COMPILER
drawbridge-1.1/doc/filtering.ps.Z
drawbridge-1.1/doc/DES
drawbridge-1.1/doc/firewall.ps.Z
drawbridge-1.1/COPYING
drawbridge-1.1/filter/
drawbridge-1.1/filter/crypt.c
drawbridge-1.1/filter/filter.8
drawbridge-1.1/filter/filter.c
drawbridge-1.1/filter/message.c
drawbridge-1.1/filter/wd.c
drawbridge-1.1/filter/filter.h
drawbridge-1.1/filter/wd.h
drawbridge-1.1/filter/filter.exe
drawbridge-1.1/filter/makefile.mak
drawbridge-1.1/fc/
drawbridge-1.1/fc/Makefile
drawbridge-1.1/fc/chario.c
drawbridge-1.1/fc/chario.h
drawbridge-1.1/fc/classes.c
drawbridge-1.1/fc/classes.h
drawbridge-1.1/fc/fc.8
drawbridge-1.1/fc/fc.c
drawbridge-1.1/fc/grammar.y
drawbridge-1.1/fc/groups.c
drawbridge-1.1/fc/groups.h
drawbridge-1.1/fc/hosts.c
drawbridge-1.1/fc/hosts.h
drawbridge-1.1/fc/lex.c
drawbridge-1.1/fc/macros.h
drawbridge-1.1/fc/ports.h
drawbridge-1.1/fc/protocols.h
drawbridge-1.1/fc/services.c
drawbridge-1.1/fc/services.h
drawbridge-1.1/fc/Sample
```

The directories fm, doc, filter, and fc are created under the drawbridge directory. In the preceding example, this directory is drawbridge-1.1. This name might change as newer versions of the drawbridge program are released.

The doc directory contains the documentation about Drawbridge. The fm directory contains the source code for the Filter Manager. The fc directory contains the source code for the Filter Compiler. The filter directory contains the source code for the Filter. The Filter program runs under DOS on a PC configured with two network interfaces.

The Filter Compiler (fc) and Filter Manager (fm) both require an ANSI C compiler. The GNU C Compiler (gcc) is recommended by the authors. The Filter requires Borland's Turbo C++ 3.0. An executable version of Filter is provided in case you do not have access to Turbo C++.

To build Filter Compiler and Filter Manager, just go into the respective directories and type the following command:

`make`

The preceding command builds the executables. To install the Filter Compiler and Filter Manager, edit the makefiles to set the destination directory, login as root user, and type the following:

`make install`

If you have the DES portion of the package, make sure to install that before typing **make**.

To build Filter, copy all of the filter directory to a PC and type **make**.

DRAWBRIDGE DESIGN

Drawbridge compares best to a filtering router firewall configuration as shown in figure 6.13. In a filtering router firewall, a router that has packet filtering support is used to filter packets to an internal network.

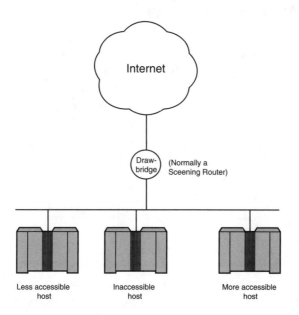

FIGURE 6.13

Drawbridge as filtering router firewall.

In figure 6.13, instead of using a screening router (firewall router), the filtering function is moved from the router into Drawbridge, which acts as a bridging filter.

One problem with packet filtering implementations is that they are difficult to configure. The simple syntax is designed so that a router can efficiently implement it, and not for a network administrator to remember the filter. In Drawbridge, the filter programming is off-loaded. Filter tables are specified using a rich and powerful language. The compiled tables are used for the dedicated filter. This allows Drawbridge to filter in terms of connections, rather than at the level of a packet.

This table design enables arbitrarily complex filters to be defined. In most conventional filtering routers, as filters are added, the performance begins to quickly drop due to how they implement the filtering rules. In Drawbridge, arbitrary numbers of complex filters can be set up, and the performance remains almost constant because simple look ups are performed and only connection establishment packets are filtered for TCP.

Drawbridge enables the testing of the configuration by enabling the administrator to see the results of a compiled configuration file, and to see if the correct filtering rules have been applied.

Drawbridge, unlike many screening routers, provides support for TCP source port filtering. Because source port filtering does allow the possibility of tunneling, Drawbridge does add the restriction that the destination port must be greater than 900. The authors selected 800 because of "broken" FTP implementations that happen to use FTP data ports beginning at around 900 rather than 1,024.

Figure 6.14 shows the steps involved in developing a filter specification. A source file containing filtering specifications in a special language is generated and maintained by an administrator. This file is then passed through the filter compiler, which generates the tables used by Filter. These tables can be loaded using a Filter Manager or by floppy disk.

FIGURE 6.14

Developing a Filter Specification.

The Filter Compiler generates four types of tables. The first is a network table, which has an entry for each host in the network. The host portion of an address determines the index into the table. The value in the table defines the "class" that is applied to a host when a TCP connection attempt or UDP packet is directed at that host. Currently, only class B and C networks are supported because class A tables would consume 16 MB of memory, and Filter does not have the capability to use any memory above 1 MB. The tables are defined in terms of *internal hosts* (hosts on the inside of Filter). No filtering is done based on the address of the host outside of the filter, except on a global basis. Filter only controls which inside host services are open, not which outside hosts may access an inside host services.

The *host class* is used as an index into the classes table. This table is composed of four subtables: TCP in, TCP out, TCP source, and UDP in. These subtables are in turn composed of lists that contain port number ranges. A *class* specifies a list out of each subtable that defines a host's filtering. TCP filtering only occurs when packets with SYN=1 and ACK=0 flags (connection initiation) are detected in a TCP header. All other packets of a TCP session are not filtered. Also, all UDP packets are filtered on an incoming basis only.

The last two tables are the allow and reject tables. The *allow table* globally allows packets out from any machine on the inside of the filter to the list of addresses in the allow table. The *reject table* globally rejects packets coming in from any machine on the outside of the filter with an address corresponding to an address in the reject table.

Figure 6.15 shows the algorithm used for filtering outgoing packets, and figure 6.16 shows the algorithm used for filtering incoming packets.

The language used by the Filter Compiler contains constructs for creating the various tables used by the filter. Constructs exist for specifying the network access on a per host basis or a network or subnetwork basis. The language enables groups of services to be created. These groups can be used in cases of related services or to group related machines.

The basic element of the language is a service specification. The service specification contains the following four pieces of information:

- ❖ The service
- ❖ The protocol
- ❖ The source or destination
- ❖ The traffic direction

The service can be either an entry from /etc/services or a numeric port. A range of port numbers also can be used. The protocol specifies the protocol that the service uses. The source or destination indicates whether the filter should use the source port or the destination port. The traffic direction indicates whether this is for outbound packets or inbound packets, or both.

FIGURE 6.15

Filtering of outgoing packets in Drawbridge.

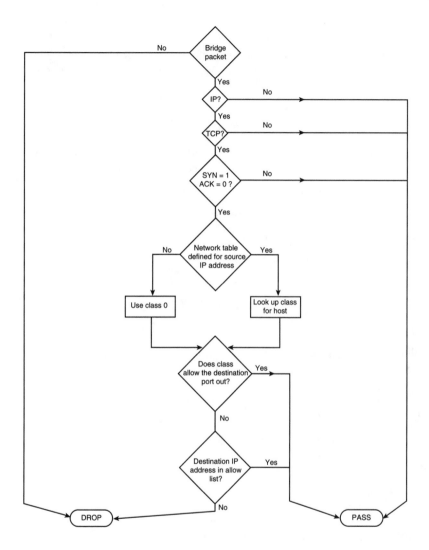

FIGURE 6.16

*Filtering of
incoming packets
in Drawbridge.*

A *group* is a list of comma-separated service specifications or other previously defined groups. Groups can be used to relate services or to categorize machines, enabling quick global changes to a category of machines. Hosts and networks can be granted network access using service specifications or group names.

DRAWBRIDGE FILTER LANGUAGE

The basic element of the language is a service specification. The service specification was described in the preceding section. The following are some sample specifications of the filter language.

Example 1 allows SMTP connections in either direction:

```
<smtp in-out>
```

Example 2 allows all outbound connections:

```
<1-65535 out>
```

Example 3 allows UDP-based network time protocol (NTP):

```
<ntp/udp in>
```

Example 4 allows data connect for ftp callback:

```
<src=ftp-data in>
```

Prefacing the service specification with an exclamation mark (!), indicates that this service is not allowed.

Example 5 does not allow TFTP:

```
<!tftp/udp in>
```

Example 6 does not permit rlogin:

```
<!login in>
```

Example 7 does not allow call to an internal NFS server:

```
<!2049/udp in>
```

Groups of service specifications can be used to repeatedly enter the same data. Groups also can be used to quickly change the access characteristics of an entire set of machines.

A *group* is a list of comma-separated service specifications or other previously defined groups, terminated by a semicolon (;).

Example 8 allows incoming mail and gopher connections.

```
define normal <smtp in>, <gopher in>;
```

The preceding example creates a group called normal that includes inbound smtp and inbound gopher. This group can be used in other groups to build up larger groups.

Example 9:

```
define server normal, <telnet in>;
```

In the preceding example, the new group server includes smtp, gopher, and telnet in.

The special group "default" is used to define access class #0, which is the default access for any machine not explicitly defined in the configuration file:

Example 10:

```
define default <1-65535 out>, <src=ftp-data in>, <smtp in>;
```

The preceding example allows all outbound connections, e-mail in, and ftp's data connections in for all machines that do not appear in the configuration file. Normally, all machines want the default services as well; therefore, group default should be added to the machines in the configuration file.

To define the access for a particular host, simply give the hostname and a comma-separated list of service specifications and group names.

Consider the following host services in Example 11:

```
    host myhost default, normal;
    host newshost default, <nntp in>;
```

Using the preceding definitions for normal and default, host myhost defines the following service definition.

```
<1-65535 out>, <src=ftp-data in>, <smtp in>,
<gopher in>, <telnet in>;
```

And host newshost defines the following service definition:

```
<1-65535 out>, <src=ftp-data in>, <smtp in>,
<gopher in>, <nntp in>;
```

If you want to specify access for an entire range of addresses, you can use the *network* command, which is similar to the host command.

Example 12:

```
network 123.45.67.0-123.45.68.255 255.255.255.0 <!1-65535 in-out>;
```

```
network 123.45.69.0 255.255.255.0 <!1-65535 in>;
```

The first entry allows no TCP connections "in" or "out" for 123.45.67.* and 123.45.68.*. The second allows no incoming connections for 123.45.69.*. Notice that the second example is an implicit range of 123.45.69.0–123.45.69.255. In the first example, you must fully specify the full range. For example, the range 123.45.67.0–123.45.68.0 would not include the hosts 123.45.68.1–123.45.68.255.

When multiple service specifications appear in a group definition or host/network command, they are merged. Service specifications are merged by doing an OR on the allowed services and keeping those explicitly disallowed, as shown in the following example:

```
define group1 <telnet in>, <!login in>, <!tftp/udp in>;
define group2 <telnet out>, <smtp in>, <login in>;
define group3 group1 group2 <tftp/udp in>;
group3 will have <telnet in-out>, <smtp in>.
```

Note that even though group2 allows <login in>, it is not possible to override the <!login in> specified in group1. Similarly it is not possible to override the <!tftp/udp in> from group1. group3 inherits the <!login in>. In other words, the actual value of group3 is as follows:

```
<telnet in-out>, <smtp in>, <!login in>, <!tftp/udp in>
```

The <telnet in> and <telnet out> in the combined group are equivalent to <telnet in-out>.

As a host's access capability is specified, either by use of a host or network command, classes of hosts are generated. All the members of a specific class have the same access allowed to them. There can be up to 256 different classes, with class 0 reserved for those hosts not specified in the configuration file. Class 0's capabilities are defined by the special group default. Each class can have up to 32 port ranges for each of incoming TCP, outgoing TCP, incoming TCP srcport, and incoming UDP.

You can break up the configuration file and include the separate files to create the filter control files, as shown in the following example:

```
include file1;
include file2;
```

Nesting of include statements is permitted.

```
reject address netmask
```

You can use the reject command to reject all incoming packets coming from a network address, as in the following example:

```
reject 18.23.0.0 255.255.255.0;
```

You can use the allow command to permit outbound packets from this destination, even if the access for the source host does not allow it. The expected use of the allow subcommand is in situations in which a restricted machine is being granted a network service. For example, if a workstation normally does not have access to the Internet, the allow subcommand can allow these machines to access a service on a specific machine/network. The syntax of the allow command is as follows:

```
allow address netmask [service-specification list];
```

After the rules are specified, you can use the compiler fc to generate the filter control tables from the source configuration file, as in the following example:

```
fc configuration-file
```

The following is a sample configuration file adapted from the Drawbridge documentation:

```
# Example config file
#--------------------------------------------------------------
#
# Defaults for any machine not listed in this file.
#
define tcpdefault <1-65535 out>, <src=ftp-data in>, <smtp in>, <auth in>,
                <gopher in>;
define udpdefault <1-65535/udp in>, <!tftp/udp in>, <!2049/udp in>,
        <!sunrpc/udp in>;
define default tcpdefault, udpdefault;
# Include 'default' in telftp since most will need defaults as well.
define telftp default, <telnet in>, <ftp in>;
# Admin requested no access in/out for these subnets
network 123.45.58.0 255.255.255.0 <!1-65535 in-out>;
network 123.45.39.0 255.255.255.0 <!1-65535 in-out>;
network 123.45.40.0 255.255.255.0 <!1-65535 in-out>;
#--------------------------------------------------------------
#
host m1.dt.tamu.edu                      telftp, <domain in>;
#--------------------------------------------------------------
# NNTP host and CSO phonebook server
host mailnews.tamu.edu                   telftp,
                                         <nntp in>, <time in>,
                                         <csnet-ns in>, <domain in>,
                                         <finger in>;
host slow.tamu.edu                       telftp;
host previous.tamu.edu                   telftp, <domain in>;
host mvt.tamu.edu                        telftp;
# IRC server on here...
host ick.tamu.edu                        <1-65535 out>, <6667 in>, <smtp in>,
<auth in>,udpdefaults;

#
# Machine (PC) in library which use tftp to do document transfers
host sender.tamu.edu                     <1-65535/udp in>;
#--------------------------------------------------------------
host h1.tamu.edu                         default, telftp;
#--------------------------------------------------------------
# These are all the VMS machines which have been cleared for telnet/ftp.
host h2.tamu.edu                         telftp;
```

```
host h3.tamu.edu                        telftp;
host h4.tamu.edu                        telftp, <domain in>; # zone transfers
host h5.tamu.edu                        telftp;
host h6.tamu.edu                        telftp;
host h7.tamu.edu                        telftp;
host h8.tamu.edu                        telftp;
host h9.tamu.edu                        telftp;
host h10.tamu.edu                       telftp;
# Research group using port 4211
host h11.tamu.edu                       telftp, <4211 in>;
host h12.tamu.edu                       telftp;
host h13.tamu.edu                       telftp;
host h14.tamu.edu                       telftp;
# NTP time server
host h15.tamu.edu                       telftp, <ntp in>,
                                        <time in>;

#-------------------------------------------------------------------
host s1.tamu.edu                        telftp;
host fast.tamu.edu                      telftp;
host dunno.tamu.edu                     telftp;
host meat.tamu.edu                      telftp, <finger in>;
# A PC FTP server
host somepc.tamu.edu                    default, <ftp in>;
# Has to have X11
host arrow.tamu.edu                     default, <ftp in>, <6000 in>;
host d2.tamu.edu                        default, <ftp in>;
host trouble.tamu.edu                   default, telftp;
#
host td.tamu.edu                        default,
                                        <ftp in>, <auth in>, <domain in>;

# No access in/out
host bee.tamu.edu                       <!1-65535 in-out>;
host g1.tamu.edu                        <!1-65535 in-out>;
host see.tamu.edu                       <!1-65535 in-out>;
host bam.tamu.edu                       <!1-65535 in-out>;
# NTP server
host bird.tamu.edu                      default, <ntp in>, <time in>;
#-------------------------------------------------------------------
# Gotta have X...
host gotta.tamu.edu                     default, <6000 in>;
host be.tamu.edu                        default, <6000 in>;
host very.tamu.edu                      default, <6000 in>;
host slow.tamu.edu                      default, <6000 in>;
#-------------------------------------------------------------------
# More name servers for subdomains
host add.tamu.edu                       default, <domain in>;
host bigadd.math.tamu.edu               default, <domain in>;
#
host dead.tamu.edu                      telftp;
#
host someone.tamu.edu                   default, <ftp in>;
```

```
# Nuclear Engineering
host hot.tamu.edu                         default, <ftp in>;
#
# Robotics Lab.  For demo. until 12/19?
host sp1.dt.tamu.edu                      telftp,
                                          <2650 in>, <2655 in>, <2700-2702 in>,
                                          <3200-3202 in>, <3300-3302 in>,
<3500-3502 in>;
# Local MUD's
host someklingon.tamu.edu                 default, <2000 in>;
host hmmmmm.tamu.edu                      default, <2000 in>;
```

DRAWBRIDGE FILTER

Filter is an executable program file called FILTER.EXE and should run on most compatibles. The FILTER.EXE is the software component of Drawbridge that runs on a 286/386/486/ Pentium PC and performs packet filtering. This module takes full control of the PC and converts it into a dedicated packet filter device. You can place a line containing the FILTER command in the AUTOEXEC.BAT file of the PC. This implies that the system should be DOS-bootable. DOS versions of 5.0 or higher can be used. By placing the Filter program in the AUTOEXEC.BAT you can ensure that the system boots automatically on power failures of system reboots initiated by the Filter Manager.

The Filter program is written using ANSI C. In its current distribution, Filter is compiled with Borland's Turbo C++ 3.0. No special settings are needed for the CONFIG.SYS file, so you can delete the CONFIG.SYS file or leave it empty. If you are using the Filter on a test PC, you may need to eliminate any device drivers that can cause conflicts. As usual with the PC world, these conflicts are hard to predict because of the many varieties of BIOS systems and device drivers.

The PC on which Filter runs should have 1 MB of memory and 5 MB of hard disk space. A 486 PC is recommended for good performance. Any memory over 1 MB is not used by the filter program because it runs in the DOS-real mode. If you are using the same PC to do the compilation, you will need more memory to modify and recompile the program with Turbo C++.

The Filter program is currently hard-coded to use only the Elite16 (8013) series of Ethernet cards from SMC. Future versions might add support for more cards. Because the PC acts as a bridge, two cards are needed for Filter. One Ethernet interface card is used for the internal network, and the other interfaces to the external network.

For those who do not intend to compile or modify Filter, an executable version of Filter is supplied with the source code. The make files (called *project files* in Borland C++) are

265

included for those who want to examine, modify, or compile the code themselves. Except for two warnings about an unused parameter in a function definition, which can be safely ignored, the compilation process should go smoothly.

The two Ethernet boards must be set as follows:

> Ethernet Card 1 [Inside (Internal) Network]
>
> > Memory Base Address: 0xD000
> >
> > I/O port address: 0x280
>
> Ethernet Card 2 [Outside (External) Network]
>
> > Memory Base Address: 0xCC00
> >
> > I/O port address: 0x300

Other considerations in setting up the hardware are as follows:

❖ Configure the cards properly for either AUI, Thin Wire, or 10BASE-T cabling.

❖ Interrupt settings are not so critical because the Filter program always polls.

❖ Depending on the model of 8013 card, you may need to set these configurations with jumpers, with the ezsetup program, or both.

For a system to be used in a production environment, you should "burn-in" a PC configuration for a week before you start using it. Other considerations are to ensure proper cooling and power regulation and protection from high humidity and dusty environments.

The Filter takes one argument, which determines which Ethernet interface is used for listening for remote Filter Manager commands. You can use the following syntax for invoking the Filter program:

```
filter [-l (inside¦outside¦both)]
```

The "inside" should be used if the commands are to be received on the internal network Ethernet interface. The "outside" should be used if the commands are to be received on the external network Ethernet interface. The "both" should be used if the commands are to be received on either internal or external network Ethernet interfaces. If no arguments are specified, the Filter does not respond to any Filter Manager commands.

A typical sample AUTOEXEC.BAT file includes the following:

```
rem Change to the "filter" directory
cd \FILTER
filter -l inside
```

In the preceding example, the FILTER.EXE has been copied to a special directory called FILTER. You can, of course, use any other directory name.

After the Filter program is loaded, all management activity occurs on the Filter Manager host. If you do not want to use the management software, you need to take the output files from Filter Compiler (using the byte reversal switch), and then copy them to the same directory on the PC on which FILTER.EXE is located.

To halt a running Filter program, type the **$** character at the PC Filter's keyboard. This causes Filter to exit and return you to the DOS prompt. If you never intend to access the Filter PC physically after it is installed, you can remove the monitor, monitor card, and keyboard, provided that you can disable the use of these devices from the BIOS so that your system does not generate errors on rebooting. If you have a keyboard attached to the system, your security policy should consider locking the keyboard or physically securing the Filter PC against accidental or intentional damage.

If you are using the Filter in conjunction with DES and lose your DES key on the Filter Manger host, you must disable the existing key. You can do this by halting the Filter program and then deleting (or replacing) the DES.KEY file in the Filter directory. This puts the Filter in a non-secure mode. You can then install a new DES key.

DRAWBRIDGE FILTER MANAGER

The Filter Manager is the tool used for managing a PC running the Filter program. The Filter Manager enables you to load new tables into the Filter and inspect them.

Currently, the Filter Manager can only run on Sun4 systems running SunOS 4.1.*x* with a kernel that has the Network Interface Tap (NIT) driver properly configured. Attempts to compile on other systems using the make files that come with the distribution produce error messages about missing critical "include" files.

If you do not have access to the hardware platform required for the Filter Manager, you can use the "sneaker-net" for distributing the filter tables to the Filter PC. You can do this by using a floppy disk to copy the output files of the Filter Compilation rules to the Filter PC.

You can build the Filter Manager by running the make program in the fm distribution directory. A binary image of the program also exists in the fm distributing directory, so you can copy it to the Filter Manager platform. The Filter Manager is written using ANSI C. The GNU C compiler is recommended.

The executable can be installed anywhere and does not need any support files. However, the Filter Manager program must be installed with SUID set for root. The Filter Manager uses root privilege only long enough to open the network interface and then changes its SUID to the real user.

The Filter Manager is an interactive program modeled after lpc. It provides more feedback and help than your typical Unix tool. The following is the syntax for using the Filter Manager:

```
fm [-i interface ]
```

If the network interface is not specified, the Filter Manager picks a likely device. You can use the following command to determine which interface to use.

```
netstat -i
```

To manage the Filter PC, you must select an interface on the same physical network to which the PC running Filter is attached. If Filter Manager's standard input is not a tty device, it does not print out any information on standard output. Instead, it sends an error message to the standard error (stderr) device.

After the Filter Manager starts, you can use commands such as help or ? to get additional help information. The commands supported include the following:

```
set (verbose¦target¦key) <args>
load (network¦classes¦allow¦reject) <filename>
show (host¦class¦allow¦reject¦target¦verbose¦key) [<args>]
query (host¦class¦allow¦reject¦stats) [<args>]
upload (networks¦classes¦allow¦reject)
write
release (classes¦allow¦reject¦network) [<args>]
ping
reboot
clear
reset
newkey <name>
genkey <name>
quit
```

A "#" at the beginning of a line comments the entire line. You can use the "!" to "escape" to the shell. The following command gives you additional information on using a specified command:

```
help command
```

To communicate with Filter PC, you need to tell the Filter Manager the Ethernet address of the Ethernet card on the PC that is connected to the same physical network. This is done using the set target command. You must specify the correct hardware address, or you cannot communicate with Filter. Filter Manager uses a nonroutable protocol to communicate with the Filter PC, so that it is not susceptible to remote attacks on routed, gated, or routing tables.

The Filter program must be started with the correct switches to enable communication with the Filter Manager. The following are examples of commands that can be used to start the Filter and enable communication with the Filter Manager:

```
filter -l inside
filter -l outside
filter -l both
```

When Filter is first started, it does not have any tables loaded (unless you used a floppy to copy the tables to the Filter PC). In this case, the default rules apply for all packet filtering. You must build a filter configuration file and use Filter Compiler to generate the filtering tables.

By default, Filter also does not use DES. You can use the newkey command in the Filter Manager to install a key in Filter to enable DES. To enable DES support, you must add additional files from a separate DES-enabled version of Drawbridge and then generate an executable using make.

When you run the newkey command, a ~/.fmkey.[name] file is created. This file holds your DES key. In this first case, the key is transmitted to the Filter PC on the network in an unencrypted form. All subsequent newkey generated keys are encrypted with the previous key. If you are extremely concerned about security, you can use the genkey command and copy the first DES key to the Filter PC using a floppy disk.

DES is only used for authentication, and it is not used to encrypt every packet. The authentication mechanism is used to prevent spoofing of the Filter Manager host or the Filter. The filter data goes across the network unencrypted, except for sequence numbers used for the authentication. Changes made to the DES key are sent with the new key encrypted with the current DES key.

The filtering tables created by the Filter Compiler are loaded into Filter Manager, using the Filter Manager load commands. Each table is loaded with separate load commands. These tables can be inspected with the show command. After the tables are loaded into the Filter Manager, you can load the information into the Filter PC using the upload command.

For example, the following command:

```
upload networks
```

uploads all the networks. When the uploaded information is successfully transferred, it is used immediately by the Filter PC. However, the uploaded information is made permanent until you issue a write command that tells Filter to write its currently loaded tables to disk.

You can inspect the currently loaded tables in the Filter PC with the query command. The use of the query command is similar to the show command for examining the tables loaded at the Filter Manager. The query command, however, queries the loaded tables in Filter PC and not the Filter Manager.

If you want to delete tables loaded into the Filter PC, you can use the release command. This command takes effect immediately and also deletes the tables from disk. The Filter PC reverts to default behavior for the deleted tables until new ones are loaded.

When the Filter Manager is started, it reads the file ~/.fmrc on startup and executes all commands in this file. Typically, the .fmrc file contains a set target command so that the Filter Manager can communicate with the Filter PC on startup, as in the following example:

```
set target 00:00:C0:04:AC:89
```

If you are using DES for authentication, you can add a set key command to the .fmrc file to avoid manually entering this command every time the Filter Manager is started.

The ~/.fmkey.* files contain DES keys so that you can manage Filter PC in a secure manner. The machine running the Filter Manager must be secured against attacks, otherwise, the key can be stolen from this machine and the Filter PC accessed by intruders. The ~/.fmrc and ~/.fmkey.* files must be set with the permission mode of 400 or the Filter Manager will complain about excessive permissions granted for these files.

You can use the Filter Manager ping command to determine if you can communicate with the Filter PC. The reboot command can be used to cause Filter PC to cold boot the PC. Therefore, the AUTOEXEC.BAT file on the PC must be configured to correctly restart the Filter PC on rebooting.

The reset and clear commands can be used to reset the Filter Manager. The reset command completely resets the Filter Manager and causes the .fmrc file to be reread. The clear command only causes the currently loaded tables to be unloaded.

SUMMARY

This chapter discussed examples of PC-based packet filters. Packet filtering enables the rejection of "suspect" packets based upon protocol information corresponding to the network and transport layers of the OSI model. The "suspect" packets are those in violation of the network security policy.

By controlling the type of network traffic that can exist on a network segment, the PC-based packet filters can control the type of services that can exist on a network segment. Services that can compromise the network security can be, therefore, restricted.

This chapter also discussed some practical tips in designing and configuring the KarlBridge and Drawbridge filters. A number of examples of packet filter specifications for Drawbridge were presented. Because screening routers operate with limited information from the network and transport layers, they are not as effective as firewall gateway solutions for controlling network traffic. However, they can be combined with firewall gateway solutions to provide a first line of defense. These solutions are discussed in the next chapter.

## CHAPTER 7

FIREWALL ARCHITECTURE AND THEORY

IN CHAPTER 4, "An Introduction to Screening Routers," you learned about screening routers and how you can use them to secure a network against intrusions. Screening routers are often used as the first level of defense against an untrusted network.

The packet-filtering technologies that are used in screening routers provide an efficient and general way to control network traffic. They have the advantage that no changes are required to client and host applications because they operate at the IP and TCP layers, and these layers are independent of application-level issues. On the other hand, packet-filtering approaches have not addressed many security requirements because they have incomplete information with which to work. Only network and transport layer (OSI model) information, such as IP addresses, port numbers, and TCP flags, is available for filtering decisions. In many packet filter implementations, the number of rules may be limited. Additionally, as the number of rules increases, there is a high performance penalty because of the extra processing needed for the additional rules.

Because of lack of context information, certain protocols such as UDP and RPC cannot be filtered effectively. Also, in many packet-filtering implementations, auditing and alerting mechanisms are missing. Many packet-filtering implementations can also suffer from poor management and user interfaces. Implementing packet filters can require a high level of understanding of communication protocols and their behavior when used by different applications.

Packet-filtering devices such as screening routers are often augmented by other devices called firewalls. *Firewalls*, because they operate at the upper layers of the OSI model, have complete information on the application functions on which to base their decisions. In this chapter, you learn the different types of firewalls that can be deployed.

There are several approaches to building a firewall. Organizations that have programming talent and financial resources often prefer to use a "roll your own" approach. This involves building custom firewall solutions to protect the organization's network. If implemented properly, this is perhaps the most effective (and also the more expensive) approach.

Other organizations prefer to use existing off-the-shelf products, and customize and configure them to meet the organization's network security policy. This book adopts the second approach. To make the discussion on firewalls more practical, several commercial firewall products are discussed in the next chapter.

EXAMINING FIREWALL COMPONENTS

The major objective of a firewall is to protect one network from another. Usually, the network that is being protected belongs to you (or is your responsibility), and the network that you are protecting against is an external network that cannot be trusted and from which security intrusions can originate. Protecting your network involves preventing unauthorized users from having access to sensitive data, while allowing legitimate users to have unencumbered access to the network resources.

Chapter 3, "Designing a Network Policy," introduced the OSI model as a means of making the distinction between screening routers and firewalls. Though the OSI model is a time-honored way of making distinctions between communication architectures and capabilities, not everyone is aware of it or makes use of it. The term firewall is used by many as a generic term that describes a wide range of functions and the architecture of devices that protect the network. Some, in fact, use the term firewall to describe almost any network security device, such as a hardware encryption device, a screening router, or an application-level gateway.

In general, a firewall is placed between the internal trusted network and the external untrusted network. The firewall acts as a choke-point that monitors and rejects application-level network traffic (see fig. 7.1). Firewalls also can operate at the network and transport layers, in which case they examine the IP and TCP headers of incoming and outgoing packets, and reject or pass packets based on the programmed packet filter rules.

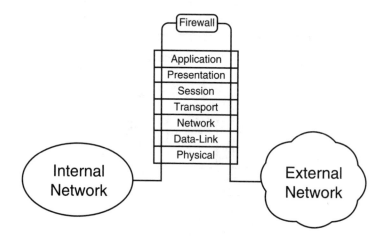

FIGURE 7.1

Firewall operation.

> The firewall is the chief instrument used to implement an organization's network security policy. In many cases, authentication, security, and privacy enhancement techniques are needed to enhance the network security or implement other aspects of the network security policy.

N O T E

The following sections describe the different types of firewalls that can be used.

DUAL-HOMED HOST

In TCP/IP networks, the term *multi-homed host* describes a host that has multiple network interface boards (see fig. 7.2). Usually, each network interface board is connected to a network. Historically, this multi-homed host also could route traffic between the network segments. The term *gateway* was used to describe the routing function performed by these multi-homed hosts. Today, the term *router* is used to describe this routing function, whereas the term gateway is reserved for those functions that correspond to the upper layers of the OSI model.

If the routing function in the multi-homed host is disabled, the host can provide network traffic isolation between the networks it connects to, and yet each network will be able to process applications on the multi-homed hosts. Furthermore, if the applications permit, the networks can also share data. A dual-homed host is a special example of a multi-homed host that has two network interfaces and has the routing functions disabled. Figure 7.3 shows an example of a dual-homed host with the routing functions disabled. Host A on Network 1 can access Application A on the dual-homed host. Similarly, Host B can access Application B on the dual-homed host. The two applications on the dual-homed hosts can even share data. It is possible for the hosts A and B to exchange information through the shared data on the dual-homed hosts, and yet there is no exchange of network traffic between the two network segments connected to the dual-homed host.

FIGURE 7.2

A classic multi-homed host.

FIGURE 7.3

A dual-homed host.

Dual-homed Host As a Firewall

The dual-homed host can be used to isolate an internal network from an external untrusted network (see fig. 7.4). Because the dual-homed host does not forward any TCP/IP traffic, it completely blocks any IP traffic between the internal and external untrusted network.

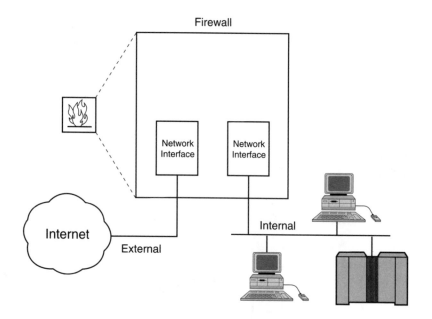

Figure 7.4

A dual-homed host as a firewall.

Many of the Internet services are essentially store-and-forward services. If these services run on the dual-homed host, they can be configured to transmit application services from one network to the other. If application data must cross the firewall, application forwarder agents can be set up to run on the dual-homed host (see fig. 7.5). Application forwarder agents are special software used to forward application requests between two connected networks. Another approach is to allow the users to log in to the dual-homed host, and then access external services from the external network interface of the dual-homed host (see fig. 7.6).

If application forwarders are used, the application traffic cannot cross the dual-homed firewall unless the application forwarder is running and configured on the firewall machine. This is an implementation of the policy "That which is not expressly permitted is prohibited." If users are allowed to log in to the firewall directly (see fig. 7.6), the firewall security can be compromised. This is because the dual-homed firewall is a central point of connection between the external network and the internal network. By definition, the dual-homed firewall is in the zone of risk. If the user selects a weak password, or allows his user account to be compromised (such as by giving away passwords), the zone of risk could extend to the internal network, thus defeating the purpose of the dual-homed firewall.

FIGURE 7.5

*A dual-homed host
with application
forwarders.*

FIGURE 7.6

*Insecurity intro-
duced with standard
user login to dual-
homed host.*

If proper logs are kept of user logins, it is possible to trace unauthorized logins to the firewall when a security breach is discovered. If users are not permitted direct login to the dual-homed firewall, however, any attempt at a direct user login will be registered as a noteworthy event and a potential security breach.

Examples of store-and-forward services are SMTP (mail) and NNTP (news). Figure 7.7 shows a situation where the dual-homed host is configured to provide discretionary forwarding of mail messages between an external untrusted network and an internal network. Figure 7.8 shows a situation where the dual-homed host is configured to provide discretionary forwarding of news messages between news servers on the external untrusted network and the internal network.

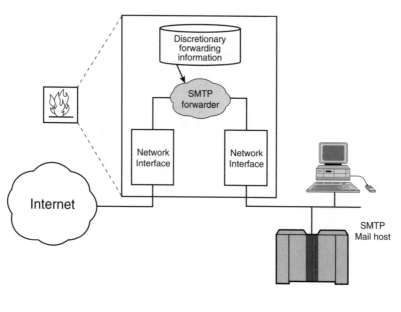

FIGURE 7.7

A dual-homed host as a mail forwarder.

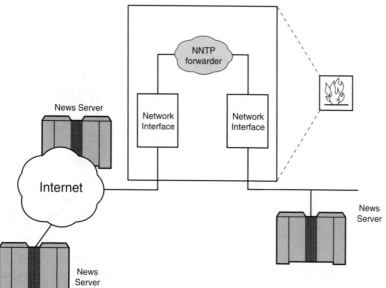

FIGURE 7.8

A dual-homed host as a news forwarder.

The dual-homed host is the basic configuration used in firewalls. The critical aspect of dual-homed firewall hosts is that routing is disabled, and that the only path between the network segments is through an application layer function. If the routing is accidentally (or by design) misconfigured so that it is enabled, the application layer functions of the dual-homed firewalls are bypassed (see fig. 7.9).

FIGURE 7.9

A misconfigured dual-homed firewall.

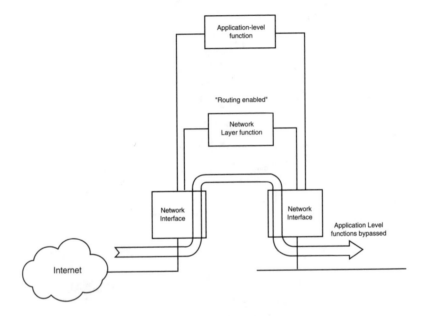

Most firewalls are built around Unix machines. On some Unix implementations, the routing functions are enabled by default. It is therefore important to verify that the routing functions in the dual-homed firewall are disabled, and if they are not, you should know how to disable them.

DISABLING ROUTING IN A DUAL-HOMED FIREWALL

Disabling routing functions in a dual-homed host based on Unix requires reconfiguring and rebuilding the kernel. This section describes that process for BSD Unix.

The Unix kernel is compiled using the make command. A command called config is used to read the kernel configuring file and generate the files that are needed to build the kernel. The kernel configuration file is in /usr/sys/conf or /usr/src/sys. In BSDI (Berkeley Systems Design, Inc.) Unix for the Intel platform, the configuration file is in /usr/src/sys/i386/conf directory.

To check to see which kernel configuration you are using, you can use the strings command on the kernel image file and look for the name of your operating system. The following shows an example of how you can check the kernel version.

```
% strings  /bsd ¦ grep BSD
BSDI $Id: if_pe.c,v 1.4 1993/02/21 20:35:01 karels Exp $
BSDI $Id: if_petbl.c,v 1.2 1993/02/21 20:36:09 karels Exp $
BSD/386
@(#)BSDI BSD/386 1.0 Kernel #0: Wed Mar 24 17:23:44 MST 1993
    polk@hilltop.BSDI.COM:/home/hilltop/polk/sys.clean/compile/GENERIC
```

The last line reveals that the current configuration is GENERIC.

You should change to the configuration directory (/usr/src/sys/i386/conf) and copy this GENERIC file into a new file suggestive of the new configuration. You can call this new file FIREWALL or LOCAL, for example.

```
cd /usr/src/sys/i386/conf
cp GENERIC FIREWALL
```

Next, edit the options parameter IPFORWARDING in the file FIREWALL and change it to −1 to represent "never forward IP datagrams." This variable has the affect of setting the *ipforwarding* kernel variable so that IP forwarding is disabled.

```
options IPFORWARDING=-1
```

On some systems, instead of the IPFORWARDING parameter, you might see the following statement in the configuration file.

```
options  GATEWAY
```

To disable forwarding of IP packets, comment this line out by placing a # as the first character in the line.

```
#options  GATEWAY
```

Also, verify that the following kernel configuration statements for TCP/IP exist.

```
options      INET          # Internet Protocol support is to be included
pseudo-device    loop      # The loop back device is to be defined
                             (127.0.0.1)
pseudo-device    ether     # Generic Ethernet support such as ARP
                             functions
pseudo-device    pty       # Pseudo teletypes for telnet/rlogin access
device we0 at isa? port 0×280  # Could be different for your Ethernet
                             interface
```

Run the config command to build the LOCAL directory and go to the directory shown in the following example.

```
config LOCAL
cd ../../compile/LOCAL
```

Next, run the make commands to create the necessary dependencies and build the kernel.

```
make depend
make
```

281

Copy the kernel image to the root directory, and then reboot.

```
cp /bsd /bsd.old
cp bsd /bsd
reboot
```

After rebooting, the machine can be set up as a dual-homed firewall.

COMPROMISING THE SECURITY OF A DUAL-HOMED FIREWALL

You should understand how the integrity of a dual-homed firewall can be compromised. With this understanding, then, you can take steps to prevent such an occurrence.

The biggest threat is if an intruder obtains direct login access to the dual-homed host. Login should always occur through an application proxy on the dual-homed host. Logins from external untrusted networks should require a strong authentication.

If the user obtains login access to the dual-homed host, the internal network is subject to intrusions. These intrusions can come through any of the following sources:

❖ Weak permissions on the file system

❖ Internal network NFS-mounted volumes

❖ Permissions granted to Berkeley r*-utilities through host equivalent files, such as .rhosts, in users home directories for user accounts that have been compromised

❖ Network backup programs that could restore excessive permissions

❖ The use of administrative shell scripts that have not been properly secured

❖ Learning about the system from older software revision levels and release notes that have not been properly secured

❖ Installing older operating system kernels that have IP forwarding enabled, or installing versions of older operating system kernels with known security problems

If the dual-homed host fails, the internal network is wide-open for future intruders, unless the problem is detected and corrected quickly.

As mentioned previously, the Unix kernel variable *ipforwarding* controls whether IP routing is performed. If the intruder gains sufficient system privileges, the intruder can change the value of this kernel variable and enable IP forwarding. With IP forwarding enabled, the firewall mechanism is bypassed.

SERVICES ON A DUAL-HOMED FIREWALL

Besides disabling IP forwarding, you should remove from the dual-homed firewall all programs, utilities, and services that could be dangerous in the hands of an intruder. The following is a partial list of some useful checkpoints for Unix dual-homed firewalls:

✤ Remove programming tools: compilers, linkers, and so forth.

✤ Remove programs with SUID and SGID permissions that you do not need or do not understand (see Chapter 2, "Security"). If things do not work, you can always put back essential programs.

✤ Use disk partitions so that an intrusion to fill all disk space on the partition will be confined to that partition.

✤ Remove unneeded system and special accounts.

✤ Delete network services that are not needed. Use the netstat -a command to verify that you only have network services that you need. Edit the /etc/inetd.conf and /etc/services files and remove unneeded service definitions.

BASTION HOSTS

A *bastion host* is any firewall host that is critical to the network security. The bastion host is the central host in an organization's network security. Because the bastion host is critical to network security, it must be well-fortified. This means that the bastion host is closely monitored by the network administrators. The bastion host software and system security should undergo regular audits. The access logs should be examined for any potential security breaches and any attempts to assault the bastion host.

The dual-homed host discussed earlier is an example of a bastion host because it is critical to the security of the network.

SIMPLEST DEPLOYMENT OF A BASTION HOST

Because bastion hosts act as an interface point to an external untrusted network, they are often subject to intrusion. The simplest deployment of a bastion host is as the first and only point of entry for external network traffic (see fig. 7.10).

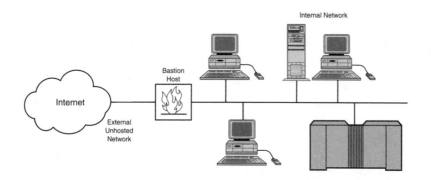

FIGURE 7.10

The simplest deployment of a bastion host (B2 configuration).

NOTATION USED TO DESCRIBE BASTION CONFIGURATIONS

The author has devised a notation that can simplify the description of a firewall configuration. In this notation, symbols are used to have the following meanings:

Symbol	Description
S	Screening router
R	Ordinary router
F1	Firewall with single network connection to the network
F2	Firewall with two network connections
B1	Bastion host with single network connection to the network
B2	Bastion host with two network connections

Using these symbols, you can describe the network configuration in figure 7.10. You can follow the path of the network traffic from the external to the internal networks:

B2

So the network in figure 7.10 is a B2 configuration.

SCREENED HOST GATEWAY

Because the bastion host is critical to the security of the internal network, another first line of defense is often introduced between the external untrusted network and the internal network. This first line of defense is usually provided by a screening router. Figure 7.11 shows the use of a bastion host with a screening router as the first line of defense. In this example, only the network interface of the bastion host is configured, and this network interface is connected to the internal network. One of the ports of the screening router is connected to the internal network, and the other port is connected to the Internet. This type of configuration is called the *screened host gateway*.

Using the notation defined in this chapter, the screened host gateway configuration shown in figure 7.11 can be described as the S-B1 configuration or just "SB1."

You must configure the screening router so that it sends all traffic received from the external networks for the internal network to the bastion host first. Before it forwards traffic to the bastion host, the screening router will apply its filter rules to the packet traffic. Only network traffic that passes the filter rules is diverted to the bastion host; all other network traffic is rejected. This architecture gives a level of confidence in the network security that is missing in figure 7.10. An intruder must first penetrate the screening router. If the intruder manages to penetrate the screening router, he must contend with the bastion host.

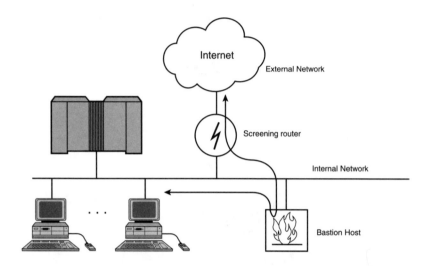

FIGURE 7.11

A bastion host with single network interface and screening router as the first line of defense (SB1 configuration).

The bastion host uses application-level functions to determine if requests to and from the external network are permitted or denied. If the request passes the scrutiny of the bastion host, it is forwarded to the internal network for incoming traffic. For outgoing traffic (traffic to the external network), the requests are forwarded to the screening router. Figure 7.12 shows the path of network traffic between the external and internal networks.

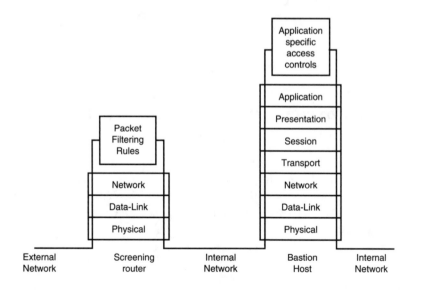

FIGURE 7.12

The path of network traffic for network with screening router and bastion host.

OFF-LOADING PACKET FILTERING TO THE IAP

Some organizations prefer to have their Internet Access Provider (IAP) provide packet filter rules for network traffic sent to the organization's network (see fig. 7.13). The packet filter still acts as the first line of defense, but you have to rely on your IAP for the correct mainte-nance of the packet filter rules.

FIGURE 7.13

The IAP provides
packet filtering to
the internal
network.

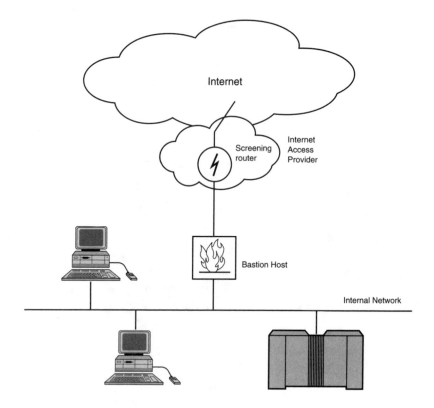

ROUTING CONFIGURATION FOR SCREENED HOST GATEWAY NETWORKS

The routing tables of the screening routers must be configured so that external traffic is forwarded to the bastion host. The routing tables in the screening router should be protected from intrusion and unauthorized change. If the routing table entry is changed so that the traffic is not forwarded to the bastion host but sent directly to the locally connected network, the bastion host is bypassed.

Figure 7.14 shows a situation where the screening router's routing table points to the bastion host. The internal network number is 199.245.180.0, and the bastion hosts IP address is 199.245.180.10. The screening router has the following entry in its routing table.

Destination = 199.245.180.0

Forward to = 199.245.180.10

All network traffic for network 199.245.180.0 is forwarded to the bastion host's IP address of 199.245.180.10.

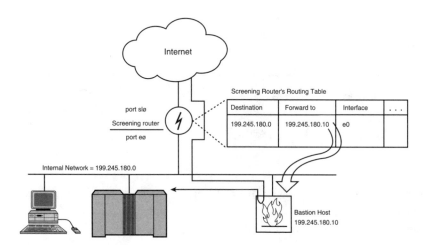

FIGURE 7.14

The normal setting of the screening router's routing table.

Figure 7.15 shows a situation where the screening router's routing tables have been subverted, and the entry for the destination network 199.245.180.0 has been removed. External traffic received by the screening router for the network 199.245.180.0 is not sent to the bastion host, but is sent directly through the local interface on the internal network. The bastion host is bypassed and the screening router is the only line of defense. Chances are that if the screening router has been subverted, other functions of the router could also be subverted, and the zone of risk will encompass the internal network.

FIGURE 7.15

The screening router's routing table is subverted.

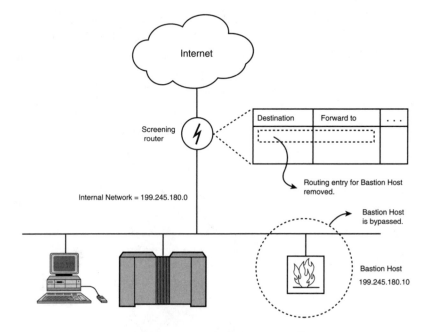

If the screening router responds to ICMP (Internet Control Message Protocol) redirect messages, it is vulnerable to false ICMP messages sent by the intruder. For this reason, response to ICMP redirect messages should be disabled.

N O T E

> If the screening router is based on Unix-derived software, you should configure the kernel to disable directed broadcasts so that broadcast packets from the internal network are not forwarded to the external network. Otherwise, information on the internal network can leak to the outside world. You can configure the kernel to disable directed broadcasts by setting the following in the configuration file:
>
> ```
> options DIRECTED_BROADCAST=0
> ```
>
> Next, you must run config on the configuration file. After this, you must run the make commands as follows:
>
> config *nameoffile*
>
> make depend
>
> make

> You should also remove unneeded network services and use static routing. Especially ensure that "routed" or "gated" daemons are not running, otherwise routes will be advertised to the external world.
>
> Also, make permanent entries in the ARP cache table to point to the bastion host. Use the following command to make permanent entries in the ARP cache.
>
> ```
> arp -s ipaddress hardware-address
> ```
>
> For example, to specify that the hardware address of the bastion host 199.245.180.10 is 0000C005564A, use the following command:
>
> ```
> arp -s 199.245.180.10 0000C004564A
> ```

You should configure the screening routers to use static routing. Static routes are not expired and changed by routing protocols. This protects the static routes from false route advertisements.

You also should disable the processing of the following at the router: ARP, ICMP redirects, proxy ARP, MOP, and ICMP unreachable messages. You can use the following configuration statements, for example, on a Cisco router.

no ip redirects

no ip route-cache

no ip proxy-arp

no ip unreachables

no mop enabled

no service finger

If your screening router supports TELNET access, you should disable it. On a Cisco router, you can set access control lists on virtual terminals to prevent remote access through TELNET.

In normal ARP operation, ARP table entries are built dynamically and are expired after a predetermined time interval. You should manually initialize the ARP cache table for the router and the bastion host. ARP entries that are made manually are never expired and act as "static" entries. With ARP processing disabled at the router, the router will not give out its hardware address.

N O T E

In BSD Unix, static routes are set up using the route command. The general syntax of this command is shown in the following example.

```
route [-n] [-q] [-v] command [-net ¦ -host] destination forward_to
```

The flags in this example have the following meanings:

-n	Prevents attempts to print symbolic names when reporting actions
-v	(verbose) Prints additional details
-q	Suppresses all output

The *command* can have the following values:

add	Adds a route
flush	Removes all routes
delete	Deletes a specific route
change	Changes aspects of a route (such as its gateway)
get	Looks up and displays the route for a destination
monitor	Continuously reports any changes to the routing information base, routing lookup misses, or suspected network partionings

To forward network traffic for the network 199.245.180.0 to the bastion host 199.245.180.10, for example, you would use the following command.

```
route add -net 199.245.180.0  199.245.180.10
```

It is best to specify all four numeric values of the dotted decimal IP address, unless you understand how partial IP addresses are interpreted. Here are some examples:

Using 130.33 without the -host or -net is interpreted as:

-host 130.0.0.33

The address 130.33.5 is interpreted as:

-host 130.33.0.5

The address -net 130.33 is interpreted as:

130.33.0.0

The address -net 130.33.5 is interpreted as:

130.33..5

290

BASTION HOST WITH BOTH NETWORK
INTERFACES CONFIGURED

Figure 7.16 shows the use of a bastion host with a screening router, but both network interfaces of the bastion host are configured. One network interface is connected to the "outside" network and the other network interface is connected to the "inside" network. One of the ports of the screening router is connected to the "inside" network and the other port is connected to the Internet. Using the notation defined in this chapter, figure 7.16 can be described as the S-B2 configuration or just as "SB2."

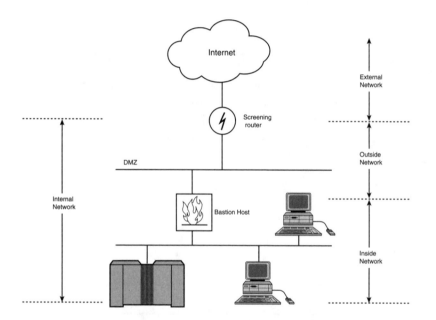

FIGURE 7.16

A bastion host with two network interfaces and a screening router as the first line of defense (SB2 configuration).

The screening router must be configured so that it sends all traffic received from the external networks for the internal network to the "inside" network interface of the bastion host. Before it forwards traffic to the bastion host, the screening router will apply its filter rules to the packet traffic. Only network traffic that passes the filter rules is diverted to the bastion host; all other network traffic is rejected. An intruder must first penetrate the screening router. If the intruder manages to penetrate the screening router, he must contend with the bastion host.

There are no hosts on the outside network, other than the screening router and one of the network interfaces of the bastion host. The outside network forms a Demilitarized Zone (DMZ). Because the DMZ has only two network connections, it can be replaced by a dedicated point-to-point link. This makes it more difficult to tap into this link using protocol analyzers. If an Ethernet or token ring network is used for the DMZ, a workstation that

291

places its network interface in the promiscuous mode can capture network traffic and access sensitive data. Normally, network interfaces only read the packet directly addressed to it. In the promiscuous mode, however, network interfaces read all packets seen by the network interface. All the organization's hosts (except for the bastion host) are connected to the inside network.

The network configuration in figure 7.16 has another advantage over the network configuration in which only one network interface of the bastion host was used (refer to fig. 7.11). This advantage is that the bastion host cannot be bypassed by attacking the screening routers routing tables. Network traffic must pass through the bastion host to reach the inside network.

USES OF TWO BASTION HOSTS AND TWO DMZS

Figure 7.17 shows the use of two bastion hosts with a screening router. Both network interfaces of the two bastion hosts are configured. Three network zones are formed in the internal network: the outside network, the private network, and the inside network. Using the notation defined in this chapter, figure 7.17 can be described as the S-B2-B2 configuration, or just "SB2B2."

FIGURE 7.17

Two bastion hosts with both network interface cards configured (SB2B2 configuration).

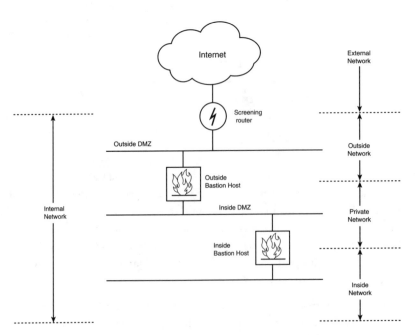

The screening router and the outside bastion host are the only two network interfaces on the outside network. The outside network forms the outside DMZ.

A private network exists between the inside and outside bastions. The private network provides a level of protection similar to that in figure 7.18. An organization could place some of its hosts on the private network and keep the more sensitive hosts behind the inside bastion host. Alternatively, an organization may want maximum security and use the private network as a second buffer zone or inside DMZ, and keep all of the hosts on the inside network.

If an organization wants to provide full access to a wide array of services, such as anonymous FTP (File Transfer Protocol), Gopher, and WWW (World Wide Web) services, it can provide certain sacrificial hosts on the outside DMZ (see fig. 7.18). The bastion hosts should not trust any traffic originating from these sacrificial hosts.

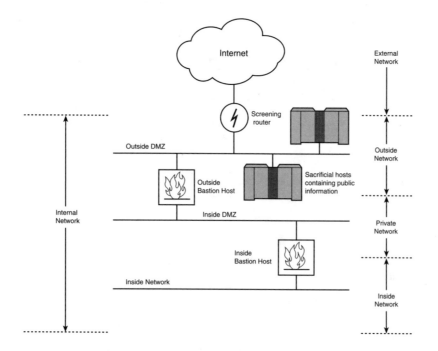

FIGURE 7.18

Sacrificial hosts on the outside DMZ.

The screening router must be configured so that it sends all traffic received from the external networks for the internal network to the inside bastion host. Before it forwards traffic to the bastion host, the screening router will apply its filter rules to the packet traffic. Only network traffic that passes the filter rules is diverted to the outside bastion host; all other network traffic is rejected. An intruder must first penetrate the screening router. If the intruder manages to penetrate the screening router, he must contend with the outside bastion host.

Even if the defenses of the outside network are breached, the intruder must penetrate the inside bastion host. If resources permit, you might want to make each bastion host the responsibility of a different administrative group. This ensures that the mistakes committed by one set of administrators will not be repeated by the other administrators. You also should

293

ensure that the two groups share information about discovered weaknesses in the bastion hosts. Figure 7.19 shows the path that the network traffic has to take between the external and internal networks.

FIGURE 7.19

The path of network traffic for the network in figure 7.17.

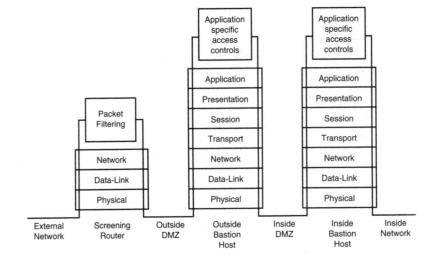

Another type of network configuration is to use two bastion hosts but only one network interface of each bastion host (see fig. 7.20). A second router called the *choke* is added between the DMZ and the inside networks. Figure 7.21 shows the path taken by network traffic between the external and internal networks.

With the network configuration of figure 7.20, you should ensure that the bastion hosts are not bypassed. You should ensure that the screening routers are using static routes. Using the notation defined in this chapter, figure 7.20 can be described as the S-B1-S-B1 configuration, or just "SB1SB1."

Other possible combinations are shown in figures 7.22 and 7.23. Whenever only a single network interface of the bastion is used, you should use static routes at the routers and properly configure the routing table entries to ensure that the bastion hosts are not bypassed. Using the notation defined in this chapter, figure 7.22 can be described as the S-B2-B1 configuration, or just "SB2B1;" figure 7.23 can be described as the S-B1-B2, or just "SB1B2."

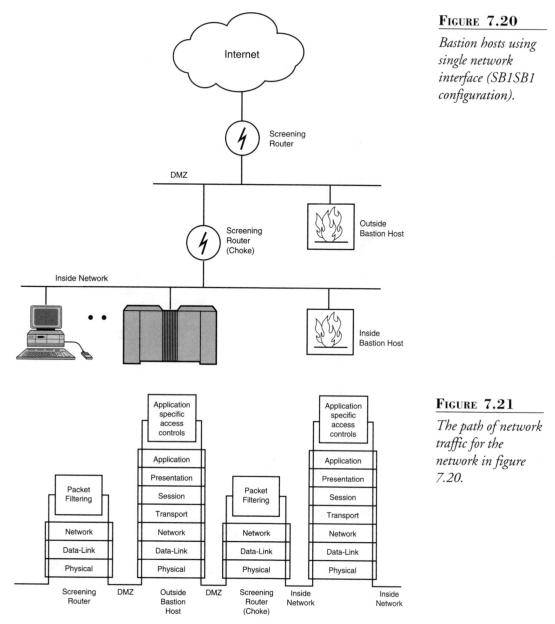

FIGURE 7.21

The path of network traffic for the network in figure 7.20.

FIGURE 7.22

A double-ended/ single-ended bastion configuration (SB2B1 configuration).

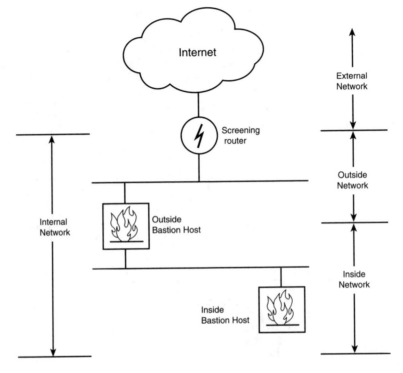

FIGURE 7.23

A single-ended/ double-ended bastion configuration (SB1B2 configuration).

SCREENED SUBNETS

In some firewall configurations, an isolated network of the type shown in figure 7.24 can be created. In this network, both the untrusted external network and the internal network can access the isolated network. However, no network traffic can flow between the untrusted external network and the internal network *through the isolated network*. The isolation of the network is performed using a combination of screening routers that are properly configured (see fig. 7.25). Such an isolated network is called a screened subnet.

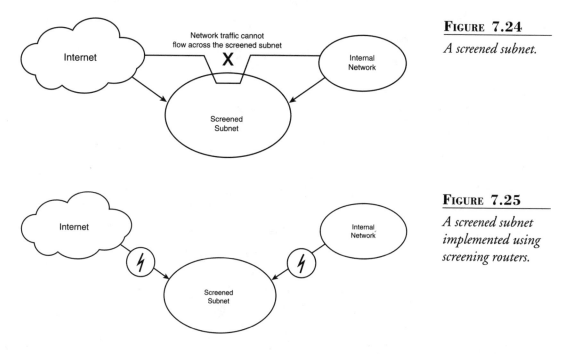

FIGURE 7.24

A screened subnet.

FIGURE 7.25

A screened subnet implemented using screening routers.

Some screened subnets may have application-level gateways on them that act as bastion hosts and provide interactive access to outside services (see fig. 7.26).

Figure 7.27 shows a screened subnet configured with a bastion host as the central access point to the screened subnet. This type of configuration is the S-B1-S, or "SB1S" configuration. Screening routers are used to connect the Internet and the internal network. The bastion host is an application gateway and denies all traffic that is not expressly permitted.

Because the only access to the screened subnet is through the bastion host, it is very difficult for an intruder to breach the screened subnet. If the intrusion comes through the Internet, the intruder would have to reconfigure the routing on the Internet, the screened subnet, and the internal network to have free access (which is made difficult if the screening routers allow access to only specific hosts). Even if the bastion host is breached, the intruder would have to break into one of the hosts on the internal network and then back into the screening router to access the screened subnet. This type of island-hopping intrusion is difficult to do without disconnecting oneself or tripping over an alarm.

FIGURE 7.26

Screened subnets with bastion hosts on the screened subnet.

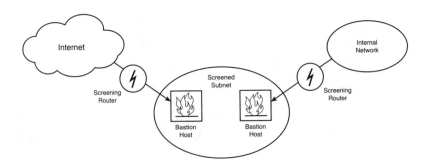

FIGURE 7.27

A screened subnet using the "SB1S" configuration.

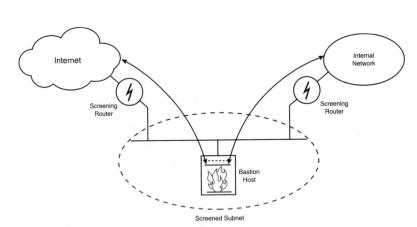

Because screened subnets do not allow network traffic to flow between the Internet and internal network, the IP addresses of the hosts on these networks are hidden from each other. This allows an organization that has not converted over to officially assigned network numbers from the NIC (Network Information Center) to access the Internet through application gateway services provided by the bastion host on the screened subnet. If these services through the application gateway are restrictive, these restrictions can act as a spur to convert the internal network to officially assigned network numbers.

APPLICATION-LEVEL GATEWAYS

Application-level gateways can handle store-and-forward traffic as well as some interactive traffic (see fig. 7.28). Application-level gateways are programmed to understand the traffic at the user application level (layer 7 of the OSI model). They can therefore provide access controls at a user level and application protocol level. Moreover, they can be used to maintain an intelligent log of all usage of the applications. The ability to log and control all incoming and outgoing traffic is one of the main advantages of having an application-level gateway. The gateways themselves can have additional security built into them as needed.

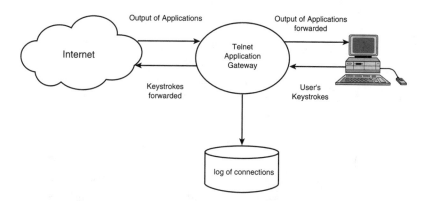

Figure 7.28

Application-level gateways.

For each application that is relayed, application-level gateways use a special-purpose code. Because of this special-purpose code, application gateways provide a high level of security. For each new type of application that is added to the network and that requires protection, new special-purpose code has to be written. Therefore, most application-level gateways provide a limited subset of basic applications and services.

To use application-level gateways, users must log in to the application gateway machine, or implement a specific client application service on every host that will utilize this service. Each application-specific gateway module can have its own set of management tools and command language.

A disadvantage of application-level gateways is that a custom program has to be written for each application. This fact is also an advantage from a security view point, though, because you cannot go through the firewall unless an explicit application-level gateway has been provided. This is an implementation of the philosophy, *That which is not expressly permitted is prohibited.*

The custom application program acts a "proxy" that accepts incoming calls and checks them against an access list of what types of requests are permitted. The proxy in this case is an application server proxy. On receiving the call—and after verifying that the call is permitted—the proxy forwards the request to the requested server. The proxy, therefore, acts as both a server and a client (see fig 7.29). It acts as a server to receive the incoming request and as a client when forwarding the request. After the session is established, the application proxy acts as a relay and copies data between the client that initiated the application and the server. Because all data between the client and server is intercepted by the application proxy, it has

299

full control over the session and can perform as detailed a log as needed. In figure 7.29, the proxy is shown as a client and server for the purposes of explaining its behavior. In most implementations, this is implemented by a single application module.

FIGURE 7.29

An application proxy as a client and server.

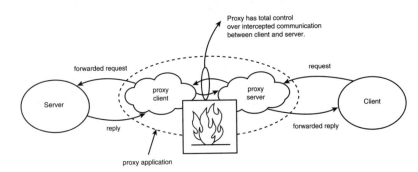

To connect to a proxy application, many application-level gateways require that you run a custom client application on your internal machines. Alternatively, you can use the telnet command to specify the port at which the proxy application service is available. If the proxy application was on host gatekeeper.kinetics.com and on port 63, for example, you would use the following command.

```
telnet gatekeeper.kinetics.com  63
```

After you connect to the port at which the proxy service runs, you should see a special prompt that identifies the proxy application. You have to run custom commands to specify the destination server. Regardless of which approach is used, the user interface to the standard application changes. If a custom client is used, the client is usually modified so that it always connects to your proxy machine and tells the proxy machine where to connect. The proxy machine then connects to the ultimate destination and passes the data through.

Some proxy application services are written so that they behave like the standard application. When the user specifies a connection target that is in a different network, the proxy application is invoked.

If you are using a custom client with the proxy application, you must install the custom client on all your internal machines that access a network through the application-level gateway. Depending on the size of the network, this can be a difficult task. If some of your users use DOS/Windows and Macintosh clients, it is usually the case that proxy versions of your client programs are not available. If you do not have the source code to these client applications (which is usually the case for Macintosh and PC client programs), you cannot modify them.

If the proxy client knows about only one application gateway server, and if this server is down, then you are vulnerable to a single point of failure. If the proxy client can be changed by the administrator to point to an alternate application gateway, the single point of failure problem can be avoided.

Because of the problems of configuring proxy clients, some sites prefer to use packet filtering for those applications such as FTP and TELNET that can be secured by proper filter rules. These sites use the proxy client approach for more complex applications, such as DNS, SMTP, NFS, HTTP, Gopher, and so forth.

If a custom client application is needed to communicate with the proxy server, some standard system calls such as connect() have to be replaced by a proxy version of these system calls. You must then compile and link the client application with the proxy versions of the system calls. A freely available library called *socks* contains nearly compatible replacements of the standard system calls such as socket(), bind(), connect(), and so on. This is available at the URL (Uniform Resource Locator) of ftp://ftp.inoc.dl.nec.com/pub/security/socks.cstc.

The proxy servers should be written in such a way as to provide a 'fail-safe' mode of operation if the properly modified client is not used. If a standard client is used to contact the proxy server, for example, then the communication should be prohibited and not cause undesirable and unpredictable behavior of the firewall and the screening routers.

Another type of application-level gateway is called the *circuit-gateway*. In circuit-level gateways, the packets are addressed to a user-application level process. A circuit-gateway is used to relay packets between the two communication end-points. The circuit-gateway simply copies the bytes back and forth between the two end points (see fig. 7.30).

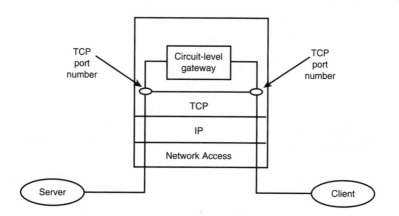

FIGURE 7.30

Circuit-level application gateways.

Circuit-level gateways are a more flexible and general approach to build application gateways. Although they may include code to support some specific TCP/IP application, this is usually limited. If they support an application, it is likely to be a TCP/IP application.

In circuit-level gateways, special client software might have to be installed, and the users might have to interact with an altered user interface or change their work habits. Installing and configuring special applications on each internal host can be time consuming and error prone for large heterogeneous networks because of the difference in hardware platforms and operating systems.

Because each packet is processed by software running at the application layer, the host performance is affected. Each packet is processed twice by all the communication layers and requires user-level processing and context switching. The application-level gateway (either a bastion-host or dual-homed host) remains exposed to the network. Other means such as packet filtering can be used to protect the application gateway host.

SUMMARY

In this chapter, you learned about different network configurations that use firewalls and screening routers to provide enhanced network security. The advantages and disadvantages of the different network configurations were discussed.

The remaining chapter, "Firewall Implementations," discusses practical implementations of firewall solutions. Some of these examples are taken from commercial firewall products and others are freely available software.

## CHAPTER 8

FIREWALL IMPLEMENTATIONS

THE PREVIOUS CHAPTER addressed firewall architecture and theory. This chapter completes the section by showing how those principles are implemented in the real world.

Several commercially available packages are discussed, as well as a shareware toolkit which allows you to construct your own firewall from scratch.

THE TCP WRAPPER

The TCP Wrapper is a freely available access control software for Unix systems. The TCP Wrapper performs the following basic functions:

✦ Logs request for internet service made through the /etc/inetd.conf file

✦ Provides an access control mechanism to control access to the services

Both of these capabilities can be used to construct a simple firewall solution. The TCP Wrapper program is available at the following URL:

```
ftp://cert.sei.cmu.edu/pub/network_tools/tcp_wrapper*.shar
```

      or

```
ftp://ftp.win.tue.nl/pub/network_tools/tcp_wrapper*.shar.Z
```

The file contains a shell archive. You must first uncompress and unarchive the files:

```
gunzip tcp_wrappers_6.3.shar.Z     # You can also use the Unix uncompress
sh tcp_wrappers_6.3.shar
make                               # You will see instructions on what to do
                                   # for building the binaries
```

The TCP Wrapper program is created in a file called *tcpd*. Place this file in a directory such as /usr/local/bin. Next, edit the /etc/inetd.conf file and place under the control of tcpd the services that you want to log and control. Suppose that you want to log and control telnet sessions to the host. The entry for telnet in the inetd.conf file should be similar to the following:

```
telnet    stream    tcp    nowait    root    /usr/libexec/telnetd    telnetd
```

To monitor access to telnet, replace the sixth field by the /usr/local/bin/tcpd program, as shown:

```
telnet    stream    tcp    nowait    root    /usr/local/bin/tcpd    telnetd
```

You can make similar changes to monitor any other services such as ftpd, tftpd, rlogind, rexecd, rshd, fingerd, and so forth.

After making the changes, restart inetd:

```
ucs# ps -aux ¦ grep inetd
root       82 0.0  0.0   652  124 ??  Is    3:17AM    0:00.27 inetd
ucs# kill -HUP 82
```

When the inetd program receives a request for the telnet service, the program tcpd is started, instead of the normal program telnetd. The tcpd program logs the request and checks the access control information in two files:

/etc/hosts.allow

/etc/hosts.deny

The hosts.allow file contains a list of hosts that are allowed access to the service. The hosts.deny file contains a list of hosts that are denied access. If these files do not exist, tcpd logs the request and allows all hosts access to the service. The tcpd program first checks the file hosts.allow, then the file hosts.deny. If a match is found for a service, it stops further examination of these files. This means that access granted through the hosts.allow cannot be overridden by the hosts.deny file.

The format of the entries for each file is as follows:

```
service-list: host-list [:shell-cmd]
```

The *service-list* is a comma-separated list of services defined in the /etc/services file.

The *host-list* is a comma-separated list of host names, IP addresses, network names, network numbers, domain names or NIS netgroups.

If a match occurs in the hosts.allow file, the listed systems are allowed access, and if a match occurs in the hosts.deny file, the listed systems are denied access.

Consider the following examples:

EXAMPLE 1

Take following entry in the hosts.allow file:

```
fingerd, telnetd: 144.19.74.1, 144.20
```

This means that hosts 144.19.74.1 and all hosts on class B network 144.20.0.0 are allowed access to telnet and finger services.

EXAMPLE 2

In the following entry in the hosts.deny file, all hosts in the domain HACKER.ORG are denied access to telnet and finger services:

```
fingerd, telnetd: .hacker.org
```

EXAMPLE 3

The keyword ALL can be used to match any service or any host. The keyword LOCAL can be used to match any host on the locally connected network:

Note the following entry in the hosts.allow file:

```
ALL: LOCAL, .KINETICS.COM
```

This means that all hosts on the locally connected network that are in the domain KINETICS.COM are allowed access to *all* services.

EXAMPLE 4

Consider the following entry in the hosts.deny file:

```
ALL: ALL
```

This means that all hosts on the network are denied access to all services, if there are no matching entries in the hosts.allow file. Remember that hosts.allows is processed before hosts.deny.

The definition of ALL is limited to those services that are invoked through inetd and are under the control of the tcpd wrapper program.

THE FIREWALL-1 GATEWAY

The FireWall-1 is a commercial gateway product, available from Internet Security Corporation. The product currently runs on SUN SparcStations.

The FireWall-1 uses the following two methods to establish network security.

❖ Application gateway

❖ Packet filtering

The configuration of the FireWall-1 gateway is done using graphical interfaces such as OpenLook for SunOS operating systems. The FireWall-1 gateway provides the following features:

❖ Secure packet filtering

❖ Adding context information to stateless connections

❖ Auditing and alerting

❖ Ability to define and add new protocols and services

- ❖ Authenticated telnet and FTP sessions
- ❖ Creating encrypted channels

A unique aspect of FireWall-1 is that, although it uses packet filtering as its basic mechanism, the packet filtering is done at layers 2 to 7 of the OSI model. Protocols that lack context information, such as UDP, are handled by building context information within the FireWall-1 gateway.

RESOURCE REQUIREMENTS FOR FIREWALL-1

Before investing resources in evaluating a product to see if it is suitable for your network environment, it is helpful to know details such as the hardware and software and training resources needed to implement the product. This information is provided for your reference. The FireWall-1 can currently run on the following platform/ operating systems:

Hardware platform:	Sun Sparc-based systems
	Intel running Solaris 2.4 or higher
Operating System:	SunOS 4.1.3 or Solaris
	NetWare server platforms
Graphical Interface:	X11R5/Open Look
	(Open Windows 3)
Disk space requirements:	5 MB
Memory requirements:	16 MB control module
Network Interface:	Standard SUN workstation interfaces
	Access List support for Cisco routers(version 9.1 or higher) and Wellfleet routers (version 8.0 or higher)

OVERVIEW OF FIREWALL-1 ARCHITECTURE

The FireWall-1 gateway acts as a secure router between an organization's internal network and an external network (see fig. 8.1). All the network traffic between the organization's network and an external, untrusted network is sent through the FireWall-1 gateway. Each packet exchanged between the external network and internal networks thus can be verified to comply with the organization's internal security.

FIGURE **8.1**

The FireWall-1 gateway.

Internet

Firewall - 1

External
Untrusted
Network

Internal
Trusted
Network

The FireWall-1 is composed of two major components, as follows:

❖ Packet-filter modules

❖ Control modules

A single control module can be used to control and monitor multiple packet filter modules. The packet filter module operates independently of the control module and can be placed on additional Internet gateways and servers to provide compartmentalized zones of risk. The control module is placed in the control workstation. The control module and packet filter module can reside on the same or different hosts. If they are placed on different hosts, communication between the control and packet filter modules are authenticated with a one-time password authentication.

The packet filter module implements the secure router functions between networks and is situated between the data link and network layers of the OSI model. Figures 8.2 and 8.3 show the packet filter operations implemented for incoming and outgoing packets, respectively. The data link layer is implemented by the network board, and the network layer is the IP protocol layer of the TCP/IP stack in the gateway.

For both incoming and outgoing packets, the packet headers are checked to see if they match a packet filtering rule. If no match takes place, the next rule is tried. For matched packets, a log/alert of the packet can optionally be done. After the log, a decision is made to pass the packet or drop it as specified in the packet filter rule.

If the packet cannot be matched, it is dropped in accordance with the security policy *That which is not expressly permitted is prohibited.*

A unique feature of FireWall-1's packet filtering is that it provides an effective way for filtering UDP and RPC traffic. This packet filtering is done by building context information for packets that are not part of a virtual circuit.

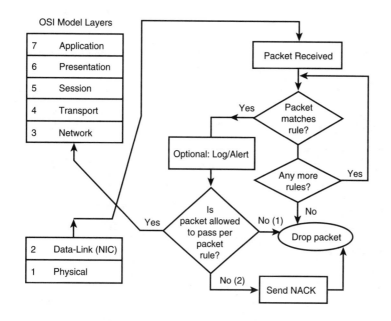

FIGURE 8.2

A FireWall-1 packet filter module operation on incoming packets.

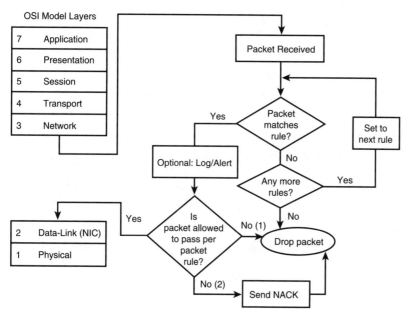

FIGURE 8.3

A FireWall-1 packet filter module operation on outgoing packets.

Other capabilities of FireWall-1's packet filtering follow:

- ✤ **LISTS AND OBJECTS.** Networks and services are represented by objects, which can be grouped together and referenced in access lists, allowing filter rules to be specified at a higher level than most packet filters.

- ✤ **FULL DATA ACCESS.** The packet filtering rules can filter on addresses and header information for any of the layers 2 to 7 of the OSI model. Filtering on upper layer protocol information allows the specification of more intelligent rules based on more complete information. This allows the implementation of security policies based on application knowledge.

- ✤ **PROTOCOL INDEPENDENCE.** High-level definitions can be used to define new protocols and applications, making the packet filter module more generic and flexible.

- ✤ **AUDITING AND ALERTING.** Packets that are matched can be audited in a log or used to generate alerts. The log and alert formats and actions are user-configurable. The standard formats contain source and destination addresses, the protocol used, the service attempted, time and date, and the action carried out. Alerts can be programmed to run user-defined scripts to perform actions, such as triggering alarms and pager alerts, opening windows, and sending e-mail. Alerts can also be sent using SNMP to a SNMP Manager. The status report can be viewed using SNMP or through the Status System Monitor software.

- ✤ **STATUS REPORTING.** A summary of status information on network traffic is available in the System Status Monitor. This information is also available through an SNMP manager.

- ✤ **KERNEL MODULE.** The packet filter module is a dynamically loadable kernel module, meaning that upgrades are simple to implement. Because the packet filter operated inside the kernel, it is not hampered by context switching overheads, which would exist if the module existed as a user process. In general, running inside the kernel has the advantage of negligible processing overheads, and is more efficient.

- ✤ **OPTIMIZATION.** Packet filter optimizers are used to reduce the time spent processing packet filter rules. Techniques such as caching and hashing tables are used to unify multiple instances of objects and to access the data efficiently.

FireWall-1 Control Module

The Control Module is used to implement the network security policy and the control packet filter modules (also called communication gateways). The Control Module can also be used as a central facility to view logging and control information.

The control workstation uses the OpenLook X11R5 GUI. Alternatively, a set of command line utilities can be used that permit a simpler computer terminal to perform management functions. The command line tools also enable the writing of script files to perform specialized control functions.

The overall architecture of the control module is shown in figure 8.4.

You can use FireWall-1 to define a global security policy for the network. Figure 8.5 shows the user interface for setting the security policy parameters.

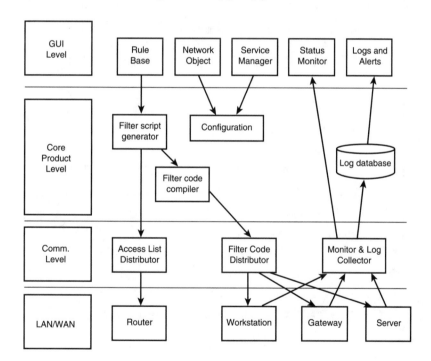

FIGURE 8.4

The FireWall-1 Control Module.

FIGURE 8.5

*The FireWall-1
control properties.*

FireWall-1 Control Properties

Security Policy

    Apply Gateway Rules to Interface Direction   ☑ Inbound

☑ Enable UDP Replies [Essential for NIS/RPC]   ☑ First

    Reply Timeout: <u>40</u>   0 ●━■▭▭▭▭▭▭300 sec

☑ Enable Established TCP Connections [Essential]   ☑ First

☑ Enable Response of FTP Data Connections   ☑ First

☑ Enable RIP [Common]   ☑ First

☑ Enable Domain Name Queries (UDP) [Essentials]   ☑ First

☑ Enable Domain Name Download (TCP)   ☑ First

☑ Enable Loopback UDP packets [Essential for NIS/RPC]   ☑ First

☑ Enable Loopback TCP connections   ☑ First

☑ Enable RPC Control   ☑ First

☑ Enable ICMP [Common]   ☑ First

☑ Enable Outgoing Packets [Common]   ☑ Last

Logging and Alerting

    Excessive Log Grace Period: <u>62</u>   0 ●━━━━━■▭▭ 90 sec

    Mail Alert Command: <u>Mail -s 'FireWall-1 Alert' root</u>

    PopUp Alert Command: <u>alert</u>

    User Defined Alert Command: <u>alert</u>

(Apply) (Reset)

NETWORK OBJECTS MANAGER

The Network Objects Manager is used to define objects that are specified in the security policy. These include the following object types:

✤ Networks and sub-networks

✤ Servers and workstations

✤ FireWall-1 hosts and gateways

✤ Routers

✤ Internet daemon

Figure 8.6 shows the Network Object Manager screen that can be used to define objects of the type discussed in this section. You can view the networks by types (internal, external) and type of objects (host, network, router, gateway, domain, group). All the object types in this figure are selected.

FIGURE 8.6

The FireWall-1 Network Object Manager screen.

Every network object has attributes, such as IP addressees and subnet masks, that define the characteristics of that object. These object attribute values are initialized from information

313

stored in network databases. These network databases include files such as the /etc/hosts, /etc/networks, /etc/services, /etc/gateways. SUN-base networks may have the *Network Information Services* (NIS) databases. The information about various network objects can be extracted by polling SNMP (Simple Network Management) agents running on these devices. Objects can be combined in groups to create higher level object abstractions and hierarchies.

Figure 8.7 shows the attributes of a Host Object. This figure shows that some of the host properties are its IP address, location (internal or external), whether it is a host or gateway, whether FireWall-1 is installed on the host, and information on its network interface. The SNMP MIB (Management Information Base) variables for this host can be set, and you can define parameters such as the SNMP community name used to access the MIB variables in this host.

FIGURE 8.7

The FireWall-1 host properties.

314

SERVICES MANAGER

The Services Manager defines the services that are known to the system and that are specified in the network security policy. All network services are screened and controlled. FireWall-1 comes pre-loaded with definitions for over 40 TCP/IP and Internet services that include the following:

- ✤ Standard services: Telnet, FTP, SMTP, and so on

- ✤ Berkeley r* services: rlogin, rsh, rcp, rexec, rwho, ruptime, and so on

- ✤ SunRPC services: NIS, NFS

- ✤ Internet search tools: HTTP (Hyper Text Transfer Protocol), Gopher, Archie, WAIS (Wide Area Information Services)

- ✤ IP services: ICMP, RIP

- ✤ Management services: SNMP

The Services Manager can be used to define a new service by selecting the service type. The service types include the following choices:

- ✤ TCP

- ✤ UDP

- ✤ RPC

- ✤ Others: This enables definition of other services and protocols that are not standard.

Services can be grouped into families and hierarchies, such as the NFS group that includes NFS-server, Lock Manager, and Mount Program. Another example is Mosaic (WWW) that includes HTTP, Archie, Gopher, and others.

Figure 8.8 shows the Services Manager. You can use this screen to define new services or edit existing ones. Figure 8.9 shows the service properties of a standard service such as Telnet.

FIGURE 8.8

*The FireWall-1
Services Manager.*

FIGURE 8.9

*The FireWall-1
TCP Services
Properties.*

RULES-BASE MANAGER

The Rules-Base Manager is a software component that is used for managing the packet filter rules for FireWall-1. After you define the network objects and services, you can define the rules that make these services for implementing the security policy. When the rules are compiled and installed, they act as a packet filter. The Rules-Base editor is used for making changes to the packet filter rules. Figure 8.10 shows the Rules-Base editor for FireWall-1. This figure shows that rules can be entered in a table that has columns for source, destination, services, action, track, and "install on."

In figure 8.10, Rule 1 accepts an SMTP service packet from any source to a group of hosts defined by the group "mailservers." The action is to accept these SMTP services on the installed gateways.

Rule 2 allows any host on the network to access any service on any network. This rule is installed on the gateway. Additionally, a short log entry is created for matching packets.

Rule 3 blocks any attempt by any external source to the local network. This rule is implemented on the gateway. Additionally, alert messages are sent with the occurrence of such attempts.

FIGURE 8.10

The FireWall-1 Rule Base Editor.

FireWall-1 Rule Base Editor: /etc/fw/conf/intro.W

File ▽) (Rule ▽) (Filter ▽) (Router ▽) (Utilities ▽) (Properties...)　　(Help ▽)

Windows: ☑ Network Objects ☑ Services ☑ System View 　 Log Viewer

No.	Source	Destination	Services	Action	Track	Install on
1	Any	Mailservers	SMTP	Accept		Gateways
2	Localnet	Any	Any	Accept	Short	Gateways
3	Any	Localnet	Any	Drop	Alert	Gateways

3 rules read 　　　　　　　　　　　　 Copyright©1993 Checkpoint Technologies, Ltd.

These rules are a high-level definition that consists of four parts: match, action, track, target. These parts are explained as follows:

✣ **MATCH.** Specifies the communication attempt in the rule. It includes the source and destination of the services involved in the communication.

✣ **ACTION.** Specifies how the communication attempt should be handled. Communication attempts can be accepted or rejected, and a negative-acknowledgment generated or simply dropped.

317

❖ **TRACK.** Specifies the type of auditing or alerting that should be performed, including the following:

No logging

Short format record

Long format record

Send e-mail message

Generate a SNMP trap

Activate a user defined procedure

Generate Alert message, such as a pop-up window on the system manager's workstation.

❖ **TARGET.** Used to specify which packet filter module on the network should implement the filter rule. This mechanism can be used to implement enterprise-wide security rules. Rules can be enforced on all gateways, destination servers and gateways, and on source gateways and hosts.

Every communication attempt is matched against the Rules-Base. Rules are matched in the order they are specified, enabling predictable behavior of the packet filtering system. If no rules are matched, the packet is rejected, thus implementing the *That which is not expressly permitted is prohibited* security policy.

Rules are verified for correctness. This verification mechanism includes:

❖ Heuristic tests

❖ Definition inconsistencies

❖ Redundancy and order checking

The complete Rules-Base is used to generate a filter script. The *filter script* describes the objects and rules using the CheckPoint's filter definition language. These scripts can be used to implement sophisticated security policies.

You can view the filter scripts that are generated. Figure 8.11 shows an example of viewing a filter script generated from a Rules-Base.

FIGURE 8.11

The FireWall-1 Filter View.

```
                              Filter View

  ( File  ∇ ) ( Update View )

  // Filter Generated by marius@monk at 4Jan94 19:51:28 Rule-base intro
  // Prologue Begin

  // Define Log Preferences
  //
  #define LOG_TIMEOUT 62
  #define UDP_TIMEOUT 40
  #define LOG_MAILCMD     "![MaiL] -s 'FireWall -1 Alert' root"
  #define LOG_ALERTCMD   "![Alert] alert"

  #include  "fwui_head.def

  // Default Filtering Code
  //
  eitherbound lo0@all { accept ;}
  ftpdata_code;
  accept_tcp_established;
  accept_rip;
  accept_icmp;
  rpc_code;
  udp_code;
  accept_domain_udp;
  accept_domain_tcp;
  // Prologue End

  // Filter Code Start

  ADDR_host(mailserver, 50.7.0.2)
  ADDR_net(localnet,  192.114.50.0,  255.255.255.0)

  intro.pf                          Copyright©1993 Checkpoint Technologies, Ltd.
```

ROUTER ACCESS LIST

The packet filter rules that are defined for routers are sometimes called router access lists by router vendors. The FireWall-1 supports both Cisco and Welfleet router access lists.

If Cisco routers with release level 9.1 (or higher) and Welfleet routers with release 8.0 (or higher) are used, they can be programmed with access lists that are generated from the Rules-Base. The rules for the routers are implemented using the router object definitions. The rules are verified and sent to the Access List Distributor module, which distributes it to the different routers.

Figure 8.12 shows an access list created from the filter script for a Cisco router. You might recognize these commands from the discussion of the access list commands for Cisco router in Chapter 5, "Packet Filters."

FIGURE 8.12

*The FireWall-1
access list for
Cisco routers.*

Most routers do not implement many of the capabilities required for secure packet filtering because they look at TCP/UDP/IP headers only. A protocol such as UDP is stateless, and the routers do not keep track of the context of previous packets.

STATUS MONITOR

The Status Monitor is a software component of FireWall-1 that is used to monitor the status of the FireWall-1 filter module. A system status window can be activated to display a snapshot of all the FireWall-1 filter modules at any time interval (see fig. 8.13). The status includes packet statistics such as the number of packets dropped, passed, logged, and so forth. The status of the filter modules is displayed as well.

The packet filtering modules support an SNMP agent that can be used for exporting information to other SNMP managers.

FIGURE 8.13

The FireWall-1 system status.

LOG VIEWER

The *Log Viewer* can display the events that have been logged, such as communication attempts, system shutdowns, firewall installations, and so on (see fig. 8.14). The event information includes date and time of event, originating machine, source and destination of communication, services attempted, action taken, and log alert types.

FIGURE 8.14

The FireWall-1 Log Viewer.

The Log Viewer can hide or display any of the information that has been logged (see fig. 8.15). A search facility enables you to locate rapidly any event of interest to you (see fig. 8.16). Reports are generated by applying selected criteria to the log fields. Reports can be viewed and exported to ASCII or PostScript. You can monitor communication activities and alerts in real-time. Nodes that appear in the log and that have SNMP agents can be probed from within the Log Viewer for SNMP information.

FIGURE 8.15

The FireWall-1 Log Viewer Selection Manager.

FIGURE 8.16

The FireWall-1 Search Log Entry.

EXAMPLES OF FIREWALL-1 APPLICATIONS

This section explains how FireWall-1 can be used to handle Internet Protocols and applications by performing secure packet filtering.

UDP APPLICATIONS

The problem of filtering UDP applications was discussed in detail in Chapter 5. Briefly, the problem with UDP, as it relates to packet filtering, is that it is a connection-less protocol. Unlike connections-oriented protocols such as TCP, there is no inherent distinction between the originator and request of the response. Because of this UDP source, port numbers can be easily "spoofed." UDP-based applications such as TFTP, DNS, and WAIS are difficult to filter in a secure manner. Some packet filtering solutions avoid this problem by not doing anything about it, thereby exposing the internal hosts to attacks through UDP ports, or by completely eliminating access to UDP ports.

FireWall-1 packet filtering solves the UDP packet filtering problem by maintaining context information on top of the UDP connection. You might think of this additional context information as representing an internal virtual-circuit in the firewall on top of the UDP connection. Every UDP request packet that is permitted to cross the firewall is recorded. Each incoming UDP packet is checked against a list of pending connections. Only when the packet is a response to a pending request is it delivered. Forged UDP packets pretend to be a response to a previous request. Because no such request is pending, the forged UDP packet is rejected.

OUTBOUND FTP CONNECTIONS

Although the FTP is a common application on the Internet, it still provides a level of complexity that can be difficult to handle. Briefly, the problem is that after the FTP client initiates a connection, the FTP server establishes a new back-connection (also called *call-back connection*) to the FTP client. The connection request originates from the FTP server, which may be outside the firewall boundary, to a dynamically allocated port on the FTP client. The dynamically allocated port is not known in advance. Many FTP clients specify new port numbers for each data transfer connection. Some older FTP clients open up the entire range of high-numbered ports, greater than 1,023, to back-connection requests. Unless a protection mechanism is implemented, the high-numbered ports are exposed to intruders.

> The call-back connection initiated by the FTP server exposes the entire range of high-numbered ports greater that 1,023 to "spoofed" back-connection requests.

323

FireWall-1 handles FTP data connections by examining application level data. When the client generates a request for a back-connection (through the FTP PORT command), the firewall records this request. When the back-connection is attempted, it is checked against the pending FTP PORT command. Only the back-connection that specifies the port number in the pending FTP port command is allowed. All other attempts to connect from the FTP_DATA port number 20 are rejected. The list of pending connections is maintained dynamically, so only the required FTP ports are opened during an FTP session.

RPC-BASED PROBLEMS

RPC-based services, such as NFS, use dynamic port number assignments. The client program contacts, with the name of a service, the portmapper program that listens on UDP port 111. Other services register with the portmapper so that the portmapper has a record of all the services registered with it. The portmapper, on being contacted for an RPC-based service by a client, maps the service name to the registered port number and sends this information back to the client. Because of dynamic port assignments, you do not know which port numbers are in use, making it difficult to protect the port numbers.

FireWall-1 keeps track of RPC port numbers, and extracts application specific information from the packet. This information is used to identify the program and source using the service. It also keeps track of the UDP packets and builds context information for these circuits. By using a combination of these approaches, FireWall-1 protects the RPC-based services from attack.

MOSAIC, WWW, AND GOPHER

Clients, such as Gopher clients and Mosaic front-ends to the World Wide Web (WWW), pose a new set of problems for securing networks. Mosaic front-ends, in particular, can access a number of application services, such as HTTP, FTP, WAIS, Archie, and Gopher, through a unified front-end. These expose the network to the security risks of the underlying protocols, such as UDP, TCP, and FTP.

Because FireWall-1 can handle the underlying protocols, such as TCP, UDP, and FTP, it can be used for securing the network when used with Mosaic.

PERFORMANCE OF FIREWALL-1

Because FireWall-1 employs several optimization techniques, the performance degradation for most applications is negligible. These optimization techniques include the following:

❖ Running inside the operating system kernel reduces processing overhead and avoids context switching overheads.

❖ Packet filter optimization reduces the time spent performing filtering actions.

❖ Memory management techniques such as caching and hashing provide rapid access to network resource objects. These techniques can unify multiple instances of objects, which allows for more efficient sharing of memory.

The Internet Security Corporation reports that tests done on low-end Sparcstations showed negligible degradation over Ethernet at 10 Mbps. Performance degradation on lower speed links will be even less because WAN links operating at 56 Kbps or 1.544 Mbps (T1) are slower, and the bottleneck is the speed of the WAN link and not the packet filtering overhead.

FIREWALL-1 RULES LANGUAGE

You can use a text editor to write filter rules directly, using theFireWall-1 rules language. You might want to do this to have greater control over the packet filtering specifications. The following examples are presented to give you an overview of the FireWall-1 rules language.

The file std.def must be included in each rules set. This file contains definitions for standard macros, aliases, log formats and TCP packet structure.

EXAMPLE 1

The following rule checks inbound packets at all interfaces on ucs.xyz.com and allows any host to send smtp mail to ucs.xyz.com.

```
#include "std.def"
inbound all@ucs.xyz.com accept dst in ucs.xyz.com, smtp;
```

EXAMPLE 2

The following rule checks inbound packets at all interfaces on ucs.xyz.com and allows all hosts on the local net to do ftp or telnet sessions to ucs.xyz.com.

```
#include "std.def"
inbound all@ucs.xyz.com accept src in local_net, dst in ucs.xyz.com, (ftp or
telnet);
```

EXAMPLE 3

The following rule allows all hosts to access any other local host for services that are defined in the list locally_allowed. The list locally_allowed is user defined.

```
#include "std.def"
eitherbound all@all accept src in local_net, dst in local_net, service in
locally_allowed;
```

325

EXAMPLE 4

The following rule checks packets coming in through the sl0 serial interface of gateway GW1 and enables clients in TRUST.COM to send smtp mail to the local network.

```
#include "std.def"
inbound sl0@GW1 accept src in .trust.com, dst in local_net, smtp;
```

EXAMPLE 5

This rule checks outgoing packets on serial interface sl0 of the gateway GW1 and allows the local network to access services on hosts in the university BERKELEY.EDU.

```
#include "std.def"
outbound sl0@GW1 accept src in local_net, dst in .berkeley.edu;
```

EXAMPLE 6

The following rule checks incoming and outgoing packets on serial interface sl0 of the gateway GW1 and rejects all packets coming from .hacker.org to the local network. All such attempts that match the rule are logged and reported immediately to the systems manager.

```
#include "std.def"
eitherbound sl0@GW1 reject log <"! alert"> short src in .hacker.org and dst
in local_net
```

EXAMPLE 7

The first rule that follows logs the first packet of every attempt to establish a telnet connection through serial interface sl0 of gateway GW1, whether it succeeds or not. Clients must be in the user-defined list trusted_hosts to make the connection.

The second rule allows packets to travel in either direction once a TCP connection is established.

```
#include "std.def"
inbound sl0@GW1 accept src in trusted_hosts,  dst in local_net, telnet,
first. log short;
eitherbound sl0@GW1 accept tcp, established;
```

EXAMPLE 8

This rule checks incoming packets on serial interface sl0 of the gateway GW1 and blocks all packets coming from .hack.org to the hosts defined in the list protect_list. All such attempts that match the rule are logged and reported immediately to the systems manager though e-mail.

```
#include "std.def"
inbound sl0@GW1 drop src in .hack.org dst in protect_list log <"!mail -s FW-1
alert root"> short;
```

OBTAINING INFORMATION ON FIREWALL-1

Additional information on FireWall-1 can be obtained from the following:

> Internet Security Corporation
> Phone: (617)863-6400
> Fax: (617)863-6464
> Email: info@security.com

or

> CheckPoint Software Technologies
> Phone: (617)859-9051
> Fax: (617)863-0524

ANS INTERLOCK

The FireWall-1 is a commercial gateway product, available from Advanced Network Services (ANS). The product currently runs on IBM AIX 3.2 (or higher) workstations or SparcStations (Solaris 2.3 or higher).

The ANS InterLock provides an application-level firewall gateway between an organization's internal network and an untrusted external network. The ANS InterLock can also be used to control access between segments of an internal TCP/IP network. This situation is shown in figure 8.17 where the InterLock service is deployed at the boundaries of the internal network. In this figure, the InterLock services running on host A is used to secure access to the Internet. The InterLock service running on host B limits access from a supplier (vendor) network. The InterLock service running on host C limits access from users of the Accounting department network, and the InterLock service running on host D limits access from users of the R&D department network.

The ANS InterLock gateway provides the following capabilities:

❖ Access control mechanisms

❖ Auditing and logging information

❖ Information hiding

❖ Mail Gateway services

327

FIGURE 8.17

*Multiple ANS
InterLock
connections.*

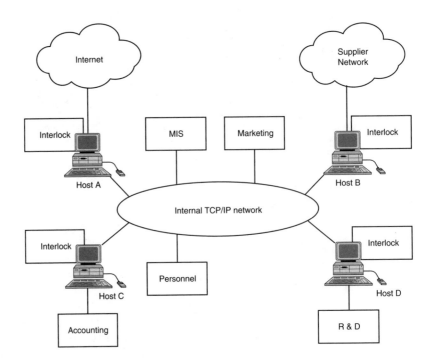

The Access control mechanism provides the ability to control access between any two networks based on a flexible criteria. Access control can be specified in terms of type of service, source, destination, and time of day the services are allowed. For example, one can specify that FTP access from external sites will be allowed from 9 a.m. to 5 p.m., Monday through Friday. You can also impose a requirement that users must authenticate themselves using a SecurID card (made by Security Dynamics Technologies, Inc.). This type of authentication can be used instead of the Unix user login, or to augment the Unix login.

The InterLock can be used to generate detailed logs and reports on authorized and unauthorized network connections. The logs accumulate usage statistics on a per user, per IP address, or per service basis. The data includes information on the duration of connection, bytes transferred, file names and sizes of files. Run-time data reduction tools are used to specify the level of detail and the amount of information logged for each service. Post run-time reporting tools can be used to generate usage statistics.

The InterLock does not reveal information about the internal network to the external network. The InterLock runs on a host with routing functions and IP forwarding disabled. As a result of this, information, such as host names, IP addresses, and network structure, is hidden from the external network. Although not recommended, it is possible to use non-NIC-assigned IP addresses to the internal network, because these addresses are hidden from the outside world.

RESOURCE REQUIREMENTS FOR INTERLOCK

Before investing resources in evaluating a product to see if it is suitable for your network environment, it is helpful to know details such as the hardware and software and training resources needed to implement the product. This information is provided for your reference.

The ANS InterLock runs on a dedicated platform based on R6000 IBM workstations or SUN SparcStations. The R6000 workstations run a modified version of the AIX operating system, and the SUN Sparcstations run a modified version Solaris. The modified workstations are pre-configured and can be purchased as a leased "turn-key." Alternatively, a leased software version (running on customer-provided hardware) and a software-only version can be purchased with an annual support contract.

The operating system modifications are done to prevent security holes that can exist because of improper configuration. Instead of turning off operating systems options that can be hazardous to security, ANS has completely removed these capabilities from the operating system to eliminate the possibility of an intruder gaining access to the system and enabling features that would bypass the firewall security.

The following operating system capabilities are removed from the operating system:

❖ No IP forwarding

❖ ICMP redirects are rejected

❖ No strict or loose source routing

With IP forwarding disabled, all connection requests are handled by application proxy daemons.

ICMP redirects can be used to create false entries in router tables, which can lead to denial of service or to network traffic being diverted to an unsecured host.

Source routing is removed to prevent packets from bypassing the firewall. On many systems, source routed packets are forwarded even if IP forwarding is disabled. By removing source routing and IP forwarding, packets can never be routed through the network layer.

OVERVIEW OF INTERLOCK

Typical tasks that need to be performed to set up the InterLock firewall are the following:

❖ Adding, deleting, and modifying user and groups

❖ Defining a security policy in the Access Control Rule Base

❖ Monitoring logs and generating reporting statistics

❖ Customizing prompts and system messages

❖ Executing the system backup scripts

❖ Editing mail mapping databases

❖ Establishing and managing password controls

All of the previously listed tasks can be performed by a single administrator or by a number of administrators. To ease system administration tasks, InterLock offers a flexible way of assigning different privileges to administrator accounts. A user account on the InterLock gateway can be assigned a combination of the following privileges:

❖ **MAIL.** Allows configuration and control over the mail system.

❖ **SECURITY.** Maintenance of security policies implemented by the Rules-Base.

❖ **ADMIN.** Creation and maintenance of user accounts.

❖ **AUDIT.** Monitoring and data reduction of log information.

❖ **SYSTEM.** Miscellaneous privileged operations.

Separation of the security privileges enables the organization to assign specific individuals to the different security functions. A specific privilege is assigned by making a user account a member of a group. This provides the organization with a flexible and familiar way of assigning privileges.

The access controls that govern the behavior of each application gateway are implemented in the *Access Control Rule Base* (ACRB). Rules to the ACRB can be specified using a menu-driven interface or a command interface. The organization's security policy is expressed as a set of rules. Explicit rules need to be provided to enable a service. Rules can be established for individual users, groups of users, or to an entire community of users using a wildcard entry.

> Because users have similar security needs, it is easier to define groups and establish rules for the groups. The individual users, then, inherit the rules because of membership in groups.

InterLock requires that all connections should be handled by application proxy daemons running on the InterLock gateway machine. Each application-layer daemon is responsible for reading its system configuration information and rules from the ACRB. If a proxy daemon is not provided, that service will be denied. InterLock provides proxy daemons for the following services:

❖ TELNET

❖ Login service

❖ FTP

❖ SMTP

❖ X Windows systems

❖ NNTP

❖ InterLock encryption service

❖ InterLock Generic Protocol Daemon (GPD)

❖ Network Time Protocol

CONFIGURING INTERLOCK

Before the InterLock gateway can be used, it must be configured with some site-specific information, which is defined in the file with the following path name:

/interlock/config/ILconfig

A sample ILconfig file follows:

```
#
# Interface names
#
    Public_Interface            en0
#   Private_Address             145.122.12.22
#   Public_Address              193.34.33.53
#Counters
#
    Max_TELNET_login failures   3
    Max_FTP_login failures      3
#
#Timers
#
    StartX_timeout_minutes              3
    X_Inactive_timeout_minutes          10
    Telnet_Inactivity_Timeout_minutes   20
    Telnet_Inactivity_Warning_minutes   5
#
#NNTP Configuration options
#
    NNTP_Public                 server.pubcorp.net
    NNTP_Private                news.xyz.com
    NNTP_DomainName             disguise.com
    NNTP Post_Header_Mapping    On
    NNTP_Use_Mailmaps           Off
#
#Authentication options
#
    Authentication_List         unixpassword
```

The `Public_Interface` field is used to define which network interface is attached to the public network. The public network is the untrusted external network.

The `Private_Address` and `Public_Address` are commented out and are not configurable by the InterLock administrator.

The `Max_TELNET_Login_Failures` is the number of times a user will be allowed to attempt an unsuccessful TELNET login attempt before InterLock will close the connection.

The `Max_FTP_Login_Failures` is the number of times a user will be allowed to attempt an unsuccessful FTP login attempt before InterLock will close the connection.

There is currently no provision to lock-out an intruder for a period of time. Also, if specific TELNET and FTP connections are to be allowed or blocked, these must be specified by the Access Control Rule Base (ACRB).

The `StartX_timeout_minutes` defines the number of minutes the InterLock proxy X-daemon will listen for an X connection on the TCP port associated with the pseudo-terminal display number. If a connection does not occur in the specified time period, the InterLock X-daemon will close the connection and not accept any connections to the display number. When the value is set to zero, timeouts are disabled.

The `X_Inactive_timeout_minutes` defines the number of minutes that a X session can be inactive before the connection is closed. When the value is set to zero, timeouts are disabled.

The `Telnet_Inactivity_Timeout_minutes` is the number of minutes that a Telnet session can be inactive before the connection is closed. When the value is set to zero, timeouts are disabled.

The `Telnet_Inactivity_Warning_minutes` is the number of minutes that a Telnet session can be inactive before a warning message is issued. When the value is set to zero, warnings are not sent.

The `NNTP_Public` is used to define the host on the public (external) network that acts as a news server. If you have an internal news server that exchanges messages with the public news server, you must define this field.

The `NNTP_Private` is used to define the host on the private (internal) network that acts as a news server. This is the destination to which NNTP news originating from the external network will be directed.

The `NNTP Post_Header_Mapping` can be set to On or Off. When set to On, the NNTP proxy daemon will attempt to map the header portion of postings from internal users with the domain name specified in the `NNTP_DomainName` field. Remapping involves replacing the lines in the news header that contain references to internal hosts.

The NNTP Post_Use_Mailmaps can be set to On or Off. This field is defined only when the NNTP Post_Header_Mapping is On. When set to On, the NNTP proxy daemon will use the mail mapping database (/interlock/config/maild.mf derived dbm file) when changing the user part of the post headers. If Off, the user will query the database built from the file derived from /interlock/config/nntpd.mf.

Authentication_List is the list of available authentication types that are supported in a specific InterLock gateway. The default authentication type is Unix passwords (unixpasswd). You can use values of "securid" or "pinpad" to specify support for Security Dynamics' SecurID and Pinpad cards (optional services).

> The ILconfig file can be edited to change any of the parameter values just discussed. After editing this file, you can run the makeconfig command, which reads the entries in the configuration file and stores them in the binary database /interlock/config/config.bin.

THE INTERLOCK ACRB

The rules that govern the actions to be performed on packets, by an InterLock proxy application, are specified in the ACRB.

The first portion describes the situations in which the rule is to be enforced. Rules that do not match a particular situation (such as being outside the valid time range for which a service can be accessed) can be configured by the administrator to deny access or remain inactive.

The second part of the rule specifies what rule constraints should be enforced. You can define different levels of logging with each rule. For example, the logging levels could be low, medium, high, or debug, for each rule.

The rules can specify combinations of any of the following:

✦ **USERNAME OR GROUP.** This is the site-defined user name or group name. A wildcard (*) can represent any user. A special user name called "trust" can be used when the internal user's identity is not required from a specific host or network. This enables users on the internal network to use authenticated services TELNET and FTP without having to enter their user name and password.

✦ **PROTOCOL NAME.** This is the name of a service, such as LOGIN, TELNET, FTP, FTP-DATA SMTP, NNTP, X, or a customer-defined service. The port number can be used instead of the service name.

333

❖ **PRIVATE NETWORK OR HOST NAME.** This is the network or host on the inside (protected) network. The host's IP address or the network IP address (example: 144.19.0.0) can be used. A wildcard (*) matches all hosts on the internal network.

❖ **PRIVATE NETMASK.** This is the range of host IP addresses on the inside (protected) network. This mask value is not the subnet mask value.

❖ **PUBLIC NETWORK OR HOST NAME.** This is the network or host on the external (untrusted) network. The host's IP address or the network IP address (example: 144.19.0.0) can be used. A wildcard (*) matches all hosts on the external network.

❖ **PUBLIC NETMASK.** This is the range of host IP addresses on the external (untrusted) network. This mask value is not the subnet mask value.

❖ **START TIME.** This specifies the time when the rule will take effect, in a 24-hour format.

❖ **STOP TIME.** This specifies the time when the rule stops being in effect, in a 24-hour format. Existing connections are not shut down at the stop time; however, new connections are not allowed.

❖ **DAY-OF-THE-WEEK.** This specifies the day or range of days that the rule is in effect.

❖ **DIRECTION.** This defines in which directions the connections are allowed to flow.

❖ **ENCRYPTION.** This is defined only if encryption is provided as part of the package.

❖ **AUTHENTICATION TYPE.** This specifies the type of authentication mechanisms that are used. Valid authentication types are described in the ILconfig file described in the previous section.

The Username or group field and the Protocol name field cannot both be wildcards (*) in the same rule. The security policy of *That which is not expressly permitted is prohibited* is used. Therefore, at a minimum, there will be *N* rules if *N* applications are to be supported across the InterLock gateway.

To define the rules, a program called *rulebase* (located in the /interlock/security directory) is run. The user interface is simple to use, as shown in the following list. The subsequent list shows the choices (in bold) for adding a new rule. This rule defines that user ksiyan is allowed to telnet from any host on the private network to the host maclean.spy.com on the public (external) network. It also allows ksiyan to telnet from host MACLEAN.SPY.COM to any host on the private network. The user ksiyan is required to use the Unix password authentication. Telnet access is allowed only from 9 a.m. to 5 p.m., from Monday through Friday. Telnet access for this user is denied at all other times.

The following is the InterLock ACRB for Version 1.2:

```
<A>dd a new rule
<D>elete an existing rule
<M>odify an existing rule
<T>oggle remote login access for root
<S>how which rules apply
<C>heck user permissions
<W>rite text verson of rules base to a file
<Q>uit
```

This list shows the Add New Access Control Rule settings:

```
Group or username: ksiyan
Protcol name: telnet

Private network or host name: *

Public network or host name: maclean.spy.com
Is MACLEAN.SPY.COM a host name (y,n)? y

What direction is access permitted?
From MACLEAN.SPY.COM to ANY private host [y,n] ? y
From ANY private host to MACLEAN.SPY.COM [y,n] ? y

What type of user authentication is required on this connection?
Authentication type (unixpasswd,securid,pinpad,*): u

What type of encryption is required on this connection?
Encryption type (software,hardware,*,both,none): n

Should this rule be enforced all of the time (y,n) ? n
Days of week (su,m,tu,w,th,f,sa,*) [*]: m-f
Starting at time (00:00 - 23:59): 0900
Ending at time (00:00 - 23:59): 1700
Should KSIYANs TELNET access be DENIED all other times (y,n) ? y
```

INTERLOCK PROXY APPLICATION GATEWAY SERVICES

This section discusses some of the application gateway proxy services provided by the InterLock gateway. Examples are shown using the command line interface to these services.

INTERLOCK TELNET PROXY SERVICES

Figure 8.18 shows a typical deployment of the InterLock gateway. Users on either side of the InterLock gateway must first connect to the InterLock gateway and authenticate themselves.

FIGURE 8.18

FIGURE 8.18

Typical InterLock gateway deployment.

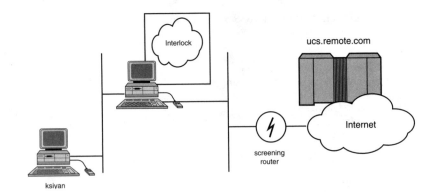

The InterLock gateway runs a telnet daemon that listens to well-known ports associated with these services. If desired, the organization can change the port associated with these services.

In this example, assume that the user ksiyan wants to establish a Telnet session from an internal host to a remote host on the Internet. The Telnet session must go through the InterLock gateway. The user must first initiate a telnet session to the InterLock gateway. The Telnet daemon on the InterLock receives this request and queries its ACRB to see if a Telnet session is allowed at the current time and day of week. If a connection is allowed, the user is prompted for a user name and password. If the InterLock service was configured with a SecurID option, prompts similar to that follow appear:

```
telnet interlock.kinetics.com
Trying...
Connected to interlock.kinetics.com
Escape character is ^[
InterLock login: ksiyan
ksiyans PIN: PIN entered is not displayed
ksiyans CARDCODE: cardcode entered is not displayed
```

After a successful login, you can see the InterLock gateway message. You must enter the remote destination to connect to.

```
InterLock Telnet Gateway N.0 (interlock.kinetics.com)
Destination: ucs.remote.com
```

The ACRB is queried again to determine if Telnet access to the specified destination is permitted. If access is allowed, connection is established by the proxy Telnet daemon to the remote host, and the user sees the login prompt for the remote host. If the ACRB checks fail (rules do not match), Telnet access is denied.

INTERLOCK FTP PROXY SERVICES

FTP works in a manner similar to Telnet. First an FTP connection to the InterLock gateway is established. The ACRB is consulted to see if a connection is allowed. The InterLock FTP server prompts the user for login name and authentication information. The user then issues the USER command to specify the user and host name for the desired destination. The InterLock FTP consults the ACRB to see if a connection is allowed.

If a connection is allowed, an FTP connection is established by InterLock FTP to the remote. The user is prompted for a password on the destination host. The following list shows a sample FTP session.

```
% ftp interlock.kinetics.com
Connected to interlock.kinetics.com
220 interlock.kinetics.com InterLock FTP Gateway N.0 ready at Wed Nov 16
12:34:33 1994
Name (interlock.kinetics.com:ksiyan): ksiyan
331 Password required for ksiyan
Password: password is not displayed
230- You are authorized as InterLock user ksiyan. Specify your remote user
230  and destination with the USER command (for example: USER
remoteuser@remotehost)
ftp> user anonymous@ucs.remote.com
331- ucs.remote.com  FTP server (Version 5.60) ready
331  Guest login ok, send ident as password
Password: password is not displayed
```

INTERLOCK SMTP GATEWAY SERVICES

The InterLock can act as a store-and-forward SMTP gateway. There is no password authentication of a user's SMTP session. The InterLock mailer, by default, consults a mapping database to determine where to deliver incoming mail from public hosts. This database also determines if the address in the FROM: line in the message header is allowed to send mail. An example mapping entry from this database follows:

```
ksiyan: karanjit@rama.kinetics.com, karan@shiv.kinetics.com
```

The entry before the colon defines the mailbox known to the outside network for this user. This is the user's external e-mail address. Mail to this user can be sent from the outside world to the address ksiyan@kinetics.com. The entries after the colon are valid sending internal e-mail addresses for the user. Mail sent to user ksiyan@kinetics.com is mapped to karanjit@rama.kinetics.com. Mail which arrives from karanjit@rama.kinetics.com or karan@shiv.kinetics.com is mapped as if it originated from the user ksiyan@kinetics.com. Therefore, the internal e-mail addresses are not known to the outside world. This is important for security reasons because internal e-mail addresses indicate the names of the hosts on the network.

An attempt made to send e-mail to the user at karanjit@rama.kinetics.com or karan@shiv.kinetics.com will fail because there is no such entry in the SMTP mapping database. A side benefit of this approach is that the remapping provides a common e-mail naming convention for the entire organization.

Rules can be specified to allow or block SMTP traffic between hosts or networks. Mail can also be configured to pass through the InterLock without requiring mapping. But in this case, replies will reveal the internal host names on the outbound headers.

INTERLOCK X SERVICES

The InterLock X daemon acts as a combination of a pseudo-X server and X-client. Suppose that an internal user wants to run an X-application that resides on a remote host (ucs.remote.com) on a local workstation (ws.kinetics.com). This situation is shown in figure 8.19. The user must telnet to the InterLock system where the user will receive the standard destination prompt after authentication. The user then runs the startX command and specifies the display number:

```
!startX ucs.kinetics.com:0
```

The exclamation mark (!) before the startX command tells the telnet daemon to run the command instead of specifying a destination host.

FIGURE 8.19

InterLock X services.

The following shows a typical X-session:

```
Destination [interlock.kinetics.com]: !startX ws.kinetics.com:0
interlock.kinetics.com will now accept X connections for screen 108.
```

```
Telnet to the machine which has your X client and use this host
and screen number in the display argument of your X client. e.g.:

      xterm -display interlock.kinetics.com:108

The server will shutdown if not used within the next 3 minutes.

The server will shutdown after 20 minutes of inactivity.
```

The user must then Telnet to the remote host on which the X client application resides by specifying the host name at the destination prompt. The user must then execute the xterm command at the remote host within the next three minutes, as follows:

```
Destination [interlock.kinetics.com]: ucs.remote.com
ucs% xterm -display interlock.kinetics.com:108
```

The InterLock X daemon then reads the X-packets from the host ucs.remote.com on port 6108 (X uses 6000 + *pseudo_screen_ number*), and display the graphics on ws.kinetics.com:0. The user must also give the InterLock gateway access permissions to his X-server, using the following command:

```
xhost +interlock.kinetics.com
```

Before establishing the X-sessions, the InterLock gateway checks its ACRB to see if the user has appropriate permissions for using Telnet and X-sessions to the remote host.

For security reasons, the InterLock gateway monitors the telnet session for inactivity. If there is no activity for 20 minutes, the session and the X-server shuts down. The time-out is configured in the ILconfig file discussed earlier.

INTERLOCK NNTP (NETWORK NEWS TRANSFER PROTOCOL) SERVICES

Under normal circumstances, when there is no InterLock firewall connecting to the external network, the news readers in the local network point to the local news servers, as shown in figure 8.20. On Unix systems, this is done by setting the NNTPSERVER environment variable to the news server host. A typical setting to run the news reader might be the following:

```
% setenv NNTPSERVER 194.23.34.5    # set the news environment variable
% xrn                              # Run the newsreader
```

With the InterLock gateway positioned between the internal hosts and the Internet, the news server must be contacted through the firewall (see fig. 8.21). The InterLock firewall does not allow direct news traffic between the internal and external networks. The internal users must, therefore, specify the InterLock gateway as their news server:

```
% setenv NNTPSERVER interlock.kinetics.com    # set the news environment
variable to point to firewall
% xrn                                          # Run the newsreader
```

FIGURE 8.20

*New Reader
configuration with
no InterLock
firewalls.*

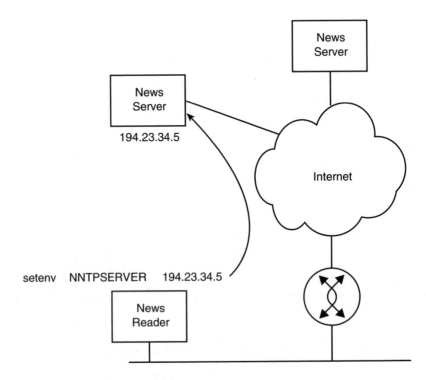

The InterLock gateway has a local application (/interlock/bin/nntpd) that listens for NNTP connection requests. When it gets a request, *nntpd* performs the following actions:

❖ It determines if the connection originated from the internal or external network.

❖ Checks the ACRB to see if the connection request is authorized. Unauthorized connection requests are logged in the file nntpd.log.

❖ If connection is authorized, nntpd opens a second connection request to the appropriate NNTP server. If the connection originated from the external network, and if an internal news server is defined, it will establish a connection to the internal news server defined by the field NNTP_Private in the ILconfig file. Similarly, if the connection originated from the internal network, nntpd will establish a connection to the external news server defined by the field NNTP_Public in the ILconfig file.

❖ nntpd reads data from one interface and copies it to the other interface, thus, acting as a circuit-gateway. If the Post_Heading_Remapping in the ILconfig file is set to On, it performs mapping operations in the posting header fields of the news messages. As a result of these mapping operations, it appears as if the news originated from the firewall, and all references to internal host names are remapped to the firewall host name. To perform this mapping, the nntpd can use a separate database (files nntpd.mf.dir, nntpd.mf.pag) or the same database used by SMTP mail (files smtpd.mf.dir, smtpd.mf.pag).

The InterLock gateway does not require password identification for users accessing the NNTP service because the NNTP protocol currently does not support any authentication. However, the InterLock can deny or allow access to services based on the value of the From: field in the news message post header.

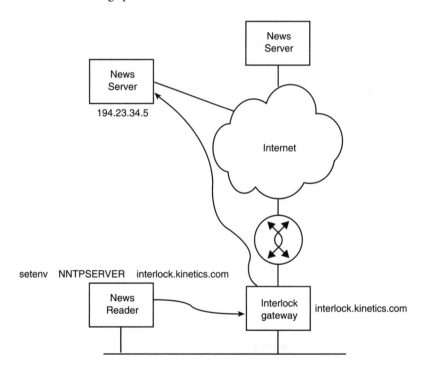

FIGURE 8.21

News Reader configuration through InterLock firewalls.

INTERLOCK HTTP (HYPER TEXT TRANSPORT PROTOCOL) SERVICES

The InterLock gateway can act as a HTTP forwarder by providing WWW proxy agents on the gateway. The InterLock forwarder can also work with WWW clients that support the

CERN proxy model (such as NCSA's Mosaic and University of Kansas' Lynx). By setting the http_proxy environment variable in the WWW clients, HTTP requests are directed to the InterLock gateway for resolution.

INTERLOCK GOPHER SERVICES

To access gopher services through the InterLock firewall, users must point their gopher clients to the InterLock gateway. The InterLock gateway can act as a data-less gopher server with menu entries but no associated data, or point to a real gopher server. The gopher protocol involves the exchange of selector information between the gopher client and server. The InterLock gateway forwarder replaces the returned selector with a *Uniform Resource Locator* (URL) containing the type, selector, and port associated with the real gopher server. The host field containing internal host names are replaced with the appropriate InterLock name. These translations occur transparently.

The user needs to know how to convert the URL advertised by external gopher servers to an appropriate InterLock format; otherwise, the InterLock gateway rejects the user's requests. Most gopher clients have mechanisms to specify information on the gopher servers to connect to. The gopher protocol sends information in four fields separated by the tab character and ending in a carriage-return/line-feed combination character (see RFC 1436). An example of the entries in these four fields that are needed to contact a remote gopher server is shown as follows:

```
Type = 0            # Gopher item is a file
Name = Remote Corp Gopher
Path = 0/gopher/recipes
Host = gopher.remote.com
Port = 70
```

Because the InterLock gateway hides knowledge of public hosts from the internal network, the gopher clients cannot directly connect to the host gopher.remote.com. This host name must be replaced by the InterLock gateway (interlock.kinetics.com in this example). The gopher client must access the external gopher using the following information:

```
Type = 0            # Gopher item is a file
Name = Remote Corp Gopher
Path = gopher://gopher.remote.com:70/0/gopher/recipes
Host = interlock.kinetics.com
Port = 70
```

For sites using the data-less model, a gopher root menu is constructed on the InterLock gateway for user connection from the internal network. A different root menu can be created for users attempting connections from the external network.

INTERLOCK GENERIC PROTOCOL DAEMON SERVICES

The *Generic Protocol Daemon* (GPD) implements a TCP and UDP forwarder and is meant for those applications that are not directly supported as InterLock application gateways. The TCP and UDP forwarders query the ACRB to determine if connection requests should be granted. Because no authentication is required, no user-level access controls, such as time-of-day, day-of-week, encryption required, and so on, can be specified.

To illustrate how the GPD works, consider the following example. The security policy requires that that organization's clients on the external networks access a special application on an internal host at TCP port 81. The TCP forwarder can specify a rule that consists of the IP address of the server, and the TCP port. Users on the external network can be informed to connect to port 81 on the InterLock gateway. When a request is received for port 81, the InterLock gateway queries the ACRB and checks if this connection is allowed. If the connection is authorized, it establishes a second connection from the InterLock gateway to port 81 on the internal host.

The GPD can be used to support services such as lpr, archie, nslookup, whois, traceroute, and dig.

ADDITIONAL SOURCE OF INFORMATION ON ANS INTERLOCK

For additional information on the ANS InterLock product and related services contact:

> Advanced Network & Services, Inc.
> 1875 Campus Commons Drive
> Suite 220
> Reston, VA 22091
> Phone: (703)758-7700
> Fax: (703)758-7717
> E-Mail: info@ans.com

TRUSTED INFORMATION SYSTEMS GAUNTLET

Gauntlet is a firewall product from Trusted Information Systems, Inc. (TIS). The product can run on the Intel-made *Classic-R* system. The base system consists of a board VGA adapter connected to a WYSE monochrome VGA monitor, two serial ports, and one parallel port.

An Adaptec SCSI controller is used to connect to a 440-MB SCSI drive. Additional SCSI devices can be added through the standard Centronics "D" connector on the Adaptec SCSI card. The CPU is an Intel 486 with a 66-MHz clock, 256 KB of cache memory, and 16 MB of main memory. The system board comes with a *zero insertion force* (ZIF) socket that can be used to upgrade to the Pentium processor.

The base operating system used for the Gauntlet product is BSD Unix from Berkeley Software Design, Inc (BSDI). The Gauntlet product comes pre-installed with BSD Unix. This pre-installed version is a subset of the binaries and utilities that normally come with BSD Unix from BSDI.

In the Gauntlet system, the kernel of BSD Unix has been modified to identify and log certain network-based threats. End users can reconfigure and rebuild the kernel, but care should be exercised to ensure that the custom networking utilities are linked into the kernel.

The Gauntlet system includes a single embedded license from BSDI. This is a special low-cost license restricted for using BSDI's BSD Unix for firewall processing. The license does not extend to general use of the system. The pre-installed BSD Unix system has, in itself, the capability to be used as a general-purpose computing platform, but this type of use is in violation of the licensing policy.

The Gauntlet system provides firewall-based proxy services for the following:

- ❖ TELNET
- ❖ rlogin
- ❖ FTP
- ❖ SMTP
- ❖ NNTP
- ❖ Gopher+
- ❖ HTTP
- ❖ X-Windows

For each service, there is a separate secure forwarding server that performs protocol-specific access control and auditing.

Configuration for the different application-level services is done through a screen-based systems interface. Operational tools include those for installing binary upgrades, checking digital signatures of system files against a database of cryptographic checksum (to detect alteration in these files), tools for audit log reduction and reporting, system alerts, and trouble monitoring.

Gauntlet's base policy is that all systems, other than Gauntlet itself, are initially untrusted. Configuration, therefore, involves explicitly adding trusted systems. In its initial default configuration mode, Gauntlet does not permit any data traffic through the firewall.

CONFIGURATION EXAMPLES USING GAUNTLET

The Gauntlet system has two Ethernet interfaces. Typically, these are Intel Express boards with both Thin Wire and 10BASE-T connectors. Figure 8.22 shows a typical use of the Gauntlet firewall. The Gauntlet network interfaces are labeled as ex0 and ex1. The *ex0* interface is connected to the outside network, and the *ex1* interface is connected to the inside network. The Gauntlet acts as a firewall between the inside and outside networks.

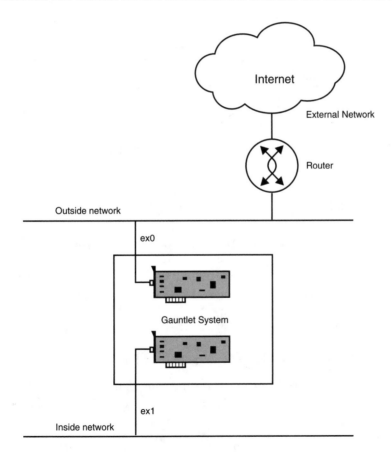

FIGURE 8.22

Typical Gauntlet firewall use.

Another possible use of the Gauntlet system is illustrated in figure 8.23. In this configuration, the Gauntlet system connects to the outside network through its network interface ex0 only. The network interface ex1 is not connected. A screening router is used to connect the outside network with the external network (Internet in this case), and another screening router is used to connect the outside and internal networks. The security of the network depends on a combined use of the screening routers and the Gauntlet system. If the screening routers are not set up correctly, the Gauntlet system could be completely bypassed.

FIGURE 8.23

The Gauntlet system using single network interface.

When setting up the routing tables for the screening routers, and the default route for the Gauntlet system, it is best to specify static routing to avoid accidental changes, and foil intruder attempts to change the routing tables. If your network policy requires that dynamic routes be used, the system can use the routed or gated daemons for providing dynamic routing.

CONFIGURING GAUNTLET

Configuration of the Gauntlet system can be done either through the menu interface or a command-line interface. A primary step is to configure the connected Ethernet interfaces with appropriate values for IP address, subnet mask, and broadcast address.

If the inside network interface, ex1, is not to be connected (see fig. 8.23), it should not be configured. Additionally, you can specify the default route, which typically is the router used to connect to the Internet. A default DNS server can be specified initially to simplify testing while the system is being installed.

The following shows Gauntlet's main management menu. This list shows the type of administration options that are available through the menu interface. These options are performed using shell scripts that invoke the Gauntlet-specific utilities and commands.

```
             Gauntlet(tm) Main Management Menu
             --------------------------------


Select option: System Backups
               System Integrity Checks
               Install Software Upgrade
               System Event/Reporting Configuration
               Trusted Network Configuration
               System Access Configuration
               User Authentication Management
               IP Address Configuration
               DNS Configuration
               Electronic Mail Configuration
               NNTP Forwarder Configuration

                   Exit Configuration Menus
                          Help
                   Menuing System Help

             To navigate, use arrow keys and Tab
           To select a highlighted item, press Enter
```

The different Gauntlet options in the previous list are briefly explained so you can form an idea of the typical administration tasks needed to configure Gauntlet.

The *System Backup* option is used to configure and perform backups of the Gauntlet system. System backups are performed by using a SCSI tape drive. The BSD Unix *dump* utility is used for backups. The dump levels that are used are levels 0, 5, and 9. Level 0 represents the full-system backup. Level 5 represents backups of all data modified since dump level 5 or lower. Level 9 represents backups of all data modified since dump level 9 or lower. If a backup device is not available for the Gauntlet system, the backup can be performed on a network tape server. The configuration for this is also completed with this option.

The *System Integrity Checks* option is used to detect files that have been modified, deleted, or replaced. It can be used to alert the system administrator if accidental or deliberate changes (to lower the security, perhaps) have been done to the Gauntlet system. After making legitimate changes, this option can be used to update the integrity of the database. The System Integrity Checks' database can be copied to different devices to protect them for later use. Options exist to copy the systems integrity database to and from a floppy disk. You can also check the system integrity against databases stored on a floppy disk or network server. You can check the system release levels against an online database, a floppy disk, or a network server.

347

The *Install Software Upgrade* option is used to implement software patches and upgrades. Floppy disk upgrades are issued in the tar archive that contains multiple archives and the file "upgrade.cat," which lists the upgrade on the floppy disk.

The *System Event/Reporting Configuration* option is used to specify Gauntlet's report configuration and event reporting options. Reports can be generated on a daily or weekly basis. You can specify the e-mail address to which reports should be mailed. Unless you configure otherwise, the reports are mailed to the alias named "firewalladmin," defined in the file /etc/aliases. Even the daily and weekly reports are disabled; they are stored in the files /var/log/daily.out and /var/log/weekly.out so you can access them at a later time. The daily and weekly reports are run from the standard daily and weekly processing scripts /etc/daily and /etc/weekly. An alarm reporting option can be enabled, which allows you to specify the times at which the logs will be scanned for "noteworthy" events.

N O T E

> Gauntlet uses an interesting approach to define that which is noteworthy. It does not attempt to list events that are noteworthy because this could leave out unexpected events that have not been defined. Instead, Gauntlet enables the administrator to define which events are ordinary. Noteworthy events are defined as those that are not ordinary. A file called /usr/local/etc/frequentcheck.ignore contains regular expression patterns defining ordinary events.

The *Trusted Network Configuration* enables you to define a list of trusted and untrusted networks, which are stored in /usr/local/etc/trusted-networks and /usr/local/etc/untrusted-networks. By default, the only network that Gauntlet trusts is its loopback interface (127.0.0.1)—that is, Gauntlet trusts only itself. The default untrusted network value is "*" (all other networks). The trusted and untrusted network files are used to build a copy of the firewall proxy permissions table file /usr/local/etc/netperm-table.

The *System Access Configuration* option is used to determine whether the administrator should be allowed to telnet or rlogin to the system. By default, these options are disabled, which means that the administrator must have physical access to the console.

The *User Authentication Management* is used to add, delete, or edit user configuration information. This screen can be used to specify the authentication mechanism that will be used for the user's login. The following authentication methods can be used with Gauntlet:

❖ **PLAIN PASSWORDS.** This is not recommended when logging in over an untrusted network.

❖ **SNK.** This is Digital Pathways Secure Net Key. Gauntlet supports the SNK authentication calculator.

❖ **S/KEY.** This is the freely available S/Key authentication system developed by Bellcore. Software for this is included, but TIS does not provide support for it.

The *IP Address Configuration* option is used to configure the network interfaces for the Gauntlet system. This option can be used to change the host name, domain name, IP address, subnet mask, broadcast address, default DNS server, and default router. If the internal network is subnetted and additional routes need to be defined for the Gauntlet system, the *route add* command can be used to add these routes in the /etc/netstart file. If the DNS software is to run on the Gauntlet system, the /etc/resolv.conf, which is used to list the DNS servers to contact for name resolution, must contain an entry for the Gauntlet system. This can be done by placing the following in the /etc/resolv.conf file:

```
nameserver 127.0.0.1
```

The *DNS Configuration* option is used to edit host tables (/etc/hosts), reload the DNS configuration from the host table, and configure DNS options. It can be used as a quick method for setting up a DNS server. For more complex configurations, you will have to edit and configure the DNS software directly, which would involve configuring the /etc/named.boot and the zone files referenced by this file.

The *Electronic Mail Configuration* option is used to specify if e-mail is to be forwarded to an internal mail hub, the postmaster for the Gauntlet system's e-mail address, or if mail headers should be modified to indicate that mail originated from the domain itself. This hides knowledge of hosts from the outside world. If there is no internal mail hub, you should not modify the mail headers; otherwise, return addresses might not be replyable.

The *NNTP Forwarder Configuration* is used to specify the internal and external NNTP servers between which news feed flows. Both internal and external news server should be configured to feed news to the Gauntlet system. The Gauntlet system uses proxy agents to forward the news.

USERS VIEW OF USING THE GAUNTLET FIREWALL

Using a firewall such as Gauntlet changes the user's interaction for some standard services, such as TELNET, FTP, and rlogin. The user must first connect to the proxy server running on the firewall, then specify the destination to connect to. The application proxy on the firewall performs the requested action on behalf of the user. Sending e-mail does not require any change in the user interface, as long as the firewall is configured properly.

349

USING *FTP* WITH THE *GAUNTLET FIREWALL*

Assume that the user wants to do an anonymous FTP session to DS.INTERNIC.NET. The user must first connect to the FTP proxy server running in the firewall, as follows:

```
% ftp gauntlet.kinetics.com
```

Once connected to the server, the user is prompted for the user name and host name to connect to the remote FTP server. You have to format this in the following RFC-822 address syntax:

username@hostname

For the example in this section, you must specify this as the following:

anonymous@ds.internic.net

A typical session through the Gauntlet system from a host on the internal network follows:

```
ucs% ftp gauntlet.kinetics.com
Connected to gauntlet.kinetics.com
220 gauntlet FTP proxy (Version N stable) ready.
Name (gauntlet:you): anonymous@ds.internic.net
331-(----GATEWAY CONNECTED TO ds.internic.net----)
331-(220 ds.internic.net FTP server (Version 5.60 ready.)
331 Guest login ok, send ident as password.
Password: password not echoed
230 Guest login ok, access restrictions apply.
ftp> dir
200 PORT command successful.
```

When you see the message GATEWAY CONNECTED TO, it means that the FTP proxy server has established connection to the remote host. From then on, all commands you enter are forwarded to the remote host by the proxy. The proxy also returns all status messages for you.

The following shows the situation when you are using the FTP from an untrusted network and want to use an FTP server on an internal host. This sequence assumes that the SNK method of authentication has been enabled at the gauntlet firewall. Assume that the DNS name of the firewall from the outside is gatekeeper.kinetics.com.

```
% ftp gatekeeper.kinetics.com
Connected to gatekeeper.kinetics.com.
220-Before using the proxy you must first authenticate
220 gatekeeper FTP proxy (Version N stable) ready.
Name (gatekeeper.kinetics.com:you):
331 SNK Challenge "81416":
Password: password not echoed
230 User authenticated to proxy
ftp> user kss@ucs.kinetics.com
331-(----GATEWAY CONNECTED TO ucs.kinetics.com----)
```

```
331-(220 ucs.kinetics.com FTP server (Version 5.60 ready.)
331 Password required for you.
Password: password not echoed
ftp>
```

USING *TELNET* WITH THE GAUNTLET FIREWALL

The user must first connect to the TELNET proxy server running in the firewall, using the following line:

% telnet gauntlet.kinetics.com

After a short pause, the command prompt for the proxy server appears. Use **connect** *hostname* of the c *hostname* command to connect to the remote host. If the system is unreachable, the proxy informs you. You can then use the quit command to break the connection to the gateway. The following commands illustrate this sequence:

```
% telnet gatekeeper.kinetics.com
Trying 199.245.180.15 ...
Connected to gatekeeper.kinetics.com
Escape character is ^].
gatekeeper telnet proxy (Version N) ready:
tn-gw-> c ucs.siyan.com
ucs BSD 386/ v1.0 (ttys1)

login: enter loginname
Password: entered password not displayed
You have mail.
```

USING rlogin WITH THE GAUNTLET FIREWALL

The user must first connect to the rlogin proxy server running in the firewall, using the following line:

% rlogin gauntlet.kinetics.com

After a short pause, the command prompt for the proxy server appears. Use the connect *hostname* or c *hostname* command to connect to the remote host. If the system is unreachable, the proxy informs you. Unlike TELNET, you do not have to authenticate the user twice.

Consider the following example where the rlogin server on ucs.siyan.com prompted for a password, because this firewall host was not in the user's .rhosts file.

```
% rlogin  gatekeeper.kinetics.com
rlogin-gw-> ?
Valid commands are: (unique abbreviations must be used)
   connect hostname
   help/?
   quit/exit
   password
```

351

```
rlogin-gw> c ucs.siyan.com
Password: entered password not displayed
Trying you@199.245.180.10
Last login: Wed Nov 16 17:45:23 from world.std.com
ucs BSD 386/ v1.0 (ttys1)

You have mail.
ucs%
```

If a user name and host name are specified, the rlogin proxy automatically reconnects to the specified remote system, as the following lines show:

```
% rlogin  gatekeeper.kinetics.com -l kss@rams.siyan.com
Trying you@199.245.180.12
Last login: Wed Nov 16 18:34:12 from world.std.com
ucs BSD 386/ v1.0 (ttys1)

You have mail.
ucs%
```

If you are logging in from an external site and the SNK authentication is used, you will see something similar to the following:

```
% rlogin gatekeeper.kinetics.com -l kss@si.kscs.com
Username: kss
SNK Challenge "23451": enter numeric code
Login Accepted
Trying you@193.25.10.3
Last login: Wed Nov 16 18:34:12 from world.std.com
ucs BSD 386/ v1.0 (ttys1)

You have mail.
ucs%
```

THE TIS FIREWALL TOOLKIT

Trusted Information Systems, Inc., the makers of the commercial Gauntlet product, also make available a free firewall package called the TIS Firewall Toolkit. Much of the functionality of the commercial Gauntlet product is built on top of this toolkit.

The TIS Firewall Toolkit is a collection of tools, from which you can pick and choose to implement the services that you need. The TIS Firewall Toolkit can be obtained by anonymous FTP from the following source:

FTP server: FTP.TIS.COM

Path: /pub/firewall/toolkit

BUILDING THE TIS FIREWALL TOOLKIT

After you have downloaded the software package from the source mentioned in the previous section, you must compute and build the firewall toolkit on your system.

The firewall toolkit is a Unix compressed tar file. In this discussion, the name of this file shall be fwtk.tar.Z.

Copy this file into a working directory on your system and use the uncompress or gunzip commands to uncompress the file. You then must extract the files from the archive. An example of these commands for BSD Unix follows:

```
uncompress fwtk.tar.Z
tar -xvBf fwtk.tar
```

The following files are extracted. They are given to be a reference of the names of the files in the toolkit.

```
fwtk/
fwtk/smap/
fwtk/smap/Makefile
fwtk/smap/smap.c
fwtk/smapd/
fwtk/smapd/Makefile
fwtk/smapd/smapd.c
fwtk/ftp-gw/
fwtk/ftp-gw/Makefile
fwtk/ftp-gw/ftp-gw.c
fwtk/tn-gw/
fwtk/tn-gw/Makefile
fwtk/tn-gw/tn-gw.c
fwtk/lib/
fwtk/lib/alldi.c
fwtk/lib/config.c
fwtk/lib/conn.c
fwtk/lib/daemon.c
fwtk/lib/enargv.c
fwtk/lib/hnam.c
fwtk/lib/lock.c
fwtk/lib/mapg.c
fwtk/lib/mapu.c
fwtk/lib/mktemp.c
fwtk/lib/nama.c
fwtk/lib/pname.c
fwtk/lib/rand.c
fwtk/lib/syslog.c
fwtk/lib/README
fwtk/lib/urg.c
```

```
fwtk/lib/Makefile
fwtk/config/
fwtk/config/netperm-table
fwtk/config/inetd.conf
fwtk/config/Makefile
fwtk/config/login-sh.conf
fwtk/config/syslog.conf
fwtk/netacl/
fwtk/netacl/Makefile
fwtk/netacl/netacl.c
fwtk/plug-gw/
fwtk/plug-gw/Makefile
fwtk/plug-gw/plug-gw.c
fwtk/tools/
fwtk/tools/client/
fwtk/tools/client/gate-ftp/
fwtk/tools/client/gate-ftp/Makefile
fwtk/tools/client/gate-ftp/README
fwtk/tools/client/gate-ftp/cmds.c
fwtk/tools/client/gate-ftp/cmdtab.c
fwtk/tools/client/gate-ftp/domacro.c
fwtk/tools/client/gate-ftp/ftp.1
fwtk/tools/client/gate-ftp/ftp.c
fwtk/tools/client/gate-ftp/ftp_var.h
fwtk/tools/client/gate-ftp/getpass.c
fwtk/tools/client/gate-ftp/glob.c
fwtk/tools/client/gate-ftp/main.c
fwtk/tools/client/gate-ftp/pathnames.h
fwtk/tools/client/gate-ftp/ruserpass.c
fwtk/tools/client/misc/
fwtk/tools/client/misc/tn
fwtk/tools/client/misc/README
fwtk/tools/client/Makefile
fwtk/tools/server/
fwtk/tools/server/ftpd/
fwtk/tools/server/ftpd/ftpd.c
fwtk/tools/server/ftpd/Makefile
fwtk/tools/server/ftpd/ftpcmd.y
fwtk/tools/server/ftpd/ftpd.8
fwtk/tools/server/ftpd/logwtmp.c
fwtk/tools/server/ftpd/pathnames.h
fwtk/tools/server/ftpd/popen.c
fwtk/tools/server/ftpd/vers.c
fwtk/tools/server/ftpd/glob.c
fwtk/tools/server/ftpd/CHANGES
fwtk/tools/server/ftpd/README
fwtk/tools/server/syslog/
fwtk/tools/server/syslog/reg/
fwtk/tools/server/syslog/reg/regerror.c
```

```
fwtk/tools/server/syslog/reg/README
fwtk/tools/server/syslog/reg/regexp.3
fwtk/tools/server/syslog/reg/regexp.c
fwtk/tools/server/syslog/reg/regexp.h
fwtk/tools/server/syslog/reg/regmagic.h
fwtk/tools/server/syslog/reg/regsub.c
fwtk/tools/server/syslog/reg/COPYRIGHT
fwtk/tools/server/syslog/reg/Makefile
fwtk/tools/server/syslog/syslogd.c
fwtk/tools/server/syslog/pathnames.h
fwtk/tools/server/syslog/syslogd.8
fwtk/tools/server/syslog/Makefile
fwtk/tools/server/syslog/syslog.h
fwtk/tools/server/syslog/syslog.conf.5
fwtk/tools/server/syslog/internal.h
fwtk/tools/server/syslog/ttymsg.c
fwtk/tools/server/syslog/strerror.c
fwtk/tools/server/syslog/daemon.c
fwtk/tools/server/syslog/logit.c
fwtk/tools/server/syslog/README
fwtk/tools/server/syslog/syslog.conf
fwtk/tools/server/syslog/sample-syslog.conf
fwtk/tools/server/syslog/syslog.ps
fwtk/tools/server/login-sh/
fwtk/tools/server/login-sh/getenv.c
fwtk/tools/server/login-sh/setenv.c
fwtk/tools/server/login-sh/README
fwtk/tools/server/login-sh/Makefile
fwtk/tools/server/login-sh/login-sh.c
fwtk/tools/server/login-sh/sample-shellfile
fwtk/tools/server/login-ts/
fwtk/tools/server/login-ts/Makefile
fwtk/tools/server/login-ts/README
fwtk/tools/server/login-ts/getenv.c
fwtk/tools/server/login-ts/login-ts.c
fwtk/tools/server/login-ts/setenv.c
fwtk/tools/server/login-ts/sample-userfile
fwtk/tools/server/aix-auth/
fwtk/tools/server/aix-auth/Makefile
fwtk/tools/server/aix-auth/README
fwtk/tools/server/aix-auth/authenticate.c
fwtk/tools/server/aix-auth/Author
fwtk/tools/server/Makefile
fwtk/tools/server/README
fwtk/tools/admin/
fwtk/tools/admin/portscan/
fwtk/tools/admin/portscan/Makefile
fwtk/tools/admin/portscan/portscan.c
```

```
fwtk/tools/admin/netscan/
fwtk/tools/admin/netscan/Makefile
fwtk/tools/admin/netscan/netscan.c
fwtk/tools/admin/reporting/
fwtk/tools/admin/reporting/Makefile
fwtk/tools/admin/reporting/today-report.sh
fwtk/tools/admin/reporting/daily-report.sh
fwtk/tools/admin/reporting/login-summ.sh
fwtk/tools/admin/reporting/smap-summ.sh
fwtk/tools/admin/reporting/netacl-summ.sh
fwtk/tools/admin/reporting/tn-gw-summ.sh
fwtk/tools/admin/reporting/ftp-summ.sh
fwtk/tools/admin/reporting/README
fwtk/tools/admin/reporting/authsrv-summ.sh
fwtk/tools/admin/reporting/weekly-report.sh
fwtk/tools/admin/reporting/http-summ.sh
fwtk/tools/admin/reporting/deny-summ.sh
fwtk/tools/admin/flog/
fwtk/tools/admin/flog/flog.c
fwtk/tools/admin/flog/Makefile
fwtk/tools/admin/flog/README
fwtk/tools/admin/progmail/
fwtk/tools/admin/progmail/progmail
fwtk/tools/admin/progmail/README
fwtk/tools/admin/Makefile
fwtk/tools/admin/README
fwtk/tools/Makefile
fwtk/tools/README
fwtk/auth/
fwtk/auth/README
fwtk/auth/authadduser.sh
fwtk/auth/authdump.c
fwtk/auth/authload.c
fwtk/auth/authmgr.c
fwtk/auth/authsrv.c
fwtk/auth/cliio.c
fwtk/auth/db.c
fwtk/auth/enigma.c
fwtk/auth/pass.c
fwtk/auth/proto.c
fwtk/auth/securid.c
fwtk/auth/skey.c
fwtk/auth/srvio.c
fwtk/auth/Makefile
fwtk/rlogin-gw/
fwtk/rlogin-gw/rlogin-gw.c
fwtk/rlogin-gw/Makefile
```

```
fwtk/x-gw/
fwtk/x-gw/child.c
fwtk/x-gw/dialog.c
fwtk/x-gw/fwd.c
fwtk/x-gw/getenv.c
fwtk/x-gw/list.c
fwtk/x-gw/pmsg.c
fwtk/x-gw/setenv.c
fwtk/x-gw/shell.c
fwtk/x-gw/sig.c
fwtk/x-gw/socket.c
fwtk/x-gw/string.c
fwtk/x-gw/sws.c
fwtk/x-gw/token.c
fwtk/x-gw/x-gw.c
fwtk/x-gw/Makefile
fwtk/x-gw/list.h
fwtk/x-gw/ulib.h
fwtk/Makefile
fwtk/README
fwtk/auth.h
fwtk/CHANGES
fwtk/LICENSE
fwtk/firewall.h
fwtk/DISCLAIMER
fwtk/fixmake
fwtk/http-gw/
fwtk/http-gw/Makefile
fwtk/http-gw/gauthd.c
fwtk/http-gw/http-gw.c
fwtk/http-gw/http-gw.txt
fwtk/http-gw/http.txt
fwtk/http-gw/version.c
fwtk/http-gw/version.h
fwtk/http-gw/http-gw.8
fwtk/http-gw/Makefile.new
fwtk/http-gw/README
fwtk/http-gw/http-gw.tbl
fwtk/http-gw/shttp.txt
fwtk/Makefile.config
```

Change the UID and GID on the extracted files to avoid any accidental access to these files. On BSD Unix systems, you can perform the following to assign the UID and GID for root and wheel.

chown -R root:wheel fwtk

Go to the fwtk directory under which the source files have been extracted. The file Makefile
references the file Makefile.config. You should change some target definitions for this file. A
listing of the Makefile.config follows:

```
#
#  Copyright (c) 1993, Trusted Information Systems, Incorporated
#  All rights reserved.
#
#  Redistribution and use are governed by the terms detailed in the
#  license document ("LICENSE") included with the toolkit.
#


#
#    Author: Marcus J. Ranum, Trusted Information Systems, Inc.
#
# RcsId: "$Header: Makefile.config,v 1.3 94/11/01 12:04:59 mjr rel $"


# Your C compiler (eg, "cc" or "gcc")
CC=     cc


# program to use for installation -- this may or may not preserve
# old versions (or whatever). assumes that it takes parameters:
# copy source dest
CP=     cp


# Options for your compiler (eg, "-g" for debugging, "-O" for
# optimizing, or "-g -O" for both under GCC)
#COPT=    -g -traditional
COPT=    -g
#COPT=    -O


# Version of "make" you want to use
#MAKE=    gnumake
MAKE=    make


# Your ranlib utility (use "touch" if you don't have ranlib)
RANLIB=    ranlib
#RANLIB=    touch


# Destination directory for installation of binaries
DEST=    /usr/local/etc
```

```
# Destination directory for installation of man pages
#DESTMAN=    $(DEST)/../man


# Names of any auxiliary libraries your system may require (e.g., -lsocket)
# If you want to link against a resolver library, specify it here.
AUXLIB= -lresolv
#AUXLIB= -lsocket


# DBM library should be specified if it is an external library or
# you with to use a different one than what is included in libc
#DBMLIB=    -lndbm
DBMLIB=


# Flags to pass to the linker (eg, -static for static binaries under GCC,
# or -Bstatic for static binaries under SunOS 4.1.x)
#LDFL=    -Bstatic
#LDFL=
LDFL= -g


# Location of the fwtk sources [For #include by any external tools needing
it]
FWTKSRCDIR=/u/b/mjr/firewall/fwtk
#FWTKSRCDIR=/usr/local/src/fwtk


# Location of X libraries for X-gw
#XLIBDIR=/usr/X11/lib
XLIBDIR=/usr/local/X11R5/lib


# Location of X include files
#XINCLUDE=/usr/X11/include
XINCLUDE=/usr/local/X11R5/include
```

You can change any of the variables defined in these configuration files, but pay special attention to the directories in which the files are referenced and installed. You should think about the settings of at least the following variables:

DEST, DESTMAN, AUXLIB, FWTKSRC, XLIBDIR, XINCLUDE

On BSDI Unix, you should change XLIBDIR to /usr/X11/lib and XINCLUDE to /usr/X11/include.

After making changes to the Makefile.config, execute the make command:

```
make
```

If you see compilation errors, make the appropriate fixes.

On BSD Unix, the author encountered the following error messages when trying to build the tools:

```
"Makefile", line 16: Need an operator
Fatal errors encountered -- cannot continue
```

This error message is caused by the fact that the "include" statements in the Makefiles in the fwtk directory and the subdirectories where the separate tools reside use a form of include that is incompatible with make on BSDI Unix. If you encounter the previous error, it is because the include statement in the Makefiles has the following syntax:

```
include name_of_file
```

You should change this to an include that uses the following syntax:

```
.include "name_of_file"
```

Another problem the author encountered was the conflict in getenv() and setenv() routines in the files in the fwtk/x-gw directory and the routines defined in the C-library. You can resolve this conflict by suitably renaming the functions that cause conflicts.

After you successfully compile and link the tools, you should run the following command from the fwtk directory:

```
make install
```

This command installs the tools in the directory specified in the DEST variable in the Makefile.config. To access these tools more conveniently, place the fwtk directory on your search path.

CONFIGURING THE BASTION HOST WITH MINIMAL SERVICES

You should configure the host on which you will be running the TIS Firewall Toolkit with only those services that are needed. This requires system-specific knowledge. The following is a partial list:

✦ Edit the system startup files, such as the /etc/rc, /etc/netstart, and /etc/rc.local (BSD Unix).

✦ Edit the operating system configuration and eliminate any undesirable kernel-based services, such as NFS, and rebuild the kernel.

✦ Edit the /etc/inetd.conf file, which specifies the internet daemon controlled services. Remove services that are not needed such as TFTP.

At each step, use the ps command to verify the services that are running. On a firewall, a reduced configuration should typically have the following processes:

```
% ps -aux
USER     PID %CPU %MEM   VSZ  RSS TT   STAT STARTED     TIME COMMAND
root       0  0.0  0.0     0    0 ??   DLs  2:35AM   0:00.00 (swapper)
root       1  0.0  0.0   652  116 ??   Is   2:35AM   0:00.11 init --
root       2  0.0  0.0     0   12 ??   DL   2:35AM   0:00.00 (pagedaemon)
root      29  0.0  0.0   608  112 ??   Ss   2:36AM   0:00.30 syslogd
root      46  0.0  0.0   520   28 ??   Ss   2:36AM   0:00.11 update
root      48  0.0  0.0   676  152 ??   I    2:36AM   0:00.38 cron
root      74  0.0  0.0   652  104 ??   Is   2:36AM   0:00.14 inetd
root      87  0.0  0.0   972  412 co   Is+  2:36AM   0:00.66 -tcsh (tcsh)
root     488  0.0  0.0   692  172 p0   R+   5:06PM   0:00.07 ps -aux
%
```

You can also use the netstat -a command to see a status of the network services that are running, as follows:

```
% netstat -a
Active Internet connections (including servers)
Proto Recv-Q Send-Q  Local Address          Foreign Address        (state)
tcp        0      0   *.time                 *.*                    LISTEN
tcp        0      0   *.daytime              *.*                    LISTEN
tcp        0      0   *.chargen              *.*                    LISTEN
tcp        0      0   *.discard              *.*                    LISTEN
tcp        0      0   *.echo                 *.*                    LISTEN
tcp        0      0   *.finger               *.*                    LISTEN
tcp        0      0   *.telnet               *.*                    LISTEN
tcp        0      0   *.ftp                  *.*                    LISTEN
tcp        0      0   *.smtp                 *.*                    LISTEN
tcp        0      0   *.sunrpc               *.*                    LISTEN
udp        0      0   *.time                 *.*
udp        0      0   *.daytime              *.*
udp        0      0   *.chargen              *.*
udp        0      0   *.discard              *.*
udp        0      0   *.echo                 *.*
udp        0      0   *.659                  *.*
udp        0      0   *.syslog               *.*
Active Unix domain sockets
Address  Type    Recv-Q Send-Q  Inode   Conn      Refs  Nextref Addr
fe46c400 dgram        0      0       0 fe396a94       0 fe3eea14
fe46c800 dgram        0      0       0 fe396a94       0 fe453994
%
```

You also can use the *portscan* tool that is in the fwtk directory under tools/admin/portscan to scan the ports on a host to see if any ports are active. You first will have to run make on the Makefile in the tools directory. Figure 8.24 shows the results of scanning ports 500 to 515 on host ucs.kinetics.com. The ports that are active on the host are displayed.

FIGURE 8.24

Using the FWTK portscan tool.

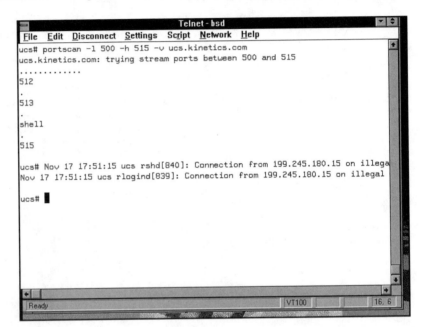

```
ucs# portscan -1 500 -h 515 -v ucs.kinetics.com
ucs.kinetics.com: trying stream ports between 500 and 515
.............
512
.
513
.
shell
.
515

ucs# Nov 17 17:51:15 ucs rshd[840]: Connection from 199.245.180.15 on illega
Nov 17 17:51:15 ucs rlogind[839]: Connection from 199.245.180.15 on illegal

ucs#
```

INSTALLING THE TOOLKIT COMPONENTS

When you run the make install command after successfully compiling the individual components, the binaries are installed in the directory specified by the DEST variable in the fwtk/Makefile.config file. The default is to install the tools in the /usr/local/etc directory.

Most of the toolkit components are invoked by the inetd daemon. The configuration for inetd is specified in the /etc/inetd.conf file. You must edit this file to invoke the firewall proxy components. The access control configuration information for the toolkit components is kept in the netperm-table file. By default, this file is found in the /usr/local/etc directory.

The following listing shows the partial contents of the /etc/inetd.conf file configured for the firewall.

```
#
# Internet server configuration database
#
#   @(#)inetd.conf   5.4 (Berkeley) 6/30/90
#
```

```
ftp        stream    tcp    nowait    root      /usr/local/etc/netacl
ftpd
ftp-gw     stream    tcp    nowait    root      /usr/local/etc/ftp-gw
ftp-gw
telnet     stream    tcp    nowait    root      /usr/local/etc/tn-gw
tn-gw
tn-admin   stream    tcp    nowait    root      /usr/local/etc/netacl
telnetd
login      stream    tcp    nowait    root      /usr/local/etc/rlogin-gw
rlogin-gw
finger     stream    tcp    nowait    nobody    /usr/local/etc/netacl
fingerd
smtp       stream    tcp    nowait    root      /usr/local/etc/smap
smap
echo       stream    tcp    nowait    root      internal
discard    stream    tcp    nowait    root      internal
chargen    stream    tcp    nowait    root      internal
daytime    stream    tcp    nowait    root      internal
time       stream    tcp    nowait    root      internal
echo       dgram     udp    wait      root      internal
discard    dgram     udp    wait      root      internal
chargen    dgram     udp    wait      root      internal
daytime    dgram     udp    wait      root      internal
time       dgram     udp    wait      root      internal
```

The netacl is a TIS firewall toolkit program that is invoked for standard ftp and administrative telnet sessions. It provides network access control for TCP-based services based on the network permissions table (/usr/local/etc/netperm-table). Usually, the netacl is configured to allow hosts on the internal network limited access to the gateway. The netacl is similar to the tcp_wrapper program discussed earlier in this chapter. This netacl program is designed to work with the network permissions table used by the TIS firewall toolkit.

If a telnet proxy gateway service has to be set up, it must be assigned the telnet standard port of 23 because the telnet program often disables options processing when connecting to a port that is different from this standard port. The telnet proxy service requires options processing so it must be connected to the standard telnet port. In the /etc/inetd.conf listing shown previously, this is done by the following entry:

```
telnet     stream    tcp    nowait    root      /usr/local/etc/tn-gw     tn-gw
```

The telnet gateway program can be found in /usr/local/etc/tn-gw . The tn-gw in the last column is the name of the service. When the /usr/local/etc/tn-gw program runs, it consults the permissions table to see if this access should be permitted or denied.

The meaning of the other fields are as follow: The *telnet* in the first column is the name of the service defined in the /etc/services file. The field *streams*, in the second column, refers to the TCP byte stream service. The field *tcp* in the third column refers to the protocol service which is TCP. The field *nowait* in the fourth column refers to the fact that when inetd

363

receives a connection request, it does not have to wait, but can easily begin listening for additional connection requests. The field *root* in the fifth column is the user name under whose permissions the service runs.

If standard port 23 is used by the telnet gateway service and administrative access to the standard telnet service is required, the standard telnet service must be defined on another port. For example, you can define the standard telnet service on port 24, and make the following entry in the /etc/services file:

```
tn-admin        24/tcp
```

Then, in the /etc/inetd.conf file, you can make the following entry:

```
tn-admin stream tcp    nowait    root    /usr/local/etc/netacl    telnetd
```

When a connection attempt is made on port 24 of the firewall, the program /usr/local/etc/netacl executes, consulting the network permissions table file /usr/local/etc/netperm-table to determine if access is allowed or not.

The FTP gateway can be configured on any port. You might want to configure the FTP gateway on a different port, if you want internal users to have access to the standard FTP server. In any case, the standard FTP services should be under the control of the netacl wrapper program which can control access to this service.

```
ftp     stream    tcp    nowait    root    /usr/local/etc/netacl    ftpd
```

The FTP gateway service can be configured, as follows, in the inetd.conf file:

```
ftp-gw    stream    tcp    nowait    root    /usr/local/etc/ftp-gw    ftp-gw
```

The following are partial contents of a sample /etc/services file that define the firewall proxy services:

```
#
# Network services, Internet style
#
#     @(#)services     5.8 (Berkeley) 5/9/91
#
echo            7/tcp
echo            7/udp
discard         9/tcp           sink null
discard         9/udp           sink null
systat          11/tcp          users
daytime         13/tcp
daytime         13/udp
chargen         19/tcp          ttytst source
chargen         19/udp          ttytst source
ftp             21/tcp
ftp-gw          22/tcp
telnet          23/tcp
```

```
tn-admin        24/tcp
smtp            25/tcp          mail
time            37/tcp          timserver
time            37/udp          timserver
rlp             39/udp          resource        # resource location
nameserver      42/tcp          name            # IEN 116
whois           43/tcp          nicname
domain          53/tcp          nameserver      # name-domain server
domain          53/udp          nameserver
```

> When debugging the firewall toolkit configuration, you must restart inetd if you make changes to the /etc/inetd.conf file. You can restart inetd by using the ps command to determine its *process identifier* (PID) and then using kill -HUP on inetd's PID. For example:
>
> ```
> % ps -aux | grep inetd
> root          76  0.0  0.0   652  128 ??  Is    5:27AM   0:00.99
>     ➥inetd
> % kill -HUP 76
> ```

N O T E

If rlogin proxy is to be installed, it must be installed on the firewall's rlogin service port (512). Rlogin requires binding to a privileged port, an operation that requires system permissions. Because of the permissive nature of rlogin security, you can set the rlogin proxy's directory option to ensure that it runs under chroot.

> The *chroot* is a mechanism under Unix where a process is confined to a single branch of the file system. After the chroot is performed, the root of the restricted branch of the file system is treated as the root directory, preventing the process from accessing critical parts of the file system, such as the /etc directory that contains the password files and other critical information, and the /dev directory that contains the device files.

N O T E

THE NETWORK PERMISSIONS TABLE

The netacl and the firewall proxies read the network permissions table file to determine if access is permitted. A sample network permissions table file (/usr/local/etc/netperm-table) follows:

```
#
# Sample netperm configuration table
#
```

```
# To get a good sample working netperm-table, just globally
# substitute YOURNET for your network address (e.g.; 666.777.888)
#

# Example netacl rules:
# -------------------
# if the next 2 lines are uncommented, people can get a login prompt
# on the firewall machine through the telnet proxy
netacl-telnetd: permit-hosts 127.0.0.1 -exec /usr/libexec/telnetd
netacl-telnetd: permit-hosts 199.245.180.9 199.245.180.10 -exec /usr/libexec/
telnetd
#
netacl-ftpd: permit-hosts 199.245.180.9 199.245.180.10 -exec /usr/libexec/
ftpd
netacl-ftpd: permit-hosts unknown -exec /bin/cat /usr/local/etc/noftp.txt
netacl-ftpd: permit-hosts * -chroot /var/anon-ftp  -exec /usr/libexec/ftpd


#
# if the next line is uncommented, the telnet proxy is available
netacl-telnetd: permit-hosts * -exec /usr/local/etc/tn-gw
#
# if the next 2 lines are uncommented, people can get a login prompt
# on the firewall machine through the rlogin proxy
netacl-rlogind: permit-hosts 127.0.0.1 -exec /usr/libexec/rlogind -a
netacl-rlogind: permit-hosts 199.245.180.* -exec /usr/libexec/rlogind -a
#
# if the next line is uncommented, the rlogin proxy is available
#netacl-rlogind: permit-hosts * -exec /usr/local/etc/rlogin-gw


#
# to enable finger service uncomment these 2 lines
netacl-fingerd: permit-hosts 199.245.180.* -exec /usr/libexec/fingerd
netacl-fingerd: permit-hosts * -exec /bin/cat /usr/local/etc/finger.txt

# Example smap rules:
# -----------------
smap, smapd:    userid 6
smap, smapd:    directory /var/spool/smap
smapd:          executable /usr/local/etc/smapd
smapd:          sendmail /usr/sbin/sendmail
smap:           timeout 3600

# Example ftp gateway rules:
# ------------------------
ftp-gw:    denial-msg    /usr/local/etc/ftp-deny.txt
ftp-gw:    welcome-msg   /usr/local/etc/ftp-welcome.txt
ftp-gw:    help-msg    /usr/local/etc/ftp-help.txt
ftp-gw:        timeout 3600
# uncomment the following line if you want internal users to be
# able to do FTP with the internet
ftp-gw:        permit-hosts 199.245.180.* -log {retr stor}
```

366

```
# uncomment the following line if you want external users to be
# able to do FTP with the internal network using authentication
ftp-gw:         permit-hosts * -authall -log { retr stor }

# Example telnet gateway rules:
# ---------------------------
tn-gw:          denial-msg    /usr/local/etc/tn-deny.txt
tn-gw:          welcome-msg   /usr/local/etc/tn-welcome.txt
#tn-gw:         help-msg    /usr/local/etc/tn-help.txt
tn-gw:          timeout 3600
tn-gw:          permit-hosts 127.0.0.1 199.245.180.* -passok -xok
# if this line is uncommented incoming traffic is permitted WITH
# authentication required
#tn-gw:         permit-hosts * -auth

# Example rlogin gateway rules:
# ---------------------------
rlogin-gw:      denial-msg    /usr/local/etc/rlogin-deny.txt
rlogin-gw:      welcome-msg   /usr/local/etc/rlogin-welcome.txt
rlogin-gw:      help-msg    /usr/local/etc/rlogin-help.txt
rlogin-gw:      timeout 3600
rlogin-gw:      permit-hosts 199.245.180.* -passok -xok
# if this line is uncommented incoming traffic is permitted WITH
# authentication required
rlogin-gw:      permit-hosts * -auth -xok


# Example auth server and client rules
# ----------------------------------
authsrv:    hosts 127.0.0.1
authsrv:    database /usr/local/etc/fw-authdb
authsrv:    badsleep 1200
authsrv:    nobogus true

# clients using the auth server
*:          authserver 127.0.0.1 7777

# X-forwarder rules
tn-gw, rlogin-gw:    xforwarder /usr/local/etc/x-gw
```

Consider the following rules from this sample configuration file for the FTP proxy:

```
ftp-gw:     denial-msg    /usr/local/etc/ftp-deny.txt
ftp-gw:     welcome-msg    /usr/local/etc/ftp-welcome.txt
ftp-gw:     help-msg    /usr/local/etc/ftp-help.txt
ftp-gw:        timeout 3600
ftp-gw:          permit-hosts 199.245.180.* -log {retr stor}
# uncomment the following line if you want external users to be
# able to do FTP with the internal network using authentication
ftp-gw:          permit-hosts * -authall -log { retr stor }
```

367

The meaning of the previous configurations statements is as follows: The hosts on the network 199.245.180.0 are permitted to use the FTP proxy. The "-log {retr stor}" indicates that logging actions for retrieval (GET) and storage (PUT) are enabled. The FTP proxy will timeout and shut the connection for a period of inactivity lasting 3,600 seconds. Also, external users can access the firewall FTP proxy if they are using authentication.

TELNET AND RLOGIN ACCESS

Normal telnet access to the firewall should generally be available to administrators only. To run the telnet/rlogin proxies, normal telnet/rlogin access cannot use the same port. You can use the following approaches for this problem:

❖ Permit administrative logins through the console of the firewall only.

❖ Run telnet/rlogin proxies on the standard service port. Run standard telnet/rlogin proxies on alternate ports, and protect them with netacl.

❖ Use netacl to switch services, depending on the origin of the request.

The first solution might be very restrictive to the administrators and might not always be possible.

The second solution might cause a problem with some telnet/rlogin implementations that do not work properly when connecting to a non-standard port.

The last solution is more convenient because users do not have to specify non-standard ports for standard telnet service. This solution, however, requires proper use of access controls. An example of the rules that provide this service follow:

```
#Telnet access
netacl-telnetd:    permit-hosts    127.0.0.1    -exec    /usr/libexec/telnetd
netacl-telnetd:    permit-hosts    199.245.180.10    -exec    /usr/libexec/
telnetd
netacl-telnetd:    permit-hosts    *    -exec    /usr/local/etc/tn-gw

#Rlogin access
netacl-rlogind:    permit-hosts    127.0.0.1    -exec    /usr/libexec/rlogind
netacl-rlogind:    permit-hosts    199.245.180.10    -exec    /usr/libexec/
rlogind
netacl-rlogind:    permit-hosts    *    -exec    /usr/local/etc/rlogin-gw
```

SETTING UP ANONYMOUS FTP ACCESS

Anonymous FTP user accounts have had their share of security problems, such as bugs in the FTP server implementation or misconfigurations. One approach to making Anonymous FTP more secure is to use the netacl program to "chroot" to a directory dedicated for anonymous FTP, before the FTP server is started. For example, the following lines from the sample network permissions table can be used for this purpose:

```
netacl-ftpd: permit-hosts 199.245.180.9 199.245.180.10 -exec /usr/libexec/
ftpd
netacl-ftpd: permit-hosts unknown -exec /bin/cat /usr/local/etc/noftp.txt
netacl-ftpd: permit-hosts * -chroot /var/anon-ftp  -exec /usr/libexec/ftpd
```

The first line permits only hosts 199.245.180.9 and 199.245.180.10 to connect to the FTP service. In the second line, hosts that are not known to DNS will have displayed the contents of the file /usr/local/etc/noftp.txt. Presumably, this text will have appropriate messages indicating that FTP service is not available to them. The third line permits access to any host, but it "chroots" to the /var/anon-ftp directory before executing the FTP service. When the FTP service starts, it will read the /etc/passwd file for user authentication. Because it has been chrooted to the FTP area, it will read the file /var/anon-ftp/etc/passwd, and not the main /etc/passwd file. This allows user accounts to be created and assigned that are for FTP only and that are independent of user accounts kept in the main /etc/passwd file.

SUPPORTING THE PROXY FTP SERVER AND STANDARD FTP SERVER ON THE SAME HOST

The proxy FTP gateway server can be invoked directly from the dedicated port 21 used for FTP service, or from inside a modified FTP daemon. If the proxy server is run on the standard FTP port, the standard FTP daemon cannot also run on this port, which means that standard FTP services are not available on the host that runs the FTP proxy. However, it is sometimes desirable to have both standard FTP and proxy FTP on the same host. For this reason, the toolkit supports a version of the FTP daemon that has knowledge about the FTP proxy, and invokes it when it recognizes an address in the form *user@host*. The source code for the modified daemon is in the fwtk/tools/server/ftpd directory. The Makefile in this directory defines a PROXY_PASSTHROUGH variable. The sample Makefile in this directory follows:

```
.include "../../../Makefile.config"

SRCS=    ftpd.c ftpcmd.c glob.c logwtmp.c popen.c vers.c
OBJS=    ftpd.o ftpcmd.o glob.o logwtmp.o popen.o vers.o

LIBS=    ../../../libauth.a ../../../libfwall.a


# SETPROCTITLE sets the process title to something readable
# PARANOID disables many internal FTP operations
# NOEXPORT enables TIS internal export control routines
# PROXY_PASSTHROUGH enables toolkit aware proxy switching

#CFLAGS= $(COPT) -I../../.. -DNOEXPORT -DSETPROCTITLE
#CFLAGS= $(COPT) -I../../.. -DNOEXPORT -DSETPROCTITLE
CFLAGS= $(COPT) -I../../.. -DPARANOID -DSETPROCTITLE -DPROXY_PASSTHRU=\"/bin/
ftp-gw\"
```

```
all: ftpd

ftpd: $(OBJS)
    $(CC) $(LDFL) -o $@ $(OBJS) $(LIBS) $(AUXLIB)

install: all
    $(CP) ftpd $(DEST)

clean:
    rm -f ftpd $(OBJS)
```

The PROXY_PASSTHROUGH should be set to the path name of the proxy executable, before you run make on the Makefile.

> If the modified FTP daemon is invoked after it has been chrooted to the FTP area, the PROXY_PASSTHROUGH must be relative to the FTP area, and not the root of the file system. A duplicate of the ftp-gw- and ftpd-specific rules from the netperm-table must also be installed in the ~anon-ftp/usr/local/etc/netperm-table file.

AUTHENTICATION MECHANISMS IN THE TOOLKIT

The TIS Firewall Toolkit has an optional authentication server, authsrv, that can be used to implement different types of authentication mechanisms in a mechanism-independent manner.

The authsrv program includes support for the following authentication mechanisms:

- ✤ Plaintext passwords
- ✤ Bellcore's S/Key
- ✤ Security Dynamics SecurID
- ✤ Enigma Logics Silver Card
- ✤ Digital Pathways SNK (Secure Net Key)

Plaintext passwords should not be used from untrusted networks. The authsrv should be run on a secure firewall. An administrative shell called the authmgr can be used from a remote location to manipulate the database information maintained by authsrv. The authmgr can optionally use encryption to protect its communication with the firewall.

When you compile the authsrv program, you must edit the authentication protocol bindings in the auth.h file for the authentication mechanisms specified in your network security policy.

The authsrv program supports authentication for all the interactive proxy servers used in the toolkit. Authentication can be done for both incoming and outgoing requests, and it consists of a simple challenge/response protocol that can be easily integrated in the software.

The authsrv maintains an internal user database that has a record for each user. This record contains the authentication mechanism to use for the user, user group, user long name, last successful authentication, and so on.

The users in the authsrv database can be organized in groups. Each group can have a separate administrator, who has administrative control of the group, including the ability to add and delete users to the group. Use of groups and a group administrator allows administrative responsibilities to be delegated in situations when a single firewall is shared by multiple departments in an organization.

The authsrv program is invoked for each authentication request. To configure authsrv, you must assign a free TCP port number and create entries in the /etc/services and /etc/inetd.conf files:

Use the following in the /etc/services file:

```
authsrv    7557/tcp    # Port 7557 was selected for authsrv
```

Use the following line in the /etc/inetd.conf file:

```
authsrv stream  tcp  nowait root /usr/local/etc/authsrv authsrv
```

It is not necessary to authenticate all services. You can authenticate selectively, based upon where the request originated and the type of requested operation. Consider the following example which shows the firewall gateway rules:

```
#
# FTP Firewall rules
#
ftp-gw:         authserver    127.0.0.1    7557
ftp-gw:         denial-msg    /usr/local/etc/ftp-deny.txt
ftp-gw:         welcome-msg    /usr/local/etc/ftp-welcome.txt
ftp-gw:         help-msg    /usr/local/etc/ftp-help.txt
ftp-gw:         permit-hosts    199.245.180.*    -log { retr stor } -auth
{stor}
ftp-gw:         permit-hosts    *    -authall
```

The first line identifies that the authsrv is running on the firewall (127.0.0.1 is the local host or loopback address).

The first permit-hosts statement identifies that hosts on the network 199.245.180.0 can access the FTP proxy. The file retrieval and storage options are logged. Of these, only file store operations are required to be authenticated. This is represented by the option:

```
-auth {stor}
```

The second permit-hosts statement says that all operations from external hosts will require authentication. This is represented by the following option:

```
-authall
```

To prevent intruders from probing the authentication server, the authsrv can be configured to specify which clients can connect to it. Typically, the authsrv and the proxy clients run on the same central firewall (bastion host). Because the clients and authsrv run on the same machine, it is only necessary to specify that the localhost (127.0.0.1) should be allowed to contact the authsrv. If administration is to be done from a remote workstation, the workstation's IP address should be listed. Following are some example rules for authsrv taken from the netperm-table configuration file:

```
#
# Example authsrv rules
#
authsrv:    database /var/adm/fwtk/authsrv.db
authsrv:    permit-hosts    127.0.0.1
authsrv:    permit-hosts    199.245.180.9 cipherkey
```

The database statement specifies the location of the authsrv database. This location should be secured from access by intruders. The clients on the host on which the authsrv runs are allowed access. The host at 199.245.180.9 is allowed access, presumably because this is a workstation used by the administrator. The keyword "cipherkey" indicates that communication between the workstation and authsrv is protected using DES encryption. The configuration file containing the cipher key should be protected from unauthorized access. To support encryption, two source code modules need to be replaced.

To import and export data from the authsrv database, two tools, authload and authdump, are included in the toolkit. The *authload* can be used to bulk-load the database from an ASCII text file. The *authdump* can be used to create an ASCII backup copy of the records in the database.

SUMMARY

In this chapter firewall solutions for several commercial products were discussed. These included Internet Security Corporation's FireWall-1, ANS's InterLock, and TIS's Gauntlet. The chapter also discussed how a firewall could be built using freely available toolkits such as the Trusted Information Systems (TIS), and the TCP Wrapper program tcpd.

PART III

APPENDIXES

APPENDIX A

LIST OF WORKSHEETS

This book contains several worksheets designed to assist you in determining your own firewall and security needs. The list below is included to aid in quickly locating them.

SOURCES OF INFORMATION

A vast collection of tools and vendors offer software and security products and services. Even though the term and use of firewalls is relatively new, it is quickly becoming a major part of the network security business. The author recommends that you carefully examine any publicly available code before trusting it to protect your networks, computer systems, and data. This caution is not meant to insinuate that the code itself might be questionable, but to ensure that what you think you are getting is actually what you want. Furthermore, the tools and vendors listed here are not necessarily any better than those not mentioned.

EXPLORING PUBLICLY AVAILABLE TOOLS

The list of publicly available tools is long, and the network administrator who is prepared to spend some time investigating each of them is wise. A list of some popular tools and where to get them is identified here.

Keep in mind that neither the authors of this book nor the authors of the software make any claims as to the software's usefulness. As the network administrator, you are responsible for verifying the usefulness and risks associated with any of the software listed here.

TCPWRAPPER AND PORTMAPPER

This is probably one of the best known tools for adding logging and filtering to most standard services. The tcpwrapper program supports only services that are invoked through inetd, while portmapper is used for RPC services that are invoked through the standard portmapper.

Host: FTP.WIN.TUE.NL

Path: /pub/security/tcp_wrapper

Path: /pub/security/portmap.shar

TIS FIREWALL KIT

The TIS Firewall Toolkit is a collection of software components and system configuration practices that enable you to put together an Internet firewall. Included in the kit are application proxies for ftp, telnet, and rlogin as well as tools for securing SMTP mail.

Host: FTP.TIS.COM

Path: /pub/firewalls/toolkit

BELLCORE S/KEY

S/Key is a one-time password scheme that requires no extra hardware. The user can print a list of challenges and responses prior to traveling.

Host: THUMPER.BELLCORE.COM

Path: /pub/nmh/skey

THE SWATCH LOGFILE MONITOR

Swatch is a tool that lets you associate actions with logfile entries. When logfile entries are found, the administrator can arrange for a command to be executed such as mail, finger, etc.

Host: SIERRA.STANFORD.EDU

Path: /pub/sources/swatch.tar.Z

TCPDUMP

Tcpdump is a collection of tools that can be used to capture and examine the TCP/IP packets flowing on a network. It is considered by many to be one of the best network analysis tools available on the Internet.

Host: FTP.EE.LBL.GOV

Path: tcpdump-3.0.tar.Z (as of November 5, 1994)

TAMU TIGER

The TAMU Tiger system is a collection of tools you can use to build a firewall or detect attack signatures. A collection of scripts are included that can be used to assess the security of the machines in your own network. Be advised that the anonymous FTP server at this site has some very tight restrictions governing the number of anonymous FTP users. It may take a while for you to get this code.

Host: NET.TAMU.EDU

Path: /pub/security/TAMU

COPS

COPS (Computer Oracle and Password Program) is another popular system auditing package. The COPS package is a collection of scripts and programs that can be used to evaluate the status of a system's security. It includes features to check passwords, SUID and SGID files, protected programs, and more.

Host: FTP.CERT.ORG

Path: /pub/tools/cops

CRACK

Chapter 2, "Security," discussed the use of a password-cracking program. This is one of the best known password-cracking programs, and it can be customized to use your own dictionaries.

> Host: FTP.CERT.ORG
>
> Path: /pib/tools/crack

A good set of alternate dictionaries can be found at the following:

> Host: BLACK.OX.AC.UK
>
> Path: /wordlists

FINDING COMMERCIAL FIREWALL VENDORS

Many commercial operations offer firewall software products and other security related services. Some of these vendors include the following:

- ✦ Advanced Network and Services (ANS) of Reston, Virginia
- ✦ Digital Equipment Corporation in Stow, Massachusetts
- ✦ Raptor Systems of Wilmington, Delaware
- ✦ Trusted Information Systems in Glenwood, Maryland
- ✦ Milkyway Corporation
- ✦ Seachange Corporation of Mississaugua, Ontario, Canada

EXPLORING FIREWALL AND SECURITY MAILING LISTS

A number of mailing lists and forums are available on the topics of firewalls and security in general. Some are distributed through e-mail, while others are part of the USENET News System.

FIREWALL MAILING LISTS

There are two major mailing lists for firewalls. One is hosted by GREATCIRCLE.COM, and the other is hosted by TIS.COM. To subscribe to the Great Circle mailing list, send a message to majordomo@greatcircle.com, with the body of the message reading:

```
subscribe firewalls your-email-address
```

The TIS.COM firewall list, which focuses primarily on using the TIS firewall toolkit, can be subscribed to by sending a message to fwall-user-request@tis.com, with the body of the message reading:

```
subscribe fwall-users your-email-address
```

In either case, the messages from each list will start flowing to your mailbox within a day or two.

SECURITY FORUMS

Other forums are available for the discussion of security in general, not necessarily just firewalls. These forums are generally part of the USENET News system and include the following news groups:

> comp.security.announce
>
> comp.security.misc
>
> comp.security.unix
>
> alt.security

This is not meant to be an all-inclusive list, as security-related discussions arise in many other newsgroups as well.

VENDOR LIST

The following vendors and their products represent security packages or firewall implementations:

3COM *LAN Security Architecture* is a randomly generated mask for Ethernet networks. 5400 Bayfront Plaza, Santa Clara, CA 95052; (800)638-3266.

ANS *Interlock* provides gateway protection, encryption, and firewall implementation. 1875 Campus Commons Drive, Suite 200, Reston, VA 22091; (800)456-8267.

BASELINE SOFTWARE Several products include: *Password Coach, Information Security Policies Made Easy*, and *Password Genie*. P.O. Box 1219, Sausalito, CA 94966; (800)829-9955.

BLUE LANCE *LT Auditor* provides access control for DOS, Macs, and Windows. 1700 W. Loop S., Suite 1100, Houston, TX 77027; (713)680-1187.

COMPUTER ASSOCIATES *CA-Unicenter* offers encryption capabilities for a wide range of operating systems. 1 Computer Associates Plaza, Islandia, NY 11788; (800)225-5224.

CYBERSAFE *Challenger/Kerberos* offers access control encryption. 2443 152nd Avenue N.E., Redmond, WA 98052; (206)883-8721.

IC ENGINEERING *Modem Security Enforcer* provides call-back modem protection, as well as access encryption and several other features. P.O. Box 321, Owings Mills, MD 21117; (410)363-8748.

LIVINGSTON ENTERPRISES *Portmaster*, *IRX*, and *Firewall* packages. 6920 Koll Center Parkway, Suite 220, Pleasanton, CA 94566; (800)458-9966.

M&T TECHNOLOGIES *Microsafe* offers operating system independent virus protection. 1435 N. Hayden Road, Scottsdale, AZ 85257; (602)994-5131.

PARALON TECHNOLOGIES *Path Key* provides encryption, access control, and authentication. 3650 131st Avenue S.E., Suite 210, Bellevue, WA 98006; (206)641-8338.

THE ROOT GROUP *Sudo* provides access control with on-screen and e-mail event notification. 4700 Walnut Street, Suite 110, Boulder, CO 80301; (303)447-3938.

SEMAPHORE COMMUNICATIONS *Semaphore Network Security System* adds access control, encryption, and data integrity features. 2040 Martin Avenue, Santa Clara, CA 95050; (408)980-7750.

SYNOPTICS *Lattis Secure* is access control hardware. 4401 Great America Parkway, Santa Clara, CA 95052; (800)776-6895.

J-K

Q-R

WANT MORE INFORMATION?

CHECK OUT THESE RELATED TITLES:

	QTY	PRICE	TOTAL
Inside Novell NetWare, Special Edition. This #1 selling tutorial/reference is perfect for beginning system administrators. Each network management task is thoroughly explained and potential trouble spots are noted. The book also includes a disk with an extremely easy-to-use workstation menu program, an MHS capable E-Mail program, and workgroup management tools. ISBN: 1-56205-096-6.	____	$34.95	_____
NetWare 4: Planning and Implementation. The ultimate guide to planning, installing, and managing a NetWare 4.0 network. This book explains how best to implement the new features of NetWare 4.0 and how to upgrade to NetWare 4.0 as easily and efficiently as possible. ISBN: 1-56205-159-8.	____	$27.95	_____
Downsizing to NetWare. Get the real story on downsizing with *Downsizing to NetWare.* This book identifies applications that are suitable for use on LANs and shows how to implement downsizing projects. This book lists the strengths and weaknesses of NetWare—making it perfect for managers and system administrators. ISBN: 1-56205-071-0.	____	$39.95	_____
LAN Operating Systems. Learn how to connect the most popular LAN operating systems. All major LAN operating systems are covered, including: NetWare 3.11, Appleshare 3.0, Banyan VINES 5.0, Unix, LAN Manger 2.1, and popular peer-to-peer networks. The following client operating systems are covered as well: MS-DOS, Windows, OS/2, Macintosh System 7, and Unix. This book clears up the confusion associated with managing large networks with diverse client workstations and multiple LAN operating systems. ISBN: 1-56205-054-0.	____	$39.95	_____

Name _____

Company _____

Address _____

City _____ State ____ ZIP _____

Phone _____ Fax _____

☐ Check Enclosed ☐ VISA ☐ MasterCard

Card #_____Exp. Date _____

Signature_____

Prices are subject to change. Call for availability and pricing information on latest editions.

Subtotal _____

Shipping _____

$4.00 for the first book and $1.75 for each additional book.

Total _____
Indiana residents add 5% sales tax.

New Riders Publishing 201 West 103rd Street • Indianapolis, Indiana 46290 USA

Orders/Customer Service: 1-800-428-5331
Fax: 1-800-448-3804

Fold Here

New Riders Publishing
201 West 103rd Street
Indianapolis, Indiana 46290
USA

Internet Firewalls & Network Security

REGISTRATION CARD

Fill out this card to receive information about future Internet books and other New Riders titles!

Name _____ **Title** _____

Company _____

Address _____

City/State/ZIP _____

I bought this book because: _____

_____

I purchased this book from:

☐ A bookstore (Name _____)

☐ A software or electronics store (Name _____)

☐ A mail order (Name of Catalog _____)

I purchase this many computer books each year:

☐ 1–5   ☐ 6 or more

I currently use these applications: _____

_____

_____

_____

I found these chapters to be the most informative: _____

_____

I found these chapters to be the least informative: _____

_____

Additional comments: _____

_____

☐ I would like to see my name in print! You may use my name and quote me in future New Riders products and promotions. My daytime phone number is: _____

New Riders Publishing 201 West 103rd Street • Indianapolis, Indiana 46290 USA

Fold Here

PLACE
STAMP
HERE

New Riders Publishing
201 West 103rd Street
Indianapolis, Indiana 46290
USA